… BACKGROUND TO CONT…

VOLUME II

BACKGROUND TO CONTEMPORARY GREECE

edited by
 Marion Sarafis
 Martin Eve

MERLIN PRESS
LONDON

© The Merlin Press 1990
First published 1990 by The Merlin Press Ltd
10 Malden Road, London NW5

Printed by Whitstable Litho,
Millstrood Road, Whitstable, Kent
Typesetting by Heather Hems
Tower House, Queen Street, Gillingham, Dorset

British Library Cataloguing in Publication Data
Background to contemporary Greece.
 1. Greece, 1936-
 I. Sarafis, Marion II. Eve, Martin
 949.507

ISBN 0-85036-394-2

CIP Office
The British Library, 2 Sheraton Street, London W1V 4BH

CONTENTS

VOLUME I

Greek Literature since National Independence
    Roderick Beaton

Katharevousa (c. 1800-1974)
An Obituary for an Official Language
    Peter Mackridge

The Greek Economy
    Jon Kofas

Women in Greek Society
    Janet Hart

Contemporary Greek History for English Readers: An Attempt at a Critical Analysis
    Marion Sarafis

VOLUME II

From the 'Great Idea' to Balkan Union
    Procopis Papastratis   153

The Greek Communist Party 1941–1945: The Internal Debate on Seizing Power
    Pericles Grambas   181

The Greek Civil War 1946–1949
    Christophe Chiclet   201

The Experience of Civil War in the Mountain Villages of Central Greece
    Anna Collard   223

The Colonels' Dictatorship 1967–1974
    Robert McDonald   255

The Greek–Turkish Conflict
    Heinz Richter   317

Contributors to Volume II

Procopis Papastratis is an Associate Professor of History at Panteion University of Political and Social Science, and author of *British Policy towards Greece during the Second World War, 1941-1944* (Cambridge University Press 1984) and of various articles on Modern Greek History.

Pericles Grambas is a graduate of Athens University School of Philosophy, MA School of Slavonic and East European Studies; since 1985 he has been working for his PhD on the History of the Greek Communist Party between the 1950s and 1980s at King's College, London.

Christophe Chiclet has a doctorate from the Centre for 20th Century History at the Institut des Etudes Politiques (Paris) and is a researcher at the Centre for European History of the 20th Century (FNSP). Publications: *Les Communistes Grecs dans la Guerre* (Paris: L'Harmattan, 1987).

Anna Collard is completing a PhD in Social Anthropology at the London School of Economics and teaches Social Anthropology parttime in Camden. Published writings include: 'The Inequalities of Change in a Greek Mountain Village' in *The Greek Review of Social Research*, Special Edition, CNRS, Athens, 1981; 'Investigating Social memory in a Greek Context' in *History and Ethnicity*, eds. Tonkin, E., MacDonald, M., and Chapman, M. ASA Monograph, Routledge, 1989; 'Anthropology and History: An Investigation into the question of Memory in the Greek Context' in *The Greek Review of Social Research*, Athens, 1989; 'Peoples' Justice: Peasants and the Law' to be published in *Droit et Cultures*, no. 20, Paris, 1990.

Robert McDonald is a freelance writer and broadcaster who has specialised in Greek affairs since the mid-1960s. He was for a time during the colonels' dictatorship the stringer for the British Broadcasting Corporation and several other international news networks. He is the author of *Pillar and Tinderbox*, a study of the Greek press during the dictatorship (Marion Boyars, 1983) and a monograph 'The Problem of Cyprus' (International Institute for Strategic Studies, Adelphi Paper 234, 1989). He is the current author of the *Country Report: Greece*, published quarterly by the Economist Intelligence Unit. He has contributed to numerous symposia on Greece, Turkey and Cyprus.

Heinz Richter teaches Contemporary History with special emphasis on Greece and Cyprus at the University of Konstanz. Publications: *Griechenland zwischen Revolution und Konterrevolution 1936-1946 1946* (Frankfurt: Europäische Verlagsanstalt, 1973, 623 pp. 2-volume Greek edition published in Athens 1977; *Greece and Cyprus since 1920: Bibliography of contemporary history*, Tri-lingual ed. (Heidelberg.

Nea Hellas, 1984), 437 pp.; *British Intervention in Greece: From Varkiza to Civil War* (London: The Merlin Press, 1986), 573 pp. Greek edition now appearing in Athens; *Frieden in der Ägäis? Zypern – Ägäis – Minderheiten* (Köln, Romiosini, 1989), 168 pp.

FROM THE 'GREAT IDEA' TO BALKAN UNION

Procopis Papastratis

The Great Idea went through a series of permutations over a period of a century. The term was first introduced by Prime Minister I. Kolettis in 1844. In spite of its vague meaning it immediately captured the Greek imagination well beyond the confines of the newly-created Greek state, giving vent to poorly-defined feelings of extreme irredentism.[1] The recapture of Constantinople was the main and most cherished aim of the Great Idea until the Greek-Turkish War in Asia Minor. Its more recent expression at the end of World War II advocated the readjustment of Greece's northern frontiers.

The receding nebulous and romantic nationalism of the mid 19th century and the primacy attached to economic factors in the middle 1940s do not revoke the two basic characteristics of the Great Idea; ambiguity of content and nationalistic spirit, common features in all similar ideological movements. Following on Kolettis' introduction, the Great Idea was soon established as the dominant ideology of Hellenism. It enjoyed this privileged position until the political and military repercussions of the Greek-Turkish war of 1922 and the ensuing traumatic experiences removed it from the forefront of the political spectrum without dismissing it altogether. However it still recurred especially during periods of crisis.

A typical example of such a revival — and the focal point of this paper — is the re-emergence of the Great Idea in parallel and in conjunction with the attempt at Balkan cooperation in the early 1930s, mainly to combat the effects of the world economic crisis of 1929.

The strong nationalist movements of the 19th century

Balkans — in acute contrast with the solidarity forged during previously fought common liberation struggles[2] — provided ideal conditions for the formulation of ideologies with great affinity but opposing aims. During the period when the Great Idea was captivating Greek public opinion a similar ideology was being propounded in Serbia, while in neighbouring Italy the Risorgimento was in full development.[3] Bulgaria followed suit a few years later. In this atmosphere of rising nationalism it was impossible for proposals envisaging a certain degree of Balkan cooperation to bear fruit. The Balkan people at the time, busy in establishing their own historical continuity and national identity, were in fact projecting the traits that distinguished them and not their common characteristics.

On the eve of the Balkan Wars (1912-1913) a Balkan *rapprochement* became possible through a series of mutual alliances between these countries. It was in fact an attempt to realise their respective Great Ideas at the expense of Turkey, their common foe. This limited effort to solve the Eastern Question under the watchful eye of the European Powers, was basically an attempt by the rising bourgeois classes to assert their dominant position on the Balkan political scene, taking advantage of the prevailing international situation. This cooperation however was soon confronted with their contradictory territorial claims, an obvious consequence of their deep nationalism.

The economic crisis of 1929 had undoubtedly a catalytic influence on the development of national societies in Europe. This event produced wide repercussions in the Balkan States, trying at the time to solve problems they inherited from the first World War. The European countries reacted to the economic crisis by creating economic blocks. In 1931 Britain, for example, adopted Imperial Preference but at the same time resisted the formation of other customs unions, between Germany and Austria, the Scandinavian countries, and between Belgium, the Netherlands and Luxemburg. France for her part, introduced the Tardieu plan in the spring of 1932 in an effort to reinforce even further her political and economic influence on Central Europe. The plan proposed an economic reorganization of the five Danubian states; three of them, Romania, Czechoslovakia and Yugoslavia had already formed the Little Entente under the guidance of France. It is clear that an additional French aim was to check German economic and political penetration in this area. In Northern Europe the Oslo Convention of 1930 had resulted in increased regional cooperation between the Scandinavian countries with Belgium and Holland.

This formation of the European countries into economic groups, a direct consequence of the world crisis, created in Germany a feeling of economic encirclement. The solution, already tried before, was to turn to Central Europe, the Balkans and Turkey. It was an area of obvious political and economic importance for Germany, whose political ambitions in this area were underlined by the announcement of the German-Austrian Customs Union in March 1931. Germany hoped to regain the status of a great power by creating a German-dominated economic and political block in S.E. Europe. Despite the fact that French economic pressure forced Austria to abandon the customs union, German penetration in the Balkans continued unabashed and gained new impetus with the Nazi rise to power.[4]

The world economic crisis affected Greece at this time whilst the Venizelos government was implementing an ambitious programme of foreign policy and internal reconstruction. The government's reaction to the world crisis did not differ from the reaction of other countries facing the same economic problems: a turn to autarchy and protectionism. In foreign affairs Venizelos continued his successful policy of bilateral agreements. However the basic problem that commanded the attention of the Greek government was the worsening economic situation. Therefore any solution that would help Greece out of this economic *impasse* was given due consideration, especially when the economic blocks under formation in Europe did not include Greece. This was in fact one of the main points of the proposal for Balkan Union introduced at the time by the former Prime Minister Alexandros Papanastasiou under favourable circumstances. The movement for a Balkan Locarno and the Briand project for a European Union (United States of Europe) during 1929-1930 had been positively received in the Balkans. Papanastasiou presented his proposal at the 27th Universal Congress of Peace held at Athens in October 1929. It met with enthusiastic approval. The Congress adopted wholeheartedly the resolution he drafted on this issue. It stressed the necessity for annual Balkan Conferences to study all questions of common interest to the Balkan people. The idea of a Balkan Federation had already been proposed in the past. The new and crucial element it introduced was economic cooperation. In view of the prevailing situation in the world economy it was obvious that the proposed economic measures had to be promptly evaluated. This was apparently the reason for the Venizelos Government's initial support for the Papanastasiou proposal over and above the warm and typical initial statements of all party leaders in the parliament.[5]

The government provided financial assistance to the Greek Delegation at the Balkan Conferences, it notified official documents to the Delegation and at the beginning at least it convened the Committee of Foreign Affairs to examine the policy that the Greek Delegation would advocate at the Balkan Conferences. The Greek Government tried in this way to control the activity of its delegation. The same logistical support and undoubtedly greater political control was exercised by the other Balkan governments on their delegations. It was obvious that the Balkan Conferences allowed the Governments to test the ground on a variety of issues without commiting themselves. However, disagreements on the part of the Greek government did exist. The Venizelos Government believed that, irrespective of the attempt to solve the economic situation, it was the method applied to this end that was of doubtful political value. This Balkan movement was advocating the conclusion of multilateral agreements of political and economic cooperation. This however: a) ran contrary to the Venizelos commitment to bilateral agreements; b) would have a negative influence on Greek-Italian relations because Greece would be a leading member of a group advocating 'the Balkans to the Balkan people' which would weaken Italy's status in an area Rome considered to belong to its sphere of influence; c) Balkan economic cooperation would be resented by the European powers which stood to lose a percentage of the Balkan market.

The Greek government had expressed reservations from the outset regarding the effectiveness of the Papanastasiou initiative. These soon turned to serious objections, setting aside the initial limited support.[6] The insistent references by the Bulgarian Delegation to the minorities question and its pressing advocacy for a settlement played a decisive role in sustaining the Greek government's reluctance to promote the Papanastasiou proposal for a Balkan Union. And this despite the fact that the Greek Delegation had identified completely with the official Greek attitude that international treaties on this issue had to be respected.

The minorities question was regarded as the main obstacle preventing the success of the Balkan Conferences. It was not the only one and perhaps not the most serious either. Bulgarian insistence on putting it on the agenda right from the start expressed her manifest resentment of the Balkan territorial settlement following the Treaty of Neuilly of 1919. It did however focus attention on the minorities question which in turn directly influenced the Balkan Conferences' chances of success.[7]

Papanastasiou was facing a series of objective difficulties in his effort to promote Balkan unity. It was not only the minorities question *per se* but also the mistrust and the negative atmosphere that surrounded it. During the period under examination, apart from Bulgarian intransigence and the negative attitude of Yugoslavia regarding this issue, there was also an evident irritability and lack of confidence on the part of the Greek Government due to the fact that this controversial question had once again come to the fore. The Greek Government was anxious lest the Greek Delegation to the Balkan Conferences would undertake initiatives that would offend Yugoslavian susceptibilities. An additional source of anxiety was the insistence of the Yugoslav and Bulgarian delegates at the 2nd Balkan Conference on solving their differences through direct consultation. This underlined one of the most sensitive aspects of Greek foreign policy during this period: the possibility of a *rapprochement* between Yugoslavia and Bulgaria, 'the most sensitive string of the Greek lyre' as the Italian ambassador pointed out.

Press coverage of the minorities question in the interested countries did not help disperse the already prevailing negative atmosphere. On the contrary age-old antagonisms were fostered, influencing unfavourably the discussion on all other matters. Everywhere the press was projecting the official policies of their respective governments, as was in fact to be expected if the prevailing political situation in the area were taken into account. The comments in the Italian Press, for example, were negative regarding both the minorities question and the possibility of success for the Balkan Conferences. *Macedonia* published in Bulgaria, referred to the situation in the Balkans as 'mutual mistrust'.

The Greek ambassador, N. Politis, reported from Paris that the French newspapers were showing a lively interest in the attempt for a Balkan unification, printing all relevant telegrams; articles commenting on this issue were however few. His counterpart in London, D. Kaklamanos, reported that *The Times* commented in a leader in favour of the 2nd Balkan Conference but doubted whether it could reach practical results at that stage.[8]

In Greece, the arguments against the idea of a Balkan union — but significantly not against economic cooperation in the area — were outlined in a series of articles in the influential journal *Ergasia*. One of the arguments underlined in these articles was the danger Greece would face from the formation of a strong South Slav state that would include Bulgaria. This was a direct reference to the efforts of the Agrarian government in Bulgaria, under N. Stamboliski, in the early 1920s to unify all South Slavs into a great federated state. Stamboliski had repeatedly urged *rapprochement* with Serbia on this issue. In Serbia there was indeed a widespread demand for a South Slav Federation; in Croatia the dominant Agrarian Party under S. Radich held the same views as its Bulgarian counterpart and other parties advocated the same course of action.[9] This movement had been crushed by the mid 1920s following the assassination of both Stamboliski and Radich and the ruthless suppression of their parties. Nevertheless in the early 1930s the possibility of such a federation still exercised the imagination of the opponents of a Balkan union. The Minister for Foreign Affairs in the Venizelos government was one of them; he did not fail to express his strong reservations on this issue on a number of occasions.[10]

The reservations of the Populist (Right-wing) Party regarding a Balkan Union were confined to the method to be applied towards this aim. Its leader, P. Tsaldaris, stressed this point during his programmatic statement in Parliament. Elaborating further on this issue he urged the formation of a customs union as a practical step towards the realisation of this movement.[11] Balkan unification was also viewed as a promising alternative solution by several of the liberal parties in the Greek Parliament. G. Kafandaris, the leader of Progressive Liberals pointed out in an article that this proposal tended to become the foremost plank in the post-war reconstruction of the area. The influential journal *Peitharchia* in a leader in the spring of 1930 stressed that the majority of Greeks who, following a war period of twenty years, had reached the indisputable conclusion that solidarity between peoples was an indispensable prerequisite for their prosperity, stood firmly under the banner of Balkan cooperation.[12]

To promote Balkan unification it was proposed to give priority to those issues on which the views of the individual states coincided, Papanastasiou himself being a strong advocate of this step-by-step approach. The necessary spadework for the first Balkan Conference included the preparation of a series of memoranda on which the delegations might base further discussion. The Greek memoranda covered in a remarkable degree the full range of the political, economic, social and intellectual aspects of Balkan cooperation. The contribution of the other Balkan states was much more limited. The Yugoslav memoranda dealt only with the economic aspects of the question. The only memorandum the Romanian delegation prepared advocated the establishment of an Institute of Balkan Cooperation to work for the dissemination of common political and social ideas in all the Balkan states. The Bulgarian point of view was presented in a brief study. It emphasized that the idea of confederation could only be based on complete respect for the stipulations for the protection of Bulgarian minorities in the Balkans. The preliminary memoranda submitted by the various delegations already indicated the pattern the Balkan Conferences would follow.

Papanastasiou and the Greek Delegation from the start focussed their attention on promoting mainly the following three issues a) political *rapprochement* by signing a multilateral Balkan pact of arbitration and friendship, b) economic cooperation with the creation of a partial customs union, c) the signing of an agreement on free admission, free circulation and free economic activity; this agreement would extend to all Balkan nationals throughout the peninsula, on a basis of reciprocity. Papanastasiou believed that these three agreements constituted the very essence of Balkan unification at that stage. Therefore he continued to press the Greek Minister for Foreign Affairs to sign them right up to the successful conclusion of the negotiations for the four-power Balkan Pact in late 1933 which, however, put the entire issue of Balkan cooperation in a totally different perspective.[13] These three draft agreements were eventually integrated into one project at the 3rd Balkan Conference in Bucharest in October 1932 following a proposal by the Turkish Delegation. Papanastasiou had specific reasons to insist on advocating the conclusion of these draft agreements. He considered that the agreement on free admission, circulation and economic activity had an equal if not greater importance for Greece than even the political ideal of Balkan unification. The significance of such an agreement was repeatedly stressed by Papanastasiou as well as by Professor A. Svolos, a member of its drafting committee.[14] It was however, one specific dimension of this draft agreement which Papanastasiou emphasized: its application would enable Greeks to return and work in Turkey. In a letter to the Greek Prime Minister in September 1933, Papanastasiou pointed out that a possible Turkish endorsement of this agreement, briefly in the offing in late 1932, would mean a radical solution of the demographic question, the most pressing social issue in Greece at the time.[15]

Papanastasiou was realistic enough to understand that the prevailing political situation in South-East Europe hardly encouraged the promotion of the political ideal of Balkan unification, a very difficult project in itself anyway. On the other hand the wish for economic cooperation could be put to good use. He apparently believed that the strengthening of Greek-Turkish economic relations with this agreement, following the bold Venizelos initiative to conclude a series of treaties with Turkey, would help to promote inter-Balkan economic relations. The almost pleading tone of his memoranda to Tsaldaris suggests that Papanastasiou by hinting at a Greek return to Turkey was appealing to the Prime Minister's wounded nationalism in an effort to draw his attention to the tangible economic benefits of an eventual Balkan union.[16]

Papanastasiou in fact was trying to convince a political opponent, renowned for his hesitant attitude and less than imaginative conservative thinking, actively to support a daring if not utopian plan for the reorganisation of the Balkan states based on a break with all traditional political and economic relations.

Papanastasiou's reference to a possible Greek return to Turkey nevertheless went hand in glove with a belief widespread at that time that Greek entrepreneurial activity was indispensable for invigorating the Turkish economy. This obviously simplistic approach to a complicated situation belonged more to the sphere of wishful thinking than to the domain of practical politics even at that time when the repercussions of the world crisis of 1929 were fully felt. This view however was repeatedly supported in Parliament as well as in the Press.

The draft agreement on free admission and free economic activity in the Balkans, the convention on the personal status of Balkan citizens as it became known, gained the approval of Venizelos himself, albeit belatedly. Expressing his strong criticism regarding the four-power Balkan Pact in February 1934 at the Council of Political Leaders, Venizelos emphasized the immense advantages Greece could enjoy in a Balkan Union if the principle of free admission and economic activity had been finally accepted. It was mainly this principle, coupled with Bulgaria's admission to the Balkan Union that could justify Greece's decision to guarantee the security of all Balkan states even in the face of opposition by a major power.[17]

The Economic Dimension

The economic cooperation of the Balkan States captured right from the start the attention of the Delegations to the Balkan Conferences. Greek interest was focussed on this issue mainly because a significant part of the foreign trade deficit of Greece was due to its commercial relations with the other Balkan countries.[18] The Greek memorandum on economic cooperation submitted to the 1st Balkan Conference duly underlined the basic characteristics of the Balkan economy; heavy dependence on the agricultural sector and the precarious development of inter-Balkan trade, for which the isolation and stifling protectionism the Balkan States had imposed upon themselves were partly to blame. It was a foregone conclusion that this situation would prevent these countries from building independent national economies.

The Greek memorandum put forward specific measures for the establishment of a Balkan bloc with a population of approximately 60,000,000 and 2,000,000 square kilometres.[19] A very important issue was thus introduced into the Balkan Conference which has to be viewed in the wider context of the world economic crisis of 1929. It was therefore fairly obvious that the question of a Customs Union should have played a dominant role in these deliberations following a pattern imposed by the economic crisis.

This issue, put in the proper perspective of regional economic cooperation, was indeed fervently supported in a series of articles published by members of the Yugoslav Delegation.[20] In view of the authoritarian regime imposed in Yugoslavia by the King himself a few years earlier, these articles could not but express official policy on the matter. Yugoslavia's emphasis on Balkan economic cooperation was based undoubtedly on the strong position it enjoyed in Balkan trade and its ambition to increase its activity in the port of Thessaloniki Free Zone for a host of political and economic reasons. Furthermore these Yugoslav initiatives were not in conflict with its alliance with France, the cornerstone of Belgrade's foreign policy at the time.

The Greek interest in economic cooperation was even stronger as Greek foreign trade was facing more pressing problems. Although the Greek Delegation did not have the Greek government's official support, it had however its tacit approval.[21]

Critics of the Balkan Union were quick to underline the negative aspects of such an endeavour, however the possibility for the establishment of fruitful economic relations did exist. The Balkan countries were predominantly agricultural, three-fourths of their exports being farm products. Greece and Turkey were exporting olives, olive oil, cotton and raisins and importing considerable amounts of wheat, an export commodity of Bulgaria, Yugoslavia and Romania. Tobacco on the other hand was exported by Turkey, Greece and Bulgaria. Romania needed markets for its oil production. It was obvious that economic coordination on a preferential system might result in a better-developed Balkan market and a better place in the world market for the products of the peninsula. Most Balkan trade was extra-Balkan at that time;

railway, customs and banking facilities, the necessary conditions, were lacking for inter-Balkan economic activity. Foreign capital in the Balkans was exerting considerable financial control through its presence in vital economic sectors.[22]

It was argued however that the establishment of economic relations was possible as well as advantageous, the difficulties of such an attempt notwithstanding. Seen from the Greek point of view the issue concealed multiple difficulties. Within the context of developing the limited inter-Balkan trade an answer had to be found to a long standing question of Greek finance; the means had to be found to reverse the adverse balance of trade position.[23] This difficulty was complicated by a number of factors which were bound to influence the Balkan countries adversely in their imports of Greek agricultural products which were luxuries, generally similar and inevitably competitive with what the other Balkan countries produced.

In addition to these inherent difficulties the Greek Government was anxious lest this economic cooperation might further increase imports from the Balkans. This apprehension must be taken into account in conjunction with the unwillingness to limit the considerable trade relations with the main creditor countries, such as the USA and Great Britain, which were importing substantial quantities of Greek agricultural products.

In order to deal with the economic dimension of this problem, the supporters of Balkan cooperation proposed a combination of economic measures. These were examined extensively by the specialised committees of the Balkan Conferences. The draft for a Customs Union came to the fore, an ideal shelter during periods of economic crisis, but also the first step towards political cooperation as it was succinctly pointed out. The indispensable prerequisite for its success was to balance the import–export relations between the Balkan countries. As far as Greece was concerned this meant that the other members of the future Customs Union must be persuaded to increase their import quotas of Greek products.[24] This issue was among the chief concerns of Greek industrialists; Greece enjoyed by comparison a stronger position in this sector. In a series of articles dealing extensively with the trade deficit it was argued that the increased Greek imports from the Balkan countries, mainly cereals and farm products, could be turned to the advantage of the Greek economy. They could be used as a strong card in a bargain to compel the Balkan countries to prefer Greek industrial products.[25] The unspoken assumption was that the worldwide fall in the prices of agricultural products had paved the way for such a bargain. In this proposed Balkan economic entity Greece was envisaged as the industrial partner *par excellence*, distinguished by the innate and unchallenged qualities of its people as entrepreneurs and seafarers. Such a prestigious place implied Greek superiority in comparison with the neighbouring farming, stock-breeding and wood-cutting Balkan peoples and further underpinned Greek ambitions for a future strategic position in the Balkan economy.[26]

Economic cooperation quickly attained primary importance during the Balkan Conference. Balkan cooperation however, had to face steadily rising political and economic forces which eventually succeeded in annulling the first positive steps in this direction, the establishment of a Balkan Tobacco Office and a Balkan Chamber of Commerce and Industry. The bilateral clearing agreements the Balkan countries started to sign and the French effort to consolidate political influence through the introduction of the Tardieu Plan and the reactivation of the Little Entente added to the pressure on this frail attempt to accomplish Balkan Union. The isolated and basically unofficial reactions of the supporters of Balkan cooperation could not possibly obstruct the formation of defensive alliances necessitated by developments in the international political situation.[27]

The Ideological Framework

In 1922 Greek society, at the end of a decade of wars and civil upheavals, was subjected to a sudden influx of enormous numbers of refugees; Greece was at the same time experiencing acute financial problems. The world economic crisis of 1929 added further negative repercussions to the slow evolution of the social assimilation and economic rehabilitation of approximately 1,300,000 refugees. In spite of all these problems, if not precisely because of them, Greek society seemed not to realise that the ideology of the Great

Idea now belonged definitely to the past. Arguments in favour of Greek expansionism did not cease to appear. It was obvious however that the magnitude of the Asia Minor Disaster precluded even the slightest reference to political or military activity towards this end. The emphasis was on economic penetration and subsequent domination, while Greek intellectual superiority — indispensable for the support of this new effort — was taken for granted. Greece faced an economic *impasse* following the Asia Minor *debâcle* and the simultaneous post-war slump. An alternative solution was proposed in 1923, Greece should turn to the Balkans including Turkey. It was then suggested that attention should be focussed on Balkan cooperation. The solution proposed was cooperation of a strictly economic character, more specifically a Balkan Customs Union. The advocates of such a scheme, men of extreme conservative political ideas, underlined the dominant economic and intellectual role Greece was bound to play in the Balkan peninsula. The contribution of emigration to Balkan economic cooperation was also pointed out.[28] An opposing view put forward at the same time insisted on strengthening the peasant population in Macedonia in order to secure its Greek character. In fact the diverging views differed only as to the tactics to be followed regarding the expansion of Hellenism. K. Amantos, a prominent professor of history at the University of Athens who put forward this second view, was against 'Hellenism scattered to the winds' as he put it and preferred to face the danger from the Slavs. This consolidation of Hellenism was indispensable for its further expansion. If the peasant population is not strengthened, Amantos wrote in 1923, 'we will never be able to return to Asia Minor and even when Turkey will collapse completely, most probably in two generations, the Slavs will advance there too...'[29]

The proposals to seek the solution of the problems Greece was facing in Asia Minor 'our East' increased at the time of the world economic crisis of 1929 and even before its repercussions directly affected the country. Although Venizelos' long-term policy had the same aims he was compelled by his realism to follow a course of gradual *rapprochement* with Turkey, contrary to the romantic utopia of his critics.

Widespread anxiety regarding the repercussions of the world crisis on the Greek economy might be considered as supporting Venizelos' insistent and in fact desperate exhortation for continuous and systematic work: his aim was to turn Greece into a modern state with an ever increasing national income to be justly distributed.[30]

It was however the negative aspects of the world crisis that made the most lasting impressions; it underlined the failure of much stronger countries to withstand the pressure at a time when Venizelos wanted to develop the already over-burdened Greek economy.

The resulting widespread disillusion must be seen as one of the reasons why the ongoing debate on the materialism of post-war Greek society turned to the quest for lost ideals. These were of course the national ideals which irrespective of whether they could materialize or not — the tone of discussion on this point was restrained — ought not to be abandoned.[31] Escaping to the field of ideological constructs is after all an expected reaction during periods of crisis.

Into this framework a new approach to the multifaceted crisis was introduced, pronouncements smacking of fascist social ideology, already rampant elsewhere in Europe, which was eventually to take root in Greece too. These pronouncements, in the form of concerned articles in the press, proposed a reconstruction of the productive forces along dictatorial lines and regarded the arrival of the refugees in conjunction with the abandonment of the old ideals as the main reason for the destruction of the 'national nucleus'.[32]

For an additional reason the atmopshere in Greece at the time was quite appropriate for dwelling upon ideological constructs. In 1930 the Centenary of Greek Independence was extensively celebrated with continuous references to the wars of liberation and to national claims. It was obvious that in this context the Great Idea would be prominently mentioned. However this intensification of nationalism was contrary to the foreign policy of Venizelos who, having succeeded in redressing the balance in the Balkans in favour of Greece by signing the 1929 Agreement with Italy, was then negotiating the Greek-Turkish *rapprochement*. It was therefore evident that the pursuit of peace should take precedence. Venizelos himself took the opportunity to stress this point in Parliament where anxiety was expressed lest this pursuit of peace would imbue the younger generation with materialism. Venizelos underlined the significance of the struggle for social and economic justice, physical and mental health, material and intellectual development; he pointed out that this ideal was much higher than war and much more in accordance with Greek traditions.[33]

During a speech in Thessaloniki, in May 1930, Venizelos referred to the romantic absorption of the Greek people in the Great Idea 'preventing the modernization of the state itself which would enable it one day to seek in earnest the realisation of the Great Idea'.[34] That Venizelos focussed his criticism on the insufficient preconditions for the realisation of the Great Idea — he returned to this issue a few months later in Parliament — did not avail to mitigate denounciations for the 'darkness of his materialistic policy'.[35]

These denounciations reached new heights when Venizelos chose to stress his arguments in favour of peace the day the remains of General Kolokotronis were conveyed from Athens to his native town with honours befitting the most prominent personality in the Greek War of Independence against Turkey. The Prime Minister, the principal speaker at this memorial ceremony, the culmination of the Centenary celebrations, declared that the wars of national integrity had been concluded and exhorted the younger generation to excell in the field of learning in the forthcoming framework of closer cooperation between the peoples of the Near East.[36] The reference to Turkey was obvious and the reaction of the opposition press predictable. This 'vile preaching against ideals and traditions' as part of the opposition press characterised the speech coincided with the opening of the Balkan Conference.[37] More importantly however it coincided with the conclusion of the Greek-Turkish negotiations and the signing of the Agreements by Kemal Ataturk and E. Venizelos during the latter's official visit to Ankara at the end of October 1930.

A section of Venizelos' own Liberal Party allied with the opposition in denouncing the Prime Minister's materialism, although the tone was definitely milder. The conservative daily *Proia* pointed out that in spite of the 'voluptuous torpor through materialist comfort' that Venizelos seemed to envisage for all Greeks, the Greek people 'was destined to win and dominate'.[38]

This nostalgic comment was further complemented by a series of articles in the Venizelist weekly *Peitharchia*, especially during Venizelos' visit to Turkey, with direct references to the Great Idea

> ... Mr. Venizelos is not doing the right thing by wanting to clip the wounded wings of the Great Idea which kept the Greek race upright for five centuries.[39]

In spite however of such verbal exaltation, emphasis was indeed laid on economic domination by means of a return to this area. References to Turkey as 'a country addicted to Greek exploitation for its own interest'[40] formed an integral part of a much wider argumentation expressing a clearly defined mentality that considered a return to Turkey as a natural and well-grounded solution to the *impasse* the economic crisis has imposed.

A similar proposal can be found in the quest for a solution towards Abyssinia: Turkey, it was argued, was an enemy preparing to destroy Greece, whereas Abyssinia had no political and religious differences with Greece.[41] These views were indeed challenged, though not forcibly and the arguments used to this end were self-defeating on a number of points. In his articles in *Proia* K. Karavidas demanded an end to emigration and all attention focussed on the village, his so called 'crop-community', a nucleus able to provide economic stability, social solidity, a safe reservoir for the invigoration of the civic population and finally peace and security on the 'borders towards the Slavs'.[42] He himself admitted however that the exodus of a section of the population was a probable, natural and common phenomenon. *Proia* also pointed out in a leader, that the state which encouraged emigration instead of streamlining its production, exploiting its own resources and securing markets for its products was morally bankrupt in the eyes of its citizens. This point however was contradicted in the same article which stressed simultaneously the superiority of the Greek race.

As far as emigration was concerned Abyssinia was preferable to the USA where the emigrants' children were completely americanized. This was due, according to the newspaper, to the higher grades of material civilization in the United States; it was difficult therefore for the American-born offspring of the wealthy emigrants to forsake the benefits of such a civilization in favour of the 'moral Greek

Idea'. Ethiopia was thus preferable to the USA, as 'there was of course no danger of... ethiopisation'.[43] These remarks were valid for the whole Eastern Mediterranean, an area where Greek intellectual superiority and the ability for economic domination was taken for granted. It was certain therefore that in this region the 'moral Greek idea' could not be endangered by the benefits of a non-existent superior materialistic civilization. It was in this context that the majority of the traditional political leadership expounded its views on the matter through the Press and in Parliament. A. Michalakopoulos himself, the Foreign Affairs Secretary in Venizelos Government, asked that the emigration safety valve, as he put it, should be opened. Papanastasiou's indirect approach to this issue was confronted by Sofianopoulos' direct exhortation 'to return to the natural road that our race has trodden from time immemorial and from which the present situation is nothing but a deviation'.[44]

All political party leaders stated clearly their views on this issue during the debate in Parliament in December 1930 on the two Agreements Venizelos and Ataturk had signed the previous October. The importance of emigration for the Greek economy was a common point of departure in all their speeches. 'Greece lives constantly with emigrations' pointed out P. Tsaldaris the leader of Popular Party.

Based on this self-evident and axiomatic state of affairs, the return to Asia Minor was justified not only as a salvaging solution for the Greek economy but also as an answer to the economic problems Turkey itself was facing.

G. Kafandaris, leader of the Progressive Liberal Party, stated categorically during his speech that the acceptance of a returned Greek element in Turkey

> would restore not only the population balance, which was disturbed by the wars, but would become beneficial mainly for the economic life of that country revitalizing its incalculable national wealth which remains dead.[45]

I. Sofianopoulos and A. Mylonas, the two Agrarian leaders echoed the same arguments two years later, in 1932, during another debate in Parliament. Tsaldaris, by that time Prime Minister, also expressed his concurrence with their views.[46]

We notice that the Papanastasiou proposals for free

admission and economic activity in the Balkan countries and more specifically in Turkey were developed in a definitely favourable context. All traditional political parties were in agreement and wished to promote but one issue; a Greek return and eventual economic consolidation in Turkey. This must have been a part of the long term plan of Venizelos when he initiated the Greek-Turkish *rapprochement*. He had of course to stop far short of this, although the ground work had been laid down in the Greek-Turkish Agreements of October 1930. Venizelos was confident, as he pointed out in Parliament, that he would eventually succeed in accomplishing a Greek return following the establishment of close friendly relations with Turkey.[47]

At the end of 1932 there was a brief identity of views between the Greek and Turkish Governments regarding the three basic issues of Balkan Union: the political pact, the Customs Union and the agreement on free admission and economic activity (i.e. the Convention on the personal status of Balkan citizens).

The Tsaldaris Government informed Turkey that it was willing to sign these agreements together and Turkey let it be known it wished this strengthening of bonds, obviously as a counterweight to the re-emergence of the Little Entente and to recent political developments in Europe.[48]

This was the last effort to realise the Balkan Union on a Greek-Turkish axis before the rise of Hitler to power. A direct repercussion of this event on European relations was that the securing of territorial frontiers took precedence over regional economic cooperation. The world economic crisis was gradually beginning to ebb, a development that certainly facilitated this change of emphasis. In Central and South-East Europe this change of direction was immediate. The Little Entente was transformed into a diplomatic federation in February 1933, a development that bore decisively on the ongoing negotiations for Balkan cooperation. The Balkan Conferences initiative was therefore undermined. Yugoslavia, a Little Entente member, was quick to indicate its changed attitude. In March 1933 the President of the Yugoslav Delegation at the Conference declared that the Little Entente showed the way small countries should follow to liberate themselves from Big Power influence. The same month the Turkish Foreign Affairs Secretary pointed out his country's limited interest in the Balkan Conference.

The Bulgarian reaction was that the Little Entente would deliver the death blow to the Balkan Conferences; as a counterweight to Yugoslav and Romanian participation in the Little Entente, discussions were proposed between Bulgaria, Turkey, Greece and Albania for an economic and political agreement.[49] The Tsaldaris government was paying at best lip service to the Balkan Conference and was soon to develop a keen interest and play an active role in the negotiations that led to the formation of the Balkan Entente.

In spite of the still-prevailing confusion, arising from a certain similarity in their titles and the fact that the Balkan Entente succeeded the Balkan Conference, these two initiatives served quite different purposes. The Balkan Conference had as a final aim the creation of a Balkan Federation. Until that noble, albeit utopian, goal should succeed sincere efforts were made to persuade all the Balkan states to agree on a minimum programme that would pave the way to an understanding on the outstanding questions to be settled. The Balkan Conference strove towards a fundamental and comprehensive union of all Balkan peoples in the political, economic, social and intellectual field.

The Balkan Entente was much more limited in scope. It was a political alliance designed mainly to guarantee Balkan frontiers. Aiming at maintaining the post-war *status quo* in the area, it was more than certain — even during the preliminary negotiations — that it would meet with strong reaction from Bulgaria. The Balkan Entente Pact was signed in Athens on February 1934. It stipulated that 'Greece, Yugoslavia, Romania and Turkey guarantee mutually the security of all their Balkan frontiers'.[50] Bulgaria was not included in spite of a series of initial diplomatic niceties. The pact turned out to be, along with the Little Entente, an anti-revisionist instrument.

The exclusion of Bulgaria proved however to be an inherent and in fact inevitable flaw in this pact. Nevertheless at the time of its signature it was considered a triumph for the diplomatic offensive France had mounted to pre-empt any German initiatives in the area. Beneš believed that under the influence of French policy the close relations between the Little Entente and the Balkan Entente would 'furnish one of the new important guarantees of peace'.[51] The Balkan

Entente Pact was indeed favourably received by the signatory countries and by France as was expected. It was in Greece however that very serious objections regarding its ratification were soon expressed by Venizelos. He argued that the pact would lead Greece on a collision course with any Great Power that decided to get openly involved in the Balkans. Such a situation would arise, Venizelos pointed out, in the event of Italy supporting Bulgaria's aggression against Yugoslavia. The heated political debate that followed ended with the unanimous ratification of the Pact by Parliament. Venizelos however succeeded in getting a retraction from the Foreign Affairs Secretary, D. Maximos, on this specific issue. He stated in the Chamber of Deputies that the Balkan Pact's aim was to guarantee the security of Balkan frontiers only in relation to another non-signatory Balkan state. As a result Greece in fulfilling the obligations assumed by the pact could not get involved in war with any Great Power. A similar explanatory statement was issued by the Turkish government.[52] These developments had repercussions on the attitude of Yugoslavia and Romania towards the Balkan Entente. The net result was that the significance of this pact was seriously undermined within months of its signature.

Nor did the Balkan Conference in spite of the considerable progress it had achieved, fare any better. The fourth such conference, held in Thessaloniki in November 1933, was considered as the most successful of these annual meetings. The delegations were moving towards agreement on many important issues. Following protracted negotiations the Conference was finally prepared to examine its constitution. On the economic side progress was much more evident. The approved draft agreement for a regional economic understanding would eventually pave the way for a Balkan Customs Union. Issues of common agricultural policy had been successfully examined. The Conference strongly recommended that the multilateral political pact, already adopted at the 3rd Conference, should be approved by the Balkan states. Even the always dissenting Bulgarian delegation cast its vote in favour of this recommendation;[53] a decision in fact not wholly unexpected as Bulgaria must have felt increasingly isolated by recent developments in the Balkans. The Greek-Turkish Pact of September 14, 1933 guaranteeing the inviolability of their common frontiers had reinforced the friendly relations between the two countries and the negotiations for the four-power Balkan Entente that would exclude Bulgaria had already started.

However in spite of these successes time was running out for the Balkan Conferences. A circular from the Greek Foreign Affairs Secretary, dated December 8, 1933 and addressed to all Greek embassies outlined the new priorities in S.E. Europe following the rise of Hitler to power; it left no room for the peaceful cooperation the Balkan Conferences had been striving to promote for the last four years.[54]

The matter came to a head at the meeting of the Council of the Balkan Conferences in Athens in the Spring of 1934. The Albanian Delegation notified its refusal to attend due to the signing of the Balkan Entente Pact. The Yugoslav group stressed that this pact had completed the work of the Conferences and proposed its postponement. This was also the suggestion of the Bulgarian Delegation but for quite opposite reasons: the Greek-Turkish Pact of September 1933 and the four-power Balkan Entente had undermined the *rapprochement* aimed at by these Conferences. Papanastasiou, the head of the Greek Delegation, insisted that the Balkan Entente Pact was a point of departure for official Balkan cooperation, the work of the Conferences had to be completed. He repeated his plea during the summer of 1934 but to no avail. The Fifth Conference scheduled to meet at Istanbul at the end of that year was postponed indefinitely.[55]

Since the mid 1930s Greece, Turkey, Yugoslavia and Romania, the four Balkan Entente powers, had gradually realised that they were in a serious predicament. In theory they had formed an alliance with the wholehearted support of one European power, namely France. In practice however this political armour, of increasingly dubious importance, had an inherent flaw. The economy of the region as a whole and of each country individually was too dependent on foreign markets to strengthen the resolve of the Balkan Entente powers to safeguard the *status quo* in the area. In order to remedy this situation an Advisory Economic Council was constituted for the progressive coordination of the economic interests of the four member states. Its immediate task was to prepare a report on a) intensification of economic and commercial relations among the signatories, b) development of the means of inter-Balkan communications, c) the possibility of creating a Balkan Bank and d) general tourist traffic.[56]

This decision was however quite contradictory to the economic policy each of these countries was pursuing out of necessity.

By the time these countries formed the Balkan Entente they already had extensive economic relations with Germany, in some cases formalised through clearing agreements. As a result they found themselves faced with an impossible choice: either to embark on the uncertain path of Balkan economic cooperation, fraught with difficulties at a time when the infrastructure to attempt this cooperation was lacking and the European political scene was becoming increasingly volatile; or to succumb to German pressure and further increase their economic relations with that country. The second alternative had a price attached to it: an increasing economic dependence on Germany at a time when they had just formed a political alliance to oppose the territorial revisions this country was so actively supporting. They opted for the second solution, delivering in the process a mortal blow to their political credibility. With short-term tangible advantages it was much easier to justify this decision. Furthermore it was in accordance with the appeasement policy so earnestly practised during the best part of that decade in Europe and across the Atlantic. In mitigation it must be said that the Balkan countries were trying hard to find markets for their products and in this respect both Great Britain and France were not exactly forthcoming.

Apart from hard economic facts there was also a close ideological affinity between Nazi Germany and the regimes in power in all Balkan countries at the time which must have played a part in making these countries more amenable to German economic penetration. The Greek case was the exception that justified the rule. The strong British connection in that country, clearly visible in the second part of the decade, could afford such a regime in power as long as British interests were not endangered. This was clearly but confidentially pointed out by Sir Orme Sargent, Assistant Under-Secretary of State at the Foreign Office at the time, to Lord Bessborough, Chairman of the Council of Foreign Bondholders:

What is required in Greece from the point of view of the British interests is that the Government should be as stable, efficient and honest as governments in Greece can be expected to be, and that its chief or chiefs should set store by the British connection. The present Government possesses more or less these qualifications and though we do not hold a brief for it in so far as it is a dictatorship rather than a parliamentary administration, we have had such disappointing experiences of the latter in Greece from the point of view of British interests that we are not inclined to attach very much value to that particular type of parliamentarism which is traditional in Greece...[57]

In the field of foreign policy, however, the evident reluctance of Great Britain to enter new commitments did not spare Greece the agony of extricating herself, along with other members of the Balkan Entente, from their commitment to abide by a consistent foreign policy directed in fact against the very country on whose economy they were becoming increasingly dependent.

The attempt at Balkan Union in the interwar period had come full circle. The first effort in the early 1920s had envisaged the creation of a South Slav Federation; for almost ten years it was a blend of idealism and economic interests; it then passed through a brief period of political alliance and finally, on the eve of the Second World War, it reached the stage of a diplomatic flurry which was but a face-saving exercise in futility.

NOTES

1. An analysis of this ideological construct has been only recently attempted in historiography. Books and articles examining the issue from this point of view are far from numerous and mainly written in Greek. E. Skopetea, *The 'Model Kingdom' and the Great Idea, Facets of the National Question in Greece* (1830-1880), Thessaloniki 1984, p. 432 (in Greek), is the most comprehensive work on this subject. A. Liakos, *The Italian Unification and the Great Idea*, Athens, Themelio 1985, p. 276 (in Greek). P. Kitromilidis, 'The Greek State as a National Centre' in *Synchrona Themata*, No. 13, December 1981, pp. 61-70 (in Greek). A.I. Panayotopoulos, 'The "Great Idea" and the vision of Eastern Federation: A propos of the views of I. Dragoumis and A. Souliotis-Nicolaidis', in *Balkan Studies*, Vol. 21, No. 2, 1980, pp. 331-365. G. Augustinos, *Consciousness and History: Nationalist Critics of Greek Society 1897-1914, East European Monographs*, Boulder 1977, p. 182. N. Danova, Nacionanijat v'pros v gr'ckite političeski programi prez XIX vek, Sofia 1980. See also A. Bryer, 'The Great Idea', in *History Today*, Vol. XV, No. 3, pp. 159-168. All previous – and numerous – Greek pamphlets, articles, and books referring to this issue were preoccupied, with very few exceptions, in promoting the Great Idea and justify-

ing Greek national claims.
2. In his Constitution, clearly influenced by the Declaration of the Rights of Man and the French Constitution of 1793, Rigas Ferraios from Velestino in Thessaly, the apostle and proto-martyr of Greek Independence urged the creation of a unified Balkan state and made plans for its mode of government. The new State would have a mixed Helleno-Balkan character. Greek language and culture would be predominant, due apparently to the supremacy of the Greek priests, schoolmasters and administrators at the time.
3. In 1844 the Serbian Načertanije was formulated stating the national claims of the country. This officially propounded programme remained secret but influenced the foreign policy of Serbia for decades to come. E. Skopetea, p. 403.
4. David E. Kaiser, *Economic Diplomacy and the Origins of the Second World War*, Princeton U.P., 1980, pp. 44-51; Antoine Fleury, *La penetration allemande au Moyen Orient 1919-1939, Le cas de la Turquie, de l'Iran et de l'Afghanistan*, A.W. Sijthoff-Leiden 1977, pp. 113-126; György Ranki, *Economy and Foreign Policy, the Struggle of the Great Powers for Hegemony in the Danube Valley, 1919-1939*, E. European Monographs, Columbia U.P. 1983, pp. 123-134.
5. Greek Parliament. Debates, Session No. OZ, 9 June 1930, pp. 1816-1819. R.H. Kerner and H.N. Howard, *The Balkan Conferences and the Balkan Entente 1930-1935*, Berkeley 1936 – Greenwood Reprint 1970, pp. 21-31. The most complete account of this subject with a very good bibliography especially on material published at the time. See also the journal *Les Balkans* published by the Papanastasiou group to promote the idea of the Balkan Conferences as well as the aims of the Greek Delegation. For an important collection of basic documents on the Balkan Conferences see A. Papanastasiou, *Vers l'Union Balkanique*, Publications de la Conciliation Internationale, Paris 1934, p. 284.
6. *Le Messager d'Athènes* (in general expressing unofficially the Government's views): 1 June 1930, Venizelos' statement to M. Raditza of the Yugoslav Agence Avala; A. Michalakopoulos' interview and proposals 1, 2, 29 July 1930. See also Venizelos and Michalakopoulos conversations with the British Minister in C1621 and C1121, Greece Annual Reports 1931 and 1932, P. Ramsay to Sir J. Simon. Regarding the assessment of the British Ambassador in Ankara and the views of the Turkish government on Balkan Union see E913 and E222, Turkey Annual Reports 1930 and 1931, Sir G. Clerk to Mr. A. Henderson and Sir J. Simon respectively. On a Venizelos attempt for a wider Balkan Cooperation, based on a *rapprochement* with Bulgaria, see K. Karamanlis, *O Eleutherios Venizelos and our Foreign Relations 1928-1932*, Athens, Euroekdotiki 1986, pp. 128-134 (in Greek).
7. See *inter alia* Archives of the Greek Foreign Ministry (A.G.F.M.) A/3 1930, Michalakopoulos to Papanastasiou, tel. 2793, 30 September 1930. L. Makkas, 'The Balkan Conference and the Bulgarian Torpedo', in *Ergasia*, 4 April 1931, pp. 319-320. A. Papanastasiou, 'The faithful application of the Treaties and the obstacles to *rapprochement* of the Balkan peoples', in *Ergasia*, 17 October 1931, pp. 1097, 1093-1094.
8. A.G.F.M. A/3 1931, Greek Embassy, Sofia to Athens, tel. 1640, 22 April 1931: Sakazov Statement regarding Bulgarian attitude. (Sakazov was the President of the Bulgarian Delegation).
   A.G.F.M. A/3 1931, Greek Embassy, Sofia to Athens, 25 June 1931: Sakazov Statement regarding the 2nd Balkan Conference.
   A.G.F.M. A/3 1931, Greek Embassy, Ankara to Athens, tel. 1961, 3 November 1931.
   A.G.F.M. A/3 1931, Greek Embassy, Rome to Athens, 20 November 1931.

A.G.F.M. A/3/Y 1933, Greek Embassy, Sofia to Athens, No. 1802, 28 February 1933.

A.G.F.M. A/3 1931, Greek Ambassadors in Paris and London to Athens, 3 November and 20 October 1931 respectively.

C10746. F.O. Memorandum, 1 January 1934, 'The Balkans and Turkey 1932-33'. The situation in the Balkans seen from the Foreign Office point of view.

9. M. Dendias, 'The Base and Aims of the Balkan Movement' (in Greek), a series of six articles in *Ergasia*, starting 5 December 1931. L.S. Stavrianos, *Balkan Federation, A History of the Movement towards Balkan Unity in Modern Times*, Northampton 1942, pp. 214-222.
10. Greek Parliament. Debates 1932, Session No. OZ, pp. 1216-1217.
11. Greek Parliament. Proceedings, 5th Session, 12 November 1932, p. 35.
12. *Peitharchia I*, No. 30, 11 May 1930, pp. 2-3 and G. Kafandaris, 'The Balkan Union must be sought on a political basis', pp. 7-8. The two influential weekly journals, *Ergasia* (Work) and *Peitharchia* (Discipline) appearing in the early 1930s represented two opposing factions of the Venizelist party. Leading personalities of the political and intellectual scene frequently contributed articles.
13. A.G.F.M. A/3/XIII 1933, Papanastasiou to Prime Minister Tsaldaris, 7 September 1933; R.H. Kerner and H.N. Howard, pp. 27-29.
14. *Ergasia*, 17 October 1931, pp. 1093-1094 and 7 November 1931, pp. 1178-1179.
15. A.G.F.M. A/3/XIII 1933, Papanastasiou to Tsaldaris, 9 September 1933.
16. A.G.F.M. A/3/V 1933, Papanastasiou to Tsaldaris, Strictly Confidential, 2 May 1933; on the aims of the Greek Delegations in the Balkan Conferences and the attitude of the other delegations.

A.G.F.M. A/3/XIII 1933, Papanastasiou to Tsaldaris, 7, 8, 9 September 1933.

17. K. Svolopoulos, *The Balkan Pact and Greek Foreign Policy 1928-1934*, Estia, Athens n.d., pp. 66-67 (in Greek).
18. *Ergasia*, 13 February 1932, p. 177. C. Evelpidis, *Les états balkaniques*, Paris 1930, pp. 307-308. A. Andreou, *The Foreign Commercial Policy of Greece, 1830-1933*, Athens 1933, pp. 330-335 (in Greek).
19. D. Santis, 'De la collaboration économique des États Balkaniques', Première Conférence Balkanique, Athens 5-12 October 1930. *Documents Officiels*, Athens 1931, pp. 135-147.
20. See *inter alia* Tch. Diourdievitch, 'L'union douanière en tant que solution du problème de l'union balkanique', *Les Balkans*, Vol. 1, No. 8, Mai 1931, pp. 15-18. Cv. Gregorie, 'L'entente économique des États des Balkans, du point de vue industriel', Première Conférence Balkanique, *Documents Officiels*, pp. 164-165. A.G.F.M. A/3 1931, an article in *Politica* of Belgrade, 18 May 1931 in favour of revising the existing Customs regime in the Balkans.
21. The majority of the committee drafting the memorandum on the Balkan economic cooperation are officials of the Ministry of Finance. A.G.F.M. A/3/XIII 1933, in a memorandum evaluating the Draft Plan of a Customs Union, the Ministry of Finance considers the plan as an intelligible and feasible idea. There was a timely interest in the issue of a Balkan Customs Union during this period in Greece too and the relevant bibliography attests to this. See *inter alia*, E. Avèroff, *Union Douanière Balkanique*, Athens 1932.
22. R.H. Kerner and H.N. Howard, pp. 23-25. J.R. Lampe and M.R. Jackson, *Balkan Economic History 1550-1950, From Imperial Borderlands to Developing Nations*, Indiana University Press, Bloomington 1982, pp. 457-

461.
23. Greek imports from the Balkan countries represent 50% of the total Greek imports whereas Greek exports to the Balkans amount only to 10% of total Greek exports. A. Angelopoulos, 'Problems of the Balkan Union. The Economic Preconditions', *Peitharchia I*, No. 51, 5 October 1930, pp. 9-10.
24. Ibid.
25. See the articles on this issue under the revealing title, 'Can our economic slavery in the Balkans be terminated?', in *Ergasia*, February-March 1932. Members of Parliament, the President of the Chamber of Commerce and Industry and leading industrialists from the main sectors of industry expressed their opinion.
26. See *inter alia* A.D. Sideris, 'Les données économiques pour une union balkanique', *Les Balkans*, Vol. 1, October 1930, pp. 10-14. *Peitharchia II*, No. 1, 19 October 1930, pp. 3-5.
27. *Ergasia*, 13 March 1932, pp. 338-339. C. Evelpidis, 'Bloc Danubien on bloc Balkanique?', *Les Balkans*, Vol. II, October-September 1932, pp. 345-347. A.G.F.M. A/3/XIII 1933, Papanastasiou to Tsaldaris, Memorandum, 7 September 1933: '. . . the new Little Entente Pact creates obstacles to the economic rapprochement of the Balkan states we are seeking'.
28. *Nea Politiki*, No. 3, 1 February 1923, pp. 58-61; No. 12, 1 June 1923. The views of Th. Nikoloudis and G. Rallis, No. 13, 15 July 1923. The views of A. Eftaxias. I. Tournakis, 'International Emigratory Movement and Emigratory Policy', Athens 1930 (in Greek).
29. As cited in Ch. Hatziiossif, 'Views on the Viability of Greece and the Role of Industry', in *Papers in Honour of Nikos Svoronos*, 2nd volume, University of Crete 1986, Rethymno, pp. 330-368.
30. E. Venizelos, 'How the Greek problem will be solved', in *Ergasia*, 2 January 1930. In *Proia* of 28 September 1930 Venizelos' speech on his two years of his government.
31. See *inter alia*, 'Materialism and Ideology', in *Proia*, 16 May 1930; 'In Search of the Lost Ideal', in *Peitharchia II*, No. 1, 19 October 1930. 'The Necrosis of Ideals', 'The Ideals of the New Generation', 'Our Postwar Ideals', 'Peace, Materialism, Democracy', all in *Ergasia*, 8 and 22 February, 26 April and 1 March 1930 respectively. In this selective list of articles, on this strongly debated subject, the opposing view to the revival of national ideals is also presented.
32. *Peitharchia II*, No. 7, 30 November, pp. 180-181 and No. 8, 7 December 1930, pp. 205-6. *Ergasia*, 5 April 1930.
33. 'Peace, Materialism, Democracy', in *Ergasia*, 1 March 1930.
34. *Eleftheron Vima*, 14 May 1930.
35. *Proia*, 16 May 1930. Greek Parliament. Proceedings, 22nd Session, 20 December 1930, pp. 493-494.
36. *Eleftheron Vima*, 13 October 1930 and *Tachydromos-Esperini*, 12 October 1930.
37. *Tachydromos-Esperini* and *Vradini*, 13 October 1930.
38. Regarding the opposition to the Venizelos Government of 1928-1932 by many traditional leading members of the Liberal Party see 'The Venizelist Opposition to Venizelos and the bourgeois political re-grouping in the inter war years' by Ch. Hatziiossif in *Venizelism and Bourgeois Modernization*, ed. G. Mavrogordatos and Ch. Hatziiossif, University of Crete Publications, Iraklion, 1988, p. 458 (in Greek).
39. *Peitharchia II*, No. 1, 19 October 1930, p. 6 and pp. 3-4; No. 2, 26 October 1930, pp. 35-36. *Peitharchia I*, No. 32, 25 May 1930, F. Dragoumis, 'The Great Idea and its Successor'.
40. *Ploutos XIII*, No. 20, 9 February 1930, p. 2.

41. K. Athanatos, 'Greece and the Balkans and the Aegean', *Peitharchia I*, No. 31, 18 April 1930.
42. *Proia*, 25, 26, 27 May, 1930.
43. *Proia*, 20 May 1930.
44. I. Sofianopoulos, 'Greece in the Balkans and the Aegean', in *Peitharchia I*, No. 29, 4 May 1930. He had already expressed similar views on this issue. See I. Sofianopoulos, *How I saw the Balkans*, Athens 1927 (in Greek). A. Souliotis-Nikolaides, 'La base et la raison d'une Confédération Balkanique', *Les Balkans*, Vol. II, pp. 25-29.
45. Greek Parliament. Proceedings, 22nd Session, 20 December 1930, p. 474; see also the speech of K. Zavitsianos on this issue, pp. 467-8. This question had already been widely covered in the Press.
46. Ibid., 4th Session, 12 November 1932, pp. 26-28. Greek Parliament. Debates, Session No. E, 12 November 1932, pp. 32-33.
47. Greek Parliament. Proceedings, 22nd Session, 20 December 1930, pp. 490-491.
48. A.G.F.M. A/3/V 1933, Papanastasiou to Foreign Affairs Secretary, Confidential, 2 May 1933. Turkish policy in the Balkans must be seen in conjunction with its parallel preoccupation with the threat to its security by the Italian presence in the Dodecanese Islands. Turkey repeatedly raised the question of a Mediterranean Pact to include France, Britain, Turkey, Yugoslavia, Greece and Italy. Britain however opposed such a plan, in contrast to her keen interest in the conclusion of the Saadabad Pact signed in July 1937 by Iran, Iraq, Afganistan and Turkey. L. Zhivkova, *Anglo-Turkish Relations*, London 1976, pp. 11, 15, 54-55.
49. A.G.F.M. A/3/V, Greek Embassy Belgrade to Athens, No. 2576, 27 March 1933; Greek Embassy Ankara to Athens, tel. 522, 22 March 1933; Greek Embassy Sofia to Athens, No. 1802, February 1933.
A.G.F.M. A/3/XIII, Papanastasiou to Foreign Affairs Secretary, Confidential, 24 November 1933.
50. L.S. Stavrianos, op. cit., p. 240.
51. A.G.F.M. A/3/IX, Greek Ambassador Ankara to Athens, tel. 1809, 21 October 1933.
A.G.F.M. A/3/VI, Greek Embassy Warsaw to Athens, No. 9423, 11 October, 1933.
52. As cited in R.H. Kerner and H.N. Howard, p. 144. On the negotiations leading to the signing of the Balkan Entente Pact see I. Andrikopoulos, *The European Impasse*, Athens n.d. (in Greek), pp. 189-198, 222-231.
53. R.H. Kerner and H.N. Howard, pp. 129-130. K. Svolopoulos, pp. 29-30.
54. A.G.F.M. A/3/IX, The Foreign Affairs Secretary to all Greek Embassies, Confidential, 8 December 1933.
55. A.G.F.M. A/3/8, D. Drossos to Foreign Affairs Secretary, 9 April 1934; Papanastasiou to Foreign Affairs Secretary, 14 August 1934.
56. R.H. Kerner and H.N. Howard, 'The Statutes of the Balkan Entente and of the Advisory Economic Council', pp. 234-237.
57. R7080, Sir Orme Sargent to Lord Bessborough, Strictly Confidential, 29 August 1938.

THE GREEK COMMUNIST PARTY 1941-1945: THE INTERNAL DEBATE ON SEIZING POWER

Pericles Grambas

Editorial Introduction

Of all the aspects of contemporary Greek history dealt with in this volume, the best documented for the English reader is the story of the wartime Resistance. From the British side there are authoritative accounts from the two officers who, in turn, served as Heads of the British (later Allied) Military Mission, Brigadier Myers and Colonel Woodhouse, as well as personal memoirs by other liaison officers. From the Greek side there is an English edition of ELAS *by its commander-in-chief, General Stefanos Sarafis. With so much material available — and analysed in the final paper of our first volume — we have not thought it necessary to go over the same ground. The contributor to this volume, Pericles Grambas, breaks ground which is new in his documented account of the differences within the leadership of the Greek Communist Party (KKE) — the major party in the left-wing EAM Resistance movement — and the way in which these differences resulted in conflicting policies.*

Much recent writing on the Resistance and, in particular, on the largest movement EAM and its military wing ELAS has concentrated on their more distant political aims, so that it is sometimes necessary to be reminded that ELAS was a fighting army whose main objective was to harass the occupying German, Italian and Bulgarian forces and progressively liberate the country. This is all the more necessary since information on the prolonged and successful guerrilla struggle was deliberately suppressed at the time by the British Government and, at its orders, by the BBC. To all who did not have access to inside information, it may come as a surprise to learn that, in its size and effectiveness ELAS came second only to the Yugoslav Partisans among European Resistance forces, with 50,000 men under arms in regular units at Liberation, not counting local reserves, and that it held down seven German divisions and — until their surrender — the 11th Italian Army. By the summer of 1944 it had liberated virtually the whole of mainland Greece. These impressive results were achieved by hundreds of guerrilla actions, gaining in scope as the campaign progressed.

Towards Balkan Resistance movements, Britain had two conflicting policies. Military policy, concerned with defeat of the Axis, needed the strong Left-wing partisan armies. But the Foreign Office looked towards post-war Europe and the British Empire (not realising that the latter was doomed). Here Churchill's obsession with the restoration of the Greek monarchy — heavily compromised by its connivance with the pre-war Metaxas dictatorship — needed some covering pretext. Thus emerged the allegation that EAM and KKE were planning to seize power by force; and the friction between ELAS and British-supported movements of the Right was alleged as evidence of this. It may be noted in passing that the largest of these movements, Napoleon Zervas' EDES, has been shown from German archives and from one of the Nuremberg trials to have had distinctly cosy relations with the German forces based on mutual hostility to ELAS. (See 'Lanz, Zervas and the British Liaison Officers' by Heinz Richter in The South Slav Journal, *Vol. 12, 43-4, 1989.*)

It is this issue of KKE's post-liberation intentions which is examined from their own records by Pericles Grambas who demonstrates the divided counsels which resulted in contradictory and confusing orders and in the remarkably low-key reaction to the events of December 1944, when the leaders of the battle-trained mountain ELAS were not allowed to bring their forces to the aid of the ELAS urban guerrillas facing the Greek Government and British forces in Athens.

We leave readers to draw their own conclusions as to the existence of any co-ordinated policy for the seizure of power.

During the years of resistance, from 1941–44, the Communist Party of Greece (KKE) played a decisive part, giving a lead to the political organizations of the Resistance (EAM) and its military wing ELAS.

Like all Communist parties, KKE took its political line from Moscow, meaning that at the outbreak of war it followed the Popular Front strategies adopted by the Comintern in 1934, which called for alliance with all anti-Fascist forces and support for a 'bourgeois–democratic' transition.

KKE had suffered severely under the Metaxas dictatorship, almost the entire leadership had been imprisoned, and, in illegality, any democratic discussion was made difficult, and necessitated a strict discipline.

Nevertheless, it would be wrong to think that the KKE was as monolithic as it appeared to many at the time. Its leader Zachariadis had been transferred from a Greek prison to Dachau concentration camp in 1941, not to emerge until the end of the war, in May 1945. In his absence, there was scope for conflict in the leadership, with differences which were to affect profoundly the course of events.

On the one hand was a group who had been in prison with Zachariadis at Akronafplia, led by Ioannidis – generally recognized as the spokesman for Zachariadis and the Comintern. On the other hand, the acting General Secretary Siantos came from a very different background. A popular figure, he had been identified as a member of the 'revolutionary left' of the Party. Of the rest of the Politburo, Tzimas and Hajis (later to be General Secretary of EAM) tended to be on Siantos' side, while Roussos and Hajivasiliou took Ioannidis' part. Others took different positions, influenced by the turn of events.

Initially, all shared the view that the decisive force in Greece was the proletariat of Athens and Salonica, and not the peasant guerrilla armies in the mountains. Most of the leadership remained in Athens for the whole of the war, and it was not until 1943 that any of the leaders left for the mountains.

The guerrilla army – ELAS – had been formed by individual activists, setting up small bands and beginning to mobilize the villages in the North of Greece to fight the Germans and Italians. The most famous of the guerrilla leaders, or *kapetanios* as they were called, was Aris Velouchiotis. Characteristically, he held no office in KKE, and had earned the disapproval of the Party for signing a repentance statement while in prison. This was a feature of the political repression started by the Metaxas regime: political prisoners were tortured until they signed a repentance statement which was then posted in their locality. In Greece, a country where the idea of personal honour reigned, the effect was devastating.

In September 1942, when Aris was raising partisan bands in the villages of Roumeli, Ioannidis, in Athens, denounced him as an ultra-revolutionist — and the only Politburo member who favoured the guerrilla struggle at this stage was Siantos. At the underground conference organized by the KKE in Athens in December no delegates from the mountains were invited.

During 1943, the area controlled by EAM/ELAS expanded all over Greece. In the early summer the armed bands of ELAS were formed into a guerrilla army under the command of a professional army officer, Colonel Sarafis. In September, with the collapse of Italy, the Pinerolo Division surrendered their arms to ELAS. Clashes were now common with the British-supported resistance bands of EDES. The leadership of the KKE had to come to some decision on this opening rift between the objectives of EAM and of the British, and for this purpose a conference was called in May 1943. This time there were more military delegates from ELAS including Colonel Papastamatiadis and Major Makridis. At this meeting, Ioannidis, backed by the Politburo argued that ELAS should be put under the command of Allied (i.e. British) GHQ in the Middle East. This would not only resolve the immediate problem but would pave the way for a peaceful transition after the war. Makridis opposed the subordination of ELAS to the British, but the KKE leaders overruled the objections cf the ELAS representatives, and agreement with Allied Military GHQ was duly signed in July. The doctrines that the KKE had adopted, after 1934, of a 'peaceful transition' or 'bourgeois–democratic evolution' were being applied to the Greek situation of 1943, notwithstanding that a growing area of Greece was in the hands of the political and military organization controlled by KKE. The KKE leadership expected their view to be understood and accepted by the British and that the evolution in Greece would be similar to that of France, Belgium and Italy, with Communist participation in government.

To Makridis, Hajis (EAM's General Secretary) and the *kapetanios* — including Aris — who reacted against the Agreement, the Politburo replied that everything had been done for the benefit of national unity, and that Tito was also calling for national unity in Yugoslavia. But what the KKE Politburo had not taken into account was that while national unity was vital for occupied Yugoslavia which had a tradition of problems between its various nationalities, and moreover faced an 'independent' Croatian State, national unity in occupied Greece only meant attempts to bring together two irreconcilable political worlds: the newly created Communist-EAMist one of the 'Mountains' and the traditional one, represented by the Government-in-Exile (Cairo), and by some individual politicians who stayed in Athens during the occupation (Kafantaris, Sofoulis, George Papandreou who later left for Cairo).

Meanwhile, a very different agreement was being negotiated in the mountains — Tito's emissary Tempo had been arguing a 'Yugoslav' solution, and the formation of a joint Command for the guerrilla armies of the Balkans. This proposal was eventually rejected (by EAM), but by this time events had moved on.

Instead, on the initiative of the chief British Liaison Officer, Brigadier Myers, a KKE-EAM delegation was to be flown to Cairo in August. In preparation for this a meeting was held to discuss the political line to be taken with the politicians of the Government-in-Exile.

Siantos argued that the EAM representatives should pose the question of whether the King should be restored to the throne before a plebiscite, and should ask for definite plans concerning the post-war reconstruction of Greece as their basic terms for joining the Government. He added moreover that if these terms were rejected, the delegation should return to Greece without participating in any further discussions. In fact the Cairo delegation was rebuffed and returned empty-handed. The KKE leaders now turned to the alternative strategy of approaching the politicians who had remained in Athens, but the result was the same here as in Cairo. Of this reverse, Hajis later wrote:

> . . . Glinos (Greece's leading Marxist intellectual and politburo member) with whom I carried out the meetings with the old democrats was disappointed.

In the Politburo assembly (October 1943) which discussed the results of our meetings he pointed out that we were simply wasting our time. In fact the latest events had changed Glinos. From supporting a peaceful post-war transition to socialism through the coalition with the 'old parties', he had become a revolutionary hardliner. However, Ioannidis again succeeded in imposing his 'moderate' line for continuation of the talks and Zevgos, although initially agreeing with Glinos, finally compromised: 'all right John', he said, 'let's do what you say. You know best...'

It therefore becomes clear that under Ioannidis' pressure EAM was prohibited from developing a course which could bring it to immediate power. It is true that some of the KKE/EAM leaders would have liked to overthrow the 'old regime' by carrying out a straight-forward Communist takeover. But this was not the official line of the KKE. The latter regarded ELAS as a means of wielding political pressure against Cairo rather than for winning military victory over the 'bourgeois parties'.

By the beginning of 1944 the KKE was still looking for political allies for a 'Government of the mountains', at the same time receiving suggestions from Cairo to participate in a 'Government of National Unity' stationed there. In January 1944 the 10th Plenary meeting of the KKE Central Committee took place in Athens. The introductory speech by Zevgos stated '. . . there are those who are in a hurry to make our party follow the revolutionary enthusiasm of the masses. . . these tendencies have mainly emerged in Greece. . . only with the development of a massive and organized movement in the cities can we lead the national liberation movement of the Greek people. . . the KKE wants the Greeks to be united...'

Siantos — who had come from the mountains — argued the impossibility of an agreement with the traditional parties leading to the formation of a single government either in Greece or Cairo. Instead he favoured the formation of a 'Government of National Liberation' on the part of the EAM alone. Makridis seconded Siantos, and also supported the argument that EAM/ELAS should break with the Allied GHQ and ask the officers of the Allied Military Mission to leave the ELAS territories. He suggested this bearing in mind — from his own point of view — the pro-Zervas intervention of Woodhouse and the other British liaison officers each time

a clash between ELAS and EDES developed. Zevgos and Ioannidis reacted to Makridis' position by characterizing it as 'ultra-revolutionist'. But under the pressure of Siantos some 'advanced' decisions were reached:
1. For the first time the KKE adopted an official position on the constitutional problem, asking for a Plebiscite after liberation as an essential condition for co-operation with the rest of the 'political world'.
2. The public condemnation of the pro-German anti-EAM Security Batallions and eventual punishment of those who had collaborated with the Germans was also imposed as a condition of joining any 'United Government'.
3. The KKE as well as the EAM/ELAS leaders would leave Athens and move to Free Greece.

In March 1944 the PEEA (Provisional Committee for National Liberation) was installed as the Government of Free Greece, with EAM/KKE predominant. In May 1944 the PEEA broadened, swelled by personalities like A. Svolos (a professor of constitutional law) and Angelopoulos (professor of economics), who had centre-left liberal political leanings. Svolos took the post of president of the PEEA; he was determined to influence KKE to accept participation in the government of Cairo, so that a civil war could be avoided.

Almost at the same time as Svolos assumed the presidency of the 'Government of the Mountains', Papandreou — who had recently left Athens — became prime minister of the Government-in-exile.

The traditional 'political world' of Greece had interpreted the formation of a separate government in Greece (one moreover supported by 60,000 armed men) as a mere threat. Therefore Papandreou suggested a meeting between the PEEA and the official government in order to form a united body for administration and political decision-making, as an alternative to PEEA's absolute power. Svolos immediately accepted the proposal, as did Ioannidis on behalf of the KKE. The rest of the KKE Politburo bowed to Ioannidis' opinion. Hajis on behalf of EAM and Makridis for ELAS expressed their mistrust of the 'politicians of Cairo'. Siantos did not react at all, as disagreement on his part would bring KKE into conflict with Svolos. As for Aris, he was sent to the Peloponnese and so away from the decision-making centre of Viniani, central Greece.

The PEEA delegates to the Lebanon conference of May 1944 were appointed: Roussos for the KKE, Porfyrogenis (also a KKE member) for EAM, Svolos, Askoutsis and Angelopoulos for PEEA, and Sarafis as the technical military consultant of the delegation. The terms given to the PEEA delegates were a compromise between the 'moderates' and the 'revolutionists' within the KKE; the former were assisted by Svolos who favoured 'national unity at any cost'.

1. The constitutional problem would be solved after Liberation, by a plebiscite. The King should not return to Greece before this.
2. The PEEA would provide half of the ministers of the Government of National Unity. Svolos would be vice-premier and the PEEA would, among others, receive the ministries of Military Affairs and of the Interior.
3. A unified army would be established, incorporating the Greek armed forces of the Middle East as well as the guerrilla fighters of all Resistance organizations of the Mainland.
4. The 'Security Batallions' would be denounced by the 'Government of National Unity'.

It was hardly likely that the Government-in-exile would accept these conditions, in particular yielding the key positions of the Ministries of War and the Interior. But two events undermined the bargaining power of the EAM/KKE delegation still further. The first, for which they were not responsible but for which they were blamed, was the unsuccessful mutiny of the Greek forces in the Middle East. The second was the disbanding of EKKA and the murder of Psarros. The accusations that arose from these events put the delegation on the defensive. Svolos also brought pressure to bear, threatening to resign if no agreement was reached.

By contrast, PEEA had called a National Congress in the mountains, and here the delegates were demanding the revolutionary seizing — or one might say retention — of power: even the members of the Politburo who were present found it difficult to contest this enthusiasm openly. News of the Lebanon Agreement seemed incomprehensible to the delegates of PEEA, who repudiated the agreement. *Eleftheri Ellada*, the official organ of EAM joined in the attacks on the Government-in-exile, and the KKE organization of Macedonia condemned the Agreement as an act of treason. Meanwhile the party organ *Rizospastis* took a moderate line, and the Athens KKE described the same agreement as 'a great event, very important to the further development of the people's movement'. (*Rizospastis* 25-5-44.) Ioannidis was shocked by the strength of the protests. He was afraid that Svolos might resign from the PEEA, thus initiating a flight of all the centre-left politicians who were currently co-operating with the KKE. This in turn would ruin the line of National Unity and minimize the possibility of a peaceful transition to Liberation.

These arguments were presented by Ioannidis to the Politburo meeting of 26th June, when the question of new instructions to the delegates in the Lebanon had to be settled. Siantos opposed the proposals, but accepted the eventual compromise:

1. PEEA would settle for 5 junior ministries in the Government of National Unity.
2. Trial and punishment of those involved in the Middle East mutiny must be stopped at once.
3. The Security Batallions must be denounced.
4. The constitutional question would be shelved until after the formation of the Government of National Unity.

Papandreou rejected the revised terms and the PEEA delegation returned to Greece in July 1944. Within the KKE two opposed political lines were in conflict: should the Party go it alone, or should it make as many concessions as necessary in order to maintain its participation in the Government of National Unity? In this debate Ioannidis had the support of the non-Communist PEEA members, who favoured participation in the Government at any cost. However, when Hajis was asked to pass the new KKE resolutions of the 26th June to the Central Committee of the EAM he refused to do so, leading to accusations against him for 'infringing party decisions'.

A Plenary Meeting of the Central Committee was now called by the Politburo; it was hoped that the Assembly would solve some of these problems and reach clear decisions on what should be done next. This assembly of the Central Committee took place in Petrilia in Thessaly, the small town where the Headquarters of the KKE Politburo was installed.

It lasted two days, 2nd and 3rd August 1944. During its sessions, the Soviet mission met Ioannidis — for the second time since their arrival in Greece. The ambivalent behaviour of Chernichef during that meeting led Ioannidis to the conclusion that the Soviet Union was not helping Greek Communists in their struggle 'against the political establishment of Greece'. Despite the Soviet intervention, Siantos once more argued against the Lebanon Agreement as a whole, as did V. Bartziotas, the secretary of the Athens KKE organization and a member of the Politburo. Bartziotas had no clear personal opinion on how power in Athens could be seized and he generally followed the directions of the Secretariat of the Politburo (Siantos, Ioannidis, Zevgos). Thus Bartziotas was involved in the internal confusion of his party — during late July Siantos had been instructing him to be ready to take over Athens. During the Assembly of the 2nd-3rd August, Ioannidis argued that the KKE should accept the Lebanon Agreement. Moreover, it should avoid 'revolutionary exercises' and should maintain order in Greece after the withdrawal of the German army which was expected to take place soon. In this way, the Communists would avoid anything that might provoke the British to intervene militarily. This was, according to Ioannidis, how Greece would achieve freedom and independence.

Ioannidis then read to the Central Committee members the decisions of the Politburo of the 26th June about the necessary concessions that would allow participation in the Government of National Unity, stating that these were to be the last, and that the PEEA would insist on the resignation of Papandreou.

The majority of the Central Committee members approved Ioannidis' directives with Siantos openly disagreeing. Maniatis (another KKE cadre and, at that time, secretary of the Party organizations of Roumeli — central Greece) said in his speech that: '. . . anyone who believes that the British will not fight against us is not a Communist. . .' The EAM secretary, Hajis, refusing to pass the new resolutions to the EAM Central Committee, resigned from the secretariat of the EAM. He was replaced by Mitsos Partsalides, another Central Committee member.

The Assembly ended without solving the prevailing problems. The 'moderates' under Ioannidis, backed by

Zevgos, had won for the time being. On the days following the Assembly (5th, 6th, 7th) of August 1944, *Rizospastis* devoted articles to explaining why the KKE should finally accept the Lebanon Agreement while Siantos was sending letters to ELAS *kapetanios*, urging them to be ready for a take-over as soon as specific orders reached their Headquarters. In fact, after August 1944 there was hardly a unified political line within the KKE. Ioannidis was trying to maintain control of events by using the mechanism of the Party, from his position as organizational secretary. Siantos, on the other hand, tried to counteract Ioannidis using his status as the cadre attached to ELAS on the part of KKE. Also, since April 1944 Siantos held the post of Secretary of the Interior in the PEEA government, which enabled him to influence ELAS. On the 21st August 1944 he addressed the following letter to Orestis, *Kapetanios* in Attica-Viotia: '. . . you must adapt your activities to the goal of capturing Athens as soon as you are instructed to do so... the *kapetanios* of your division must be the vanguard in the fight against the Germans and their collaborators. . .' But on 2nd September Ioannidis was instructing Partsalides, now the General Secretary of EAM, to ensure a peaceful transition in Athens. 'The mountain ELAS', he wrote, 'should not enter Athens.'

In late September 1944, the Caserta Agreement between the EAM, PEEA, KKE, EDES, the government-in-exile and the Supreme Allied Commander under General Wilson was signed. Article 1, section C, of the Agreement stated: 'In accordance with the proclamation issued by the Greek Government, the Greek guerrilla leaders declare that they will forbid any attempt by any units under their command to take the law into their own hands. Such action will be treated as a crime and will be punished accordingly.'

Under the Caserta Agreement, General Scobie was appointed Commander-in-Chief of the Greek armed forces, but a statement assigning to him the responsibility for maintaining 'law and order' was removed from the text at the insistence of the PEEA ministers prompted by General Sarafis, who did not want Scobie as Commander-in-Chief but yielded to Zevgos' insistence on this.

The appointment of Colonel Spiliotopoulos as military commander of Athens (a suspected collaborator) was accepted by the EAM delegates. The demand for the resignation of Papandreou was dropped. In this way it was hoped that there would be no British military intervention.

After the signing of the Caserta Agreement, Zevgos paid a short visit to London where he stated in a press conference: '. . . we entered the Government in pursuit of the objectives of a peaceful post-war political life with the participation of every party and of all political persuasions. . . I believe that all patriotic people will work together with the KKE and in accordance with the directions of the Government of National Unity, for the preservation of order. . . and for the normal and democratic development of the country. . .'

The moderates were in the ascendancy, and a peaceful transition with KKE participation now seemed assured. But this line was far from being accepted by the *kapetanios*.

In early October 1944, during the celebrations for the liberation of Lamia, Aris addressed the public gathered outside the local ELAS headquarters. Amongst other things he stated that ELAS would not surrender its arms until the people of Greece became 'rulers in their own country'.

On 6th to 7th October Hajis (now secretary of the KKE organizations of Roumeli) went to Athens as a representative of the 2nd ELAS Division of Attica-Viotia. He met Zevgos and asked for orders about the capturing of Athens, as it was obvious that the Germans would leave the city in a few days time. Hajis brought the following suggestion from Orestis, the *Kapetanios* of the Attica–Viotia forces: if the KKE would allow him to take over Athens before the expected arrival of the British troops, he himself would take full responsibility for his actions, accepting to be judged as in violation of the party line. Zevgos explicitly refused to give such orders and replied that these thoughts should be considered as advocating outright anarchy.

The Germans left Athens on October 12th 1944. There was no attempt on behalf of the EAM/KKE to seize power in the city. The 'Government of National Unity' was officially installed on October 17th.

During that time, the resolution of the KKE Politburo concerning the liberation of the capital was issued to the people of Athens. Among other things, the resolution stated: '. . . the heroic struggle of Athens and Piraeus gave birth and strengthened the ELAS guerrilla fighting. . .' It was of course true that the KKE organizations of Athens had grown strong throughout the Resistance years: from 1,200 members in March 1942 to approximately 150,000 members in September 1944. This was a strong argument in favour of the future development of 'People's Democracy under the leading role of the proletariat of Athens'. In their enthusiasm (caused by the development of the Communist movement in Athens), the Politburo did not see it was actually the initiation of the guerrilla struggle in the mountains and the provinces that had inspired numbers of people in the cities, and not the other way round. Moreover, the Politburo held that if the KKE managed to avoid a civil war and keep the British out of the struggle between the Greek political forces, the party cadres in Athens, Salonica and other cities would develop further and would lead the Greek people to the KKE's idea of 'victory'. The KKE leaders believed that this was much safer than relying upon the 'petty-bourgeois based' ELAS army with the thousands of non-proletarian Resistance fighters of peasant origin. For the time being the KKE had to avoid premature clashes. The same Politburo decision of 17-10-44 continued: '. . . the brave soldiers of our liberal Ally Great Britain will meet the warmest welcome and help from the Greek people. . .'

Exactly one month after the proclamation of the Politburo, Aris called the famous meeting of the *kapetanios* in Lamia (17-11-44). There he suggested that ELAS should remain in being, until a new social regime was established in the country, and that it should not hesitate to fight against the British and the Government forces. These included the Sacred Batallion and the Rimini Brigade which had arrived in Athens on 9th November 1944, as well as the Gendarmerie who now obeyed the 'Government of National Unity'.

The majority of the *kapetanios* who attended the meeting at Lamia, although anxious about the future of ELAS, did not oppose the Politburo line. Most were members of the Party and despite their 'revolutionary' sentiments, could not bring themselves to go against the leadership. Thus Aris remained inactive, unable to decide against the official KKE on his own. Siantos meanwhile had also given up efforts to persuade the Politburo that a more decisive route to the seizure of power could be followed. He kept declaring his disagreements, always adding that he made up the minority of the Politburo so could not influence events.

The 'moderate' line would have remained triumphant if the negotiations between the EAM ministers and Papandreou about the 'National Army' had not brought about a new political crisis in November 1944.

During the last phase of November 1944, the crisis of the disarmament of the guerrilla forces and the formation of the 'National Army' had developed. Consequently, a new evolution started in the KKE. Ioannidis wanted the use of ELAS's military power to exert pressure on Papandreou, thus forcing him to accept EAM terms about disarmament. Siantos on the other hand was expecting a clash with the government troops.

During the night of December 2nd-3rd 1944, the EAM ministers resigned from the Government. Svolos and Tsirimokos, unwilling to participate in the civil war that seemed likely to follow, withdrew to their homes. So the KKE remained the sole political instructor of EAM during the period of the December Events. Moreover, as Ioannidis had gone into hospital some days earlier, Siantos assumed control over the Politburo of the KKE during the first days of December 1944. There was a meeting of the Politburo on November 28th. The decision reached was for the arms '... not to be surrendered without a guarantee'. This guarantee would be the simultaneous disarmament of all the armed forces and the condemnation of the activities of the ultra-right 'X' and the Security Batallions, a guarantee which formed part of the already familiar conditions of EAM/KKE. According to another decision of the same Politburo meeting of the KKE, Zevgos would meet Papandreou so that a political solution to the crisis could be found. The Politburo agreed to meet again if a conflict arose, but it did not decide to initiate an armed struggle.

The demonstration of December 3rd 1944 was in keeping with the KKE doctrine of the vanguard action of the masses of the city. EAM had instructed its members to participate unarmed and demand 'simultaneous disarmament, freedom and democracy' according to the decisions of the KKE Politburo of 28th November. It was a demonstration aimed at a political solution. It is important to realize, however, that the events following the shooting of the EAM demonstrators (attacks against police stations and 'X' camps) were decided by local EAM/ELAS bodies and not by the Central Committee of EAM or KKE. Siantos did not reach a decision about a general confrontation before December 4th, twenty-four hours after the events of 'Bloody Sunday', December 3rd. The KKE as a whole was so confused by the contradictory forecasts about the possibility of civil war that it was unable to influence the development of events. In any case, there was no official military preparation on behalf of the EAM/KKE until the 4th of December. Only Siantos had shown activity by ordering ELAS units of Central Greece to concentrate their attention on taking Athens. (*Letters of September 1944*.) But always, after the intervention of Ioannidis, the final orders to the units concerned were for the maintenance of order and peace. The *kapetanios* — despite any personal preferences — had first and foremost to obey the Party, and consequently the EAM. In this way their confusion between 'loyalty' and 'duty' deprived them of much of their fighting effectiveness and self-confidence.

Late at night on December 3rd 1944, Siantos called a meeting of the Politburo and Central Committee members of the KKE who happened to be in Athens at that time. Roussos, Zevgos, Hajivassiliou and Bartziotas were among the participants (Ioannidis was in hospital). Siantos explained the situation and told the others that they were facing a war. He asked them to take the appropriate measures according to the instructions of the ELAS Central Committee, which, with the approval of the KKE, put forward the following military plan:

1. Reinforcements were to arrive in Athens from Central Greece (Roumeli) as soon as possible. They would consist of the 13th ELAS division. These troops would be the main buffer against the opposing forces in the capital.
2. Athens ELAS (15,000 men, not well armed) would withdraw from the central areas of the city. Together with the divisions of Attica-Viotia (2nd) and of the Peloponnese (3rd) — which were near Athens since December 1st on Siantos' orders — they would clear the suburbs of the 'X' and Security Batallion forces.
3. As soon as the 13th Division arrived, the general attack against Central Athens would develop. The government troops would be attacked and the whole city would be

taken over.
4. The GHQ of ELAS (under Sarafis and Aris) were ordered to disband Zervas' EDES to prevent a 'force of reactionaries' from threatening the rear of ELAS during the operations in Athens.

On December 5th, Siantos telegraphed Bavoudis, a KKE cadre and liaison officer with Moscow, who was active in Sofia: 'we continue struggle. As soon as reinforcements reach us we will clear Athens of Greek fascists, even of the English.'

Under Siantos the KKE seemed to have broken away from the rest of the Greek political world, following the line of a 'revolutionary' way of achieving power. Meanwhile, the Party leaders had moved from Athens to Hasia in Northern Attica, roughly 25 miles away. It was there that Ioannidis joined them after leaving hospital on December 7th, despite his poor state of health. He called a meeting of the Politburo (7-12-44) where he accused Siantos and the others of following ultra-left policies at a time when they should have kept Svolos in active co-operation with EAM and looked for a compromise to end the war.

Siantos disagreed with both these criticisms as well as with Ioannidis' directions: nevertheless, the rest of the Politburo, all of whom had some days ago accepted Siantos' preparations for a general attack, once more changed their minds after the decisive intervention of the organizational secretary. Siantos, angry and disappointed, asked to resign from his responsibilities from both ELAS and KKE. The others refused to discuss the matter.

Thus there was a shift in the policies of the Communists from 7th December onwards, at a time when fighting in the streets of Athens between ELAS and British troops had been going on since December 5th. Despite this, the first orders to reach Athens ELAS on December 7th were for the units not to fight the British but to persuade them to remain neutral. Only in the event of a British attack should the guerrillas defend themselves, without taking any further initiative. The ELAS officers of the units already in Athens and of those approaching the capital – according to Siantos' plans – were prepared for every possibility, when these revised orders reached them on December 7th. At the same time, the previous orders given to the ELAS Divisions all over Greece to be ready to disarm the various British units and

take over cities such as Salonica and Volos, were replaced with others demanding the maintenance of friendly relations with the British forces. Moreover, the reinforcements (13th Division) which were approaching Athens from the north were ordered to stop their advance. The 13th Division remained in Thebes, a town 45 miles away from Athens. As the 'battle of Athens' continued, the intentions of KKE became clearer: on December 12th, General Scobie received ELAS proposals for a cessation of hostilities. They were repeated on December 18th as there was at first no reply. ELAS offered to withdraw from Athens completely if:
1. The Security Batallions were disarmed.
2. The Caserta Agreement was properly applied.
3. The Rimini Brigade and the Sacred Batallion were disarmed, likewise ELAS.
4. The Government of National Unity was re-formed.

Only when the British launched the final attack on the ELAS units fighting in Athens (27-12-44) did the Central Committee of ELAS ask for the help of GHQ. But by now it was too late. On January 7th 1945, ELAS began evacuating Athens pursued by the British troops.

Would the outcome of the December 1944 events have been different if the KKE had carried out Siantos' plans of December 3rd; or would Greece have become a Communist-ruled country if ELAS had been ordered to seize Athens as the Germans left? (October 1944). Any answer to this question (which would also solve the puzzle of which of the post-war military-political camps would Greece join) seems mere speculation. The real fact remains that during the critical period from May to December 1944 the KKE was vacillating between the 'democratic way' of Lebanon and Caserta and the 'revolutionary path of a "Peoples Government"' as demonstrated during the sessions of the 'National Congress of Koryschades' (May 1944). The rivals of EAM/KKE, on the other hand, were united against the left forces, despite their existing differences. Also, what was probably more important, Britain was determined not to allow Greece to secede from its own sphere of influence. Thus, the time and the place of the decisive clash between the political forces in Greece was chosen by the non-Communists, while the KKE remained undecided as to the best way to influence events.

On January 11th 1945, an armistice was signed between

ELAS and General Scobie's forces. The frontier of the ELAS territories was accordingly fixed well away from Athens.

Aris had in the meantime returned from Epirus to Roumeli. In the district of Lamia, he started reorganizing ELAS units which had recently arrived – and were still arriving – from Athens. Makridis, of the GHQ command, was also there. Both he and Aris were in favour of continuing the guerrilla war, this time against the British and the 'puppet' government which was now led by General Plastiras, a politician with a republican background and strong anti-Royalist convictions.

The first *Kapetanios* of ELAS (Aris) and his sub-commander Makridis regarded the armistice of January 1945 as a lever to assist the reorganization of ELAS, for the continuation of the fighting. They believed this to be a realistic aim as the majority of the ELAS forces had remained intact, including of course the mountain ELAS (i.e. the Divisions under the orders of the GHQ which were the most experienced guerrilla forces).

This interpretation of the armistice was not shared by Ioannidis or by other moderates. Hajivasiliou, Tzimas and Bartziotas, who were also present at Trikala – the city where the new Headquarters of the Communist Party was located after the evacuation of Athens – similarly believed that a permanent cessation of hostilities should be achieved as soon as possible. Moreover, on January 15th 1945 a telegram from Tito reached the KKE leadership, advising a compromise instead of continuation of the war. As there was no doubt that this was an initiative from Stalin, Ioannidis sought to put Tito's advice into action. In early February he called a meeting of the Central Committee and Politburo members who were at Trikala. During the meeting there were reactions against Ioannidis' 'compromise' initiatives but the majority of the Communist leaders decided in favour of a quick and permanent agreement with the Government and the British.

Thus the way was clear for the signing of the Varkiza Agreement (February 12th 1945). ELAS surrendered their arms, and KKE their only bargaining card.

BIBLIOGRAPHY

Iatridis, J., *Revolt in Athens. The Greek Communist Second Round, 1944-45*. Princeton University Press, 1972.
KKE, *Episima Kimena*, Athens 1974. (Modern Greek Library, King's College, London).
KKE, *Deka Khronia Agonon, 1935-45*, Athens 1977. (Modern Greek Library, King's College, London).
Sarafis, S., *ELAS: Greek Resistance Army*, Merlin Press, 1980.
Hajis, Th., *I Nikifora Epanastasi pou Hathike*, Athens, 1977.

NOTE

All other references, used for this work, can be found under the title: *The Greek Communist Party, 1941-1945: The Internal Debate On Seizing Power*, School of Slavonic and East European Studies, University of London. (Unpublished M.A. dissertation, submitted by the author in October 1984.) Most of the books used can be found at the Libraries of SEES and King's College (old library) Modern Greek Library.

THE GREEK CIVIL WAR 1946-1949

Christophe Chiclet

For all its drama, the Resistance was a time of exaltation, of hope. The 'little men' acquired stature, the small, the anonymous, attained greatness. During the Civil War men were 'belittled', the great were forced to bow their heads, to become part of an anonymous mass. If, during the Resistance, we, the young, became conscious of our humanity; during the years which followed we were made to drink the poison of inhumanity... During the Resistance there was always a smile. But no-one can speak with humour of the years 1946-1950. The Resistance is a many-coloured picture in which the black harmonises paradoxically with the red, the blue, with all colours. The colour of the Civil War is black.[1]

— *Manolis Anagnostakis*

Editorial Introduction

Effectively, Greece knew only about two months of post-war freedom, from mid-October to the end of November 1944. The clashes of December 1944 between the returned Greek Government supported by the British and the EAM-ELAS Resistance were ended by an armistice in January 1945, followed by the Varkiza Agreement in February. Had the terms of this Agreement been honoured by the Greek Government, political life could have developed normally with the EAM Resistance Movement and the Greek Communist Party (KKE) playing a similar role to that played by the left in France and Italy. What follows is from Christophe Chiclet's book Les Communistes Grecs dans la Guerre, *supplemented from an article by the same author.*

Despite its defeat of February (i.e. Varkiza), KKE had retained considerable influence. In the trade union elections of the first quarter of 1945 it had secured 71% of the 250,000 votes. In pursuance of its new line of 'mass political struggle' it was forming new organisational structures. ERGAS (Antifascist Labour League) appeared as heir to EEAM (Labour National Liberation Front) representing the KKE trend in the General Confederation of Labour under the leadership of Kostas Theos, an old trade union militant, secretary of the GCL in 1929 and Secretary of EEAM. His electoral victory gave him control of the GCL since the 'yellow' trend, led by Fotis Makris, Secretary of the Telephonists' Union under Metaxas, had secured only 21%, with 7.5% for the Socialists and 5% for Dimitris Stratis of EEAM. Thus, EAM represented about 50% of organised Labour. KKE also retained its influence amongst the peasantry through the agricultural co-operatives.

But already there were signs of the Government's intention to reduce this influence. Whilst Tito was forming his own government, demobilised ELAS fighters paraded in Athens, having surrendered their arms but still in uniform and with clenched fist salutes. There were skirmishes with monarchist groups. What the Left would come to know as the White Terror had begun.

This terrorism was now taken over by the Government and for this it needed the endorsement of the British protector. Churchill wrote in his memoirs: 'Czechoslovakia has been engulfed. The Baltic States, Poland, Roumania, and Bulgaria have been reduced to satellite States under totalitarian Communist rule. Austria is denied all settlement. Yugoslavia has broken loose. Greece alone is saved.'[2] It was the Resistance veterans who were made to pay the price of this 'salvation'. Officially they now became 'bandits, EAMO-Bulgarians, anarcho-slavo-communists'. For a time Prime Minister Plastiras, who had been titular head of a Resistance Movement, was able to restrain this drift to persecution. So the British replaced the old Republican by an admiral, who had once been a Republican but had legitimised himself by suppressing the (pro-EAM) Middle East 'mutiny' of April 1944. On 9th April Petros Voulgaris formed a more Right-wing government.

'Monarcho-fascism' began by attacking the weakest and most unpopular. One can use the term 'monarcho-fascism' to designate the conglomeration of right-wing parties whose common factor was their monarchist objective. In fact, the majority of Venizelist Liberals and former Republicans had rallied to George II against communism; and the administration now made use of fascist elements, former followers of Metaxas, extreme royalists and even of collaborators. On 12th and 13th March there were pogroms against the 3-4,000 Albanian Chams who had returned to Epirus when it was liberated by ELAS.

The restrictive Varkiza amnesty had signalled that the hunt was on. The old Liberal Sofoulis began by whitewashing the Security Battalions[3] during the trial of the third collaborationist prime minister, Ioannis Rallis. Those who had collected taxes for the PEEA (Political Committee for National Liberation, the provisional Government of Free Greece) were now accused of theft, the judges of the Popular Justice tribunals of murders and the ELAS commanders of 'moral responsibility' for crimes. On 9th March 1945 two sailors of ELAN, the ELAS navy, Avgeris and Bourdis, and an ELAS man, Michalis Monedas, who had taken part in the battle to save the Piraeus Electricity plant on 12th October 1944 were sentenced to death for killing traitors during the Occupation. They were eventually shot on 10th and 19th June 1947. The newly-recruited police and gendarmerie were ready to leave this job of repression to fascist para-military gangs. Thus, in Thessaly and the Peleponnese, these bands which had acted as auxiliaries of the Germans resumed their work. These were the notorious 'head-hunters' who hunted down resisters wherever EAM was not in a position of strength. It was amongst these that such figures as Sourlas, Tsantoulas, Tambouras and Chavropoulos made names for themselves. Wherever they were in a minority particularly in the towns, the former leaders of ELAS had to go underground. This was the case with Markos Vafiadis and Kikitsas in Salonica. This repression was so extreme that C.M. Woodhouse wrote in his final report: 'In 1944 I saw the freedom of the Greek people endangered by the extreme Left. In 1945 I saw the freedom of the Greek people endangered by the extreme Right. That is why I am against them.'[4]

The non-Communist Left was the first victim of the polarisation of political life. Squeezed between a rampant Right and a maximalist Communist Party it could find no field for political action. The extreme Trotskyist Left — stronger than KKE in 1931, perhaps even in 1934 — had been unable to recover from the persecution it had suffered between 1936 and 1944. Hunted by the police of the dictator Metaxas from 1936 to 1941, the Trotskyists were then singled out by KKE's OPLA.[5] Having had no real participation in the Resistance, they were defined as 'Hitler-Trotskyists' and were pitilessly persecuted... The Socialist Left, though more important and better organised likewise failed completely in its effort to find a third way between Communists and Monarchists. Some having participated in the EAM Resistance and others with the 'nationalists', the socialists could not overcome this awkward legacy, nor could they find an autonomous position in the political landscape. Riven by inconsistencies, they were continually faced with a choice between the two camps: with or against KKE, with or against the Liberal-Populist coalition supported by the Anglo-Americans and supporting the monarchy...

In this group SKELD[6] was certainly the determining factor. Founded in April 1945, it had attracted those political personalities who wanted to leave EAM and distance themselves from KKE after the crisis of December 1944. It incorporated in its 'rag-bag' pro-Trotskyists like Grigoroyannis and Paraskevas, liberal Resistance fellow-travellers of KKE (Ilias Tsirimokos, Alexandros Svolos and Nikolaos Askoutsis), lifelong trade unionists (Dimitris Stratis, Yannis Kalomiris), socialists from SKE[7] (Stratis Someritis) and crypto-communists (Vangelis Machairas and Stavros Kanellopoulos). Strong in its membership in the larger towns and in Central Greece, SKELD could count on known personalities as well as on thousands of activists. But it would be ground down by the civil war, paralysed by its political opportunism and by its factional in-fighting. If, in 1945-46 it represented a real force, it was knocked out by this recurring strife, to end with only 3,500 votes in the parliamentary elections of 1951.

In the winter of 1945 an EAM delegation went round the embassies in Athens to make its complaints. A three-page memorandum was left with the ambassadors of the United Kingdom, the US and France.[8] Tsirimokos handed it in person to Jean Baelen on 16th March. This memorandum demanded the inclusion of EAM in the government, denounced the failure to respect the terms of the Varkiza Agreement (though it was of the essence of this agreement that it had permitted the repression by legalising it). The memorandum signed by Siantos, Partsalidis and Tsirimokos likewise denounced the demotion from their sees of the EAM bishops, Joachim and Antonios, the sacking from the universities of Professors Svolos, Georgalas, Kokkalis, Angelopoulos and Kitsikis and the death sentences on Avgeris, Bourdis and Monedas. But the Soviet diplomatic mission refused to receive the EAM delegation. Stalin held to his agreements.[9] The first effects of this royalist terror found expression in the flight of about 7,000 Greeks, mainly Slavo-Macedonians, into Yugoslavia. Resistance fighters in fear for their lives or wanted by the police crossed the Yugoslav or Albanian frontiers alone or with their families. The north of Greece witnessed a movement of population in all directions.

. . . The Civil War did not begin with a dateable military operation; it imposed itself — or was imposed — on KKE at the 2nd Plenum (February 1946), which is why this gathering has been the source of so much controversy. Zachariadis (the KKE General-Secretary recently returned from Dachau) always proudly claimed paternity. In May 1947, in a memorandum to Stalin, he wrote: 'The Central Committee Plenum finally took decisions which resulted in the organisation of the Greek Democratic Army. . .'[10]

Rizospastis[11] of 17th February 1946 stated the problem clearly. If EAM's demands were not acted upon, KKE would abstain at the forthcoming elections. But Markos and Kikitsas (the guerrilla leaders), in a hurry to organise self-defence groups, did not receive any instructions. This is the ambiguity of the period; Zachariadis was pushing the party towards a test by force but refused to prepare for it. In 1946 he was still hoping to exert pressure on the government by raising the spectre of insurrection.

Meanwhile EAM put into practice the KKE leadership's decisions. Aided by a stepping-up of para-military repression and by the vacillations of the government, EAM succeeded in involving the rest of the Left in the risk of non-participation in the country's political life. Svolos' and Tsirimokos' SKELD, the Left Liberals of General Grigoriadis and Hajibeis, the Progressive Party of the former minister Kafandaris and the Left Democrats of the former minister Sofianopoulos, all called for abstention on the eve of the elections.

On 31st March 1946, 27 parties contested 38 electoral

districts. 1,850,000 voters were registered which corresponded to the figure for 1936,[12] though 200,000 were known to have died. Despite the revision of the lists by AMFOGE;[13] there were more than 100,000 illegal votes. Altogether 1,108,000 voted, implying approximately 740,000 abstentions (40%). The monarchist coalition polled 611,000 votes, *i.e.* 55% and took 206 seats. The centre-right union polled 215,000 votes, *i.e.* 19.5% with 68 seats. The Liberals only 160,000 votes, *i.e.* 15% with 48 seats. Zervas[14] had 6% with 66,000 votes and 20 seats. This gave the King's supporters 80%. The support for the Left, basically for EAM, can be measured by the abstentions. If one subtracts the dead and the vote in those villages controlled by the terror, abstention probably exceeded 40%. Subtracting from this 10% for 'normal' abstention, *e.g.* old age, sickness, absence, EAM could claim to represent 30% of the population. This indicates a drop of at least 10% two years from liberation. Nevertheless, AMFOGE concluded in its report, 'The conduct of the elections was in general free and fair. The final result represents the true and candid verdict of the Greek people... The extent of political abstention was 9.3%.'[15] This fraud left the strong democratic minority at the mercy of the monarchist *revanchists.* In May the French government withdrew its participation from AMFOGE which went on to prepare the referendum for the return of George II in September 1946.

The fuse ignited at the 2nd Plenum in February exploded in the first half of July when a partisan unit attacked and routed a regular army detachment at Kilkis. By August there were already about 4,000 old and new Democratic Army guerrillas in the mountains of Thessaly and Macedonia, subsisting with the assistance of the villagers and by raids on isolated army posts. These autonomous and decentralised groups were under the direction of the local KKE secretaries following the instructions of Zachariadis who, on the principle that 'a good communist must know everything' had decided to base his army on political and not on military cadres. Bartziotas, Vlandas, Goussias, Markos would suddenly become military experts whilst the real strategists: Bakirjis, Makridis, Sarafis were distanced from the second guerrilla war despite the contrary advice of Tito and Enver Hoxha.

The summer of 1946 saw the country plunged even deeper

into poverty and misery. Over 30,000 political prisoners, 1,200 deportees on the islands, 7,000 refugees in Yugoslavia. Government forces of 126,000 (100,000 soldiers, 20,000 gendarmes, 6,000 police), to say nothing of 200 para-military bands of 'head-hunters' and 16,000 British troops, all facing 4,000 guerrillas. Industrial and agricultural production was down 20–50% by comparison with 1940. There was galloping inflation and prices were back at the level of summer 1942. Of 600,000 workers, 300,000 were unemployed and the rest were earning 7–8,000 drachmas a day, the equivalent of 1 oka (1.3 kilograms) of meat. Minor officials were even worse off with 4–5,000 drachmas a day (the equivalent of 2.5 okas of bread). Of 160,000 children examined by the Red Cross, 155,000 were in bad health.

The tragedy now took on an international dimension. On 13th January 1947 the first US Economic Mission, under Paul Porter, arrived in Athens. On the 30th January the UNSCOB (United Nations Security Commission for observing the Balkans) arrived in its turn. This consisted of five communist delegates (a Russian, a Bulgarian, an Albanian, a Yugoslav and a Pole) and six 'Westerners' (an American, an Englishman, a Frenchman, a Belgian, an Australian and a Chinese). Having installed themselves in Athens, they went to inspect the deportation camps on the islands of Aï-Strati, Ikaria and Syros. Taking advantage of their presence, in particular of the 5-member communist element, on the 20th January EAM demanded a truce to hostilities during the enquiry.

But the Government did not see things in the same way, rather the Secret Services were re-organised for greater efficiency. The Greek Section of OSS was absorbed into the Information Centre of the US Embassy which collaborated closely with their British and Greek colleagues, all under the supervision of the Greek–American, Thomas Karamessinis. The army too began to free itself from Government tutelage and to constitute itself an independent and intransigeant power-centre. In January the General Staff had already decided to eliminate KKE. But it had to wait another year for the Government to declare it illegal. On 24th January the Tsaldaris Government fell victim to the intrigues of ministers of the extreme-right and was replaced by the moderate royalist Maximos with a coalition government which, uniting the various right-wing trends, was in a better position to oppose the Democratic Army. The para-military bands of 'head-hunters' were now institutionalised as MAY (Rural Security Units), in other words the Army's peasant reserve. Their task was to inform on the presence of partisans and to stop Democratic Army recruitment in the countryside. At the same time General Rawlings devised a counter-insurgency tactic which has been imitated world-wide, to cut off the rebels from their native environment and their subsistence. He decided to evacuate the mountain villages, turning the guerrilla areas into deserts.

In February, the Democratic Army, now 10,000 strong, became more daring. In the Peloponnese it defeated the second large-scale 'monarcho-fascist' offensive, led by Zervas in person, held Sparta for half a day and liberated 215 prisoners. This renewed offensive was made possible by the reaction of the fraternal parties to Zachariadis' complaints. On 1st February Ioannidis sent the Political Bureau a considerable sum of money from Eastern Europe and from the progressive trades unions of the US and the Communist Parties of France and Britain.

The Political Bureau met in mid-February and decided to make armed struggle the main axis of Party policy. Meanwhile EAM maintained its role as a legalist façade. On the 7th it organised a demonstration for reconciliation in Athens; on the 11th it demanded that UNSCOB organise a truce and on the 17th it published a memorandum signed by Partsalidis (its Secretary-General), Gavriĭlidis (for the Agrarian Party AKE), Michail Kyrkos (Radical Democratic Party) and S. Kritikas (Democratic Union). This memorandum was drawn up by the lawyer Kostas Despotopoulos and translated into French by Octave Merlier, Director of the Athens French Institute. It demanded: recognition and guarantee of Greek neutrality, formation of a democratic government, cessation of hostilities, general amnesty, restoration of democracy and the holding of fresh elections.[16]

Whilst this was going on, the US was preparing to take over. The first direct intervention had come when Paul Porter tried unsuccessfully to re-model the Maximos Government. Two weeks later, on 27th February, Great Britain announced its withdrawal from Greece. Economic crisis and the loss of Empire obliged England to yield her place.

Eleven months of civil war had already produced a heavy reckoning. 13,000 partisans were fighting 150,000 soldiers and gendarmes. The Government forces already had 500 dead, whilst the Democratic Army had only lost 100. The armed struggle had developed rapidly since October 1946, even without total support from KKE. The following testimony of a partisan explains perfectly the increased recruitment to the ranks of the Democratic Army:

> For a whole year I was tortured, imprisoned, persecuted. I gritted my teeth. But eventually I could stand it no longer, I went to the mountains.

Zachariadis continued to use the guerrilla struggle to bring pressure for a change in political conditions. In fact, he could not do otherwise since he did not have a strong enough base to overthrow the Government by force. The failure to organise the armed struggle from July 1946 and the minimal aid received from Eastern Europe during the winter of 1946 caused the eventual defeat. Only massive Soviet aid could have counteracted the false start in summer 1946. But Stalin had other interests and was playing a more subtle game. However, the mere fact of the existence of an armed rebellion, however feeble, was enough to make KKE – and with it the whole of the 'democratic movement' – appear to both the Government and the Americans as a danger which had to be eliminated. Thus the civil war made inevitable the internationalisation of the conflict as demonstrated by the intervention of the UN and the US. The decision for armed struggle cancelled out the movement for reconciliation. Tsaldaris and Maximos no longer gave any weight to EAM's moderate statements.

This ambivalence between EAM's pacific tone and the violent acts of the KKE confused the democratic masses who had accepted KKE influence on a basis of legality. For instance, on the island of Zakynthos there was no civil war because the communists refused to take up arms and the local authorities respected the *status quo* until early 1949. Zachariadis understood perfectly the difficulties of armed struggle, hence his efforts to persuade his allies. But he did not understand that time was working against KKE. The guerrilla war had the opposite effect: the pressure it brought to bear on the State drove the latter towards the Right, not towards the Left.

Nor did the Americans remain inactive. The British Ambassador, Sir Clifford Norton, even suspected them of wanting KKE outlawed. The first US 'military advisers' arrived on 24th May, whilst there were still 15,380 British troops in Greece. International tensions found their voice through the first UNSCOB Group who presented their report on 23rd May, denouncing both the aid given to the Democratic Army by its northern neighbours and the persecution existing in Greece. The Albanian, Bulgarian and Yugoslav delegates resigned from the group; the Soviet and Polish delegates did not sign the report and assigned responsibility for the trouble to the Greek Government. France abstained and Belgium and Columbia (the other participants) expressed reservations. The delegates then returned to Salonica; but Bulgaria closed its frontiers to them.

An increase in legal repression coincided with the arrival of the Americans. On 3rd June Zachariadis was sentenced a third time in absence. On the 7th, National Solidarity (EA, the EAM welfare organisation) was dissolved. On the 12th the General Confederation of Labour suffered a final attack, the US Ambassador McVeagh having pressed Maximos to exclude the communists, the courts appointed a new provisional Executive, diminishing ERGAS participation from a half to a third. The communists refused to participate. Their leaders were soon arrested and in September the GCL was purged of all its Left-wing members. It had taken 14 months to destroy the labour movement. On the 19th, 17 ELAS men were executed for their participation in the December 1944 events.

Whilst neither side could as yet get the better of the other, within KKE the latent discord between Zachariadis and Markos Vafiadis declared itself. On 2nd December the Secretariat of the Political Bureau met and Zachariadis demanded a total break with the ELAS tradition and the formation of a 15,000 man reserve on the Grammos massif as a base for the plan to consolidate dominion over Northern Greece. Markos suggested the opposite: the continuance of guerrilla tactics since a reserve on Grammos would merely constitute an easy target. The Secretariat then insisted on the formation of a bastion on the Vitsi massif. From that

Markos had no difficulty in dissuading them in view of the unfavourable situation. But Zachariadis obstinately returned to his first idea. Markos, the Democratic Army commander, wanting to avoid rupture, consented to the Grammos reserve on the basis of increased recruitment. The politician then told the military man of his intention to establish a Provisional Democratic Government in January 1948. Before leaving for Yugoslavia Zachariadis said this would be done after the liberation of Konitsa, the future capital of a communist Greece. Markos planned the operation for 25th December with the political declaration to follow on the 26th. But Zachariadis, whose habit it was to force hands and to face friends and enemies with *faits accomplis*, stole a march on Democratic Army GHQ. On 24th December Radio Free Greece announced the formation of the Provisional Democratic Government, as follows: Markos Vafiadis (Prime Minister and War Minister), Yannis Ioannidis (Vice-Premier and Interior Minister), Miltiadis Porfyrogenis (Justice Minister), Leonidas Stringos (National Economy and Supply), Dimitris Vlandas (Agriculture), Petros Kokkalis (Health, Education & Social Welfare).

Appointing his opponent head of government was a calculated move by Zachariadis as it gave him an ideal scapegoat in the event of failure. Markos had suggested Ioannidis but Zachariadis had insisted. His own absence from the government put him above the fray and five of the appointments were his loyalists.

Markos announced his programme:
1. The Provisional Democratic Government of Free Greece is convinced that its primary aim is to raise all the people's forces for the liberation of the country from the foreign imperialists. . .
2. Establishment of popular justice.
3. Nationalisation of foreign property and of heavy industry.
4. Agrarian reform.
5. Reconciliation between all Greeks.
6. Re-organisation of the country on a democratic basis.
7. Friendly relations with the People's Democracies.
8. Equal rights for national minorities.
9. Formation of an armed force to resist foreign aggression.
10. Holding of fresh elections.[17]

At the same time the Provisonal Democratic Government published its first Legislative measure:

Article 1. The land belongs to the cultivator.

Article 2. Popular Government must allow each cultivator a minimum holding to support himself and his family...

Article 4. No cultivator may possess a holding more than eight times in excess of the minimum.[18]

50,000 acres were distributed to 3,000 families and a commission was formed to look into the problems of ethnic minorities. But, with the exception of the War Ministry, the rest of the posts were purely titular and did not involve any real work. In fact, this mountain government only controlled a tenth of the territory and a poverty-stricken population of 100–200,000.

On the 25th the Democratic Army launched its major offensive against Konitsa, 20 kilometres from the frontier with Albania. After an initial success the guerrillas came up against the obstinate resistance of the 1,200 defenders and on the 31st they moved out, with 240 dead and about 300 wounded. The defenders had lost 500 but the percentages tell a different story. The Democratic Army had lost 1% of its active strength, the government army 0.3%.

The Government and its US advisers were not rattled. On the day the Provisional Democratic Government was announced they arrested 300 communists in Athens and 70 in the Piraeus. After Partsalidis' escape from Ikaria, Sarafis, Moustérakis (and others) were taken to the Makronisos concentration camp at the end of January 1948. But the most important reaction was the outlawing of KKE and EAM on 27th December when Prime Minister Sofoulis signed Emergency Law No. 509. This law was to remain in force until 23rd September 1974. All the organisations' offices were taken over and their property confiscated.

The year 1947 ended in blood and tears with 30,000 deportees on the islands, including 12,000 soldiers and with 22,000 guerrillas attacking the northern towns, whilst 170,000 government troops exhausted themselves in attempts at encirclement which inevitably closed in upon a void. Already there were 5,000 dead of whom 2,000 were guerrillas. If in 1947 the Democratic Army had been on the increase, in 1948 it attained its zenith. Militarily, the opponents had reached stalemate but the government army was building up its strength and would be in a position to reverse this trend at the end of 1948.

From Spring 1948 the two sides were locked in a life-or-death struggle. A state of siege was proclaimed in Attica, then in the Peloponnese and from 30th October in the whole country.

During this Spring the Democratic Army attained its maximum strength. Despite its heavy reverses, it could boast 28,000 partisans of whom 25% were women. Much more prominent than in ELAS they formed 70% of the auxiliary services; the entire administration, 80% of the medical services, 50% of the telephone network. There were 116 second lieutenants, women's fighting units and mixed brigades. Another feature was the predominance of youth: 80% were between 15 and 25 years old. These adolescents had neither Resistance experience nor political education. The majority of the Democratic Army had not really known the epic days of Aris and Sarafis and saw their struggle as the successor to the Resistance. But neither the aims, the mentality, the context nor the leaders were the same. This was Greece's drama: the flower of her youth died on the peaks of Macedonia or withered in the island concentration camps. This blood-letting would fossilise Greek society for twenty years or more.

At the end of June UNSCOB submitted its final report, still a condemnation of the Democratic Army but without any mention of the Athens Government's provocations against Belgrade, Sofia and Tirana. Markos, who now foresaw eventual defeat, issued appeals for peace. On 31st May, 2nd and 11th June, as prime minister in the Provisional Democratic Government, he proposed negotiations and a start to reconciliation. The Athens Government replied with a new offensive which launched 40,000 troops against the 12,000 guerrillas on Grammos. The much-trumpeted reserve for Salonica, unit 670 of the Democratic Army, was broken from the start. The US made use of this laboratory and on 20th June the Greek guerrillas were the first victims of napalm bombing.

Spring 1948 was marked by the case of the children. This proved of the greatest profit to the US psychological warfare specialists. The Democratic Army had sent a number of children into Eastern Europe. Right-wing propaganda began to cry 'kidnapping' and 'a return of the janissaries'. In fact the US *chargé d'affairs*, Karl Rankin, wrote at the end of March 'This issue can be turned into useful anti-communist propaganda.'[19]

What exactly was all this? Faced with the bombing and the forced evacuation of villages, by all the horrors of war, KKE tried to protect the rising generation. The children of Democratic Army fighters, the orphans of the fallen and those directly in the combat zone were sent across the frontier. In the liberated zone most parents more or less voluntarily registered their children for this journey. On 6th March, the parish priest Gymnopoulos asked the Provisional Democratic Government to collect his little strayed and starving flock. In July 1948 KKE installed the central office of the Committee for Aid to Greek Children in Budapest. 12,000 children left Greece accompanied by one woman for each 25 children. These little war victims were re-grouped in Greek settlements with Greek nurses and teachers. By the end of the year there were 23,700: 10,000 in Yugoslavia, 3,800 in Romania, 3,000 in Hungary, 2,600 in Bulgaria, 2,300 in Czechoslovakia and 2,000 in Albania. If exile, especially after the defeat of 1949, was not a paradise it did at least save 20,000 little Greeks from death by starvation, cold and bullets. At the end of May Markos said in a memorandum that the children had left for safety. The Yugoslav Government noted: 'In Yugoslavia there are no children brought by force, there are only children who have left with their mothers in the face of terror, or orphans, that is children threatened with death by terror, cold and starvation.'[20]

In the West those of good faith said the same. Homer Bigart wrote in the *New York Herald Tribune*: 'This story of the kidnapped children is one of the main pillars of Greek propaganda. The children were not seized by the guerrillas but were sent by their parents to the East for safety.'[21] Kenneth Matthews of the BBC, Miss Levinsohn of the Stockholm Save the Children, Alexander Sheppard, a British Officer attached to UNRRA and Jean Blot of UNSCOB all agreed. But the 'calumny' will spread its poison far into the future.

Whilst napalm was ravaging the summits of Grammos, there was a different explosion within the Communist camp. On 28th June Yugoslavia was expelled from the Cominform.

The repercussions would be as serious as those of the US bombs. Zachariadis relied so completely on supplies from his brother communists that any dissidence in the camp could be fatal for the Democratic Army. He had broken all his bridges one by one and found himself with a regrouped Democratic Army under attack on Grammos and a Provisional Democratic Government totally unrecognised and not even able to ensure supplies of salt! Without any possibility of disengagement, KKE found itself in a tunnel, a victim of the Soviet Union's diplomatic game. In fact the Soviet Union, mobilised for the Berlin blockade, was not ready to keep the promise made to Zachariadis in Moscow in May 1947. US intervention had made things more difficult and the Titoist schism had not helped.

Yet before the second offensive prime minister Tsaldaris tried to negotiate. He sent the American journalist, Homer Bigart, as an emissary to Yugoslavia. On 15th July 1948 Bigart brought a message from Athens suggesting the opening of negotiations with Zachariadis. Markos who had never ceased from his demand that untenable positions be evacuated and for a return to guerrilla warfare, insisted that this last chance be taken to avoid a massacre. The Athens Government, too, was suffering terribly and seemed prepared to make concessions. Zachariadis, haunted by the ghost of Siantos, riposted: 'You are not going to make me negotiate in Varkiza-style, you who are the leader of the Democratic Army. . . I am not going to see this American. Tell him our conditions: we are ready to negotiate if the members of the Greek Government stand trial as war criminals.'[22]

The opposition between Markos and Zachariadis, effective since December 1947, came into the light of day on 21st August 1948. Markos was now one of the 'bad communists'. Unfortunately, the internal dissensions within KKE are still insufficiently known and defective sources permit only hypothesis. When the Democratic Army HQ withdrew temporarily into Albania on 20th-21st August, Zachariadis staged one of his calculated tantrums. He insulted and tried to provoke Markos who remained calm. The whole aim was to get rid of him. Soon afterwards he was ordered not to move to Vitsi but to remain in Albania, to 'rest'. Markos, convinced that the Titoist schism had put paid to the Democratic Army's struggle, complied. Zachariadis had won.

From Tirana Markos was removed to Moscow by the Soviet Mission.

Although the US was putting pressure on Tito, he did not listen to Truman's sirens. The Yugoslavs did not accept their expulsion and still wanted to prove themselves 'good communists' and they hoped to find an ally in KKE. According to a US journalist, Tito continued his aid to the Democratic Army until November 1948[23] and in December 1948 Democratic Army officers visited Belgrade to negotiate for its continuance. Yugoslav support never really ceased: only from Spring 1949 it was put on the 'back burner'. This change in the alignment of forces within the communist camp faced Zachariadis with a choice. He opted for loyalty to the supreme leader and added his voice to the chorus of anti-Titoist abuse from world communism. No doubt this was a difficult choice as is suggested by the 6 months between the Soviet condemnation of Tito and KKE's first anti-Titoist statements and it still took time before calumnies against Belgrade blossomed in the party press and in its leaders' speeches. At first, the condemnation was for internal consumption only, where it provided a theoretical and ideological basis for the elimination of Markos and his friends.

But this obliged KKE to take sides in the Macedonian quarrel. Because it denounced Yugoslavia, it had to align itself with Bulgarian claims. Stalin would thus be able to use both Dimitrov and Zachariadis against Tito on Macedonia. This was why the 5th KKE Plenum (January 1949) revived the old slogan of a united and independent Macedonia.[24] At his trial in 1951 Beloyannis said: 'At the 5th KKE Plenum it was not a question of Macedonian autonomy. . . The resolutions, as pronounced at the time, were intended to check Tito's aspirations with regard to Greek Macedonia.'[25] In order to align itself with the USSR KKE had to commit *hara-kiri* in the cause of Macedonian partition and this gave the Greek Slavo-Macedonians a disproportinate role in the movement. In 1947 the partisans never spoke of Macedonia; in 1949 they spoke of nothing else: even slogans on the walls in Free Greece were in the Slav language. The ELAS veterans, fiercely nationalist, were completely disillusioned; whilst Right-wing propaganda had a field-day: the communist janissaries were preparing to lop off Greek territory in favour of the Bulgarian barbarians. The democratic movement had drawn its strength from outraged national feeling against the German, Italian, British and American Occupations. The Macedonian affair gave it the *coup-de-grâce*. After the removal of Markos, the failure of the attacks on towns, followed by this propaganda on behalf of a miniscule minority, Democratic Army morale was reduced to the lowest level. Militants and sympathisers had lost hope: a black veil covered the future and the process of internal disintegration accelerated.

To give a concrete basis to its new theoretical position, KKE needed the support of Greece's 70,000 Slavs and their organisation NOF (National Liberation Front). But the majority of these favoured the Socialist Republic of Yugoslav Macedonia. Zachariadis therefore had to turn to the few disciplined pro-Bulgarians. The 5th Plenum started by purging the Titoist Slavs from KKE; then it went on to attack NOF and its 10,000 activists. Since NOF was the successor of the (wartime) SNOF of Gotsev and Mitrovski the task was a hard one. NOF held its 2nd Plenum two days after the 5th KKE Plenum. It had to define its position on Zachariadis' new policy and on the Tito–Stalin conflict. Like KKE at the end of 1948, it took no definite stand but temporised for a further two months. Eventually, in accordance with their statutes,[26] the 9-member NOF executive accepted what was on offer to them from KKE: the right to their schools, their press and their churches and they prepared to undertake responsibilities within the Democratic Army and the Provisional Democratic Government (2 ministries). For these Macedonian autonomists it signified a recognition of their rights, their existence and their work since 1944. The frictions and affrays with their Greek comrades in 1944 and 1945 were forgotten. But they, for their part, forgot that this recognition went hand-in-hand with the excommunication of Tito and assent to the Bulgarian position. It took the pro-Bulgarians within NOF just two months to liquidate the pro-Yugoslavs.

The Tito–Stalin schism had provided KKE with an *a posteriori* justification for the elimination of Markos but at the price of resurrecting the old demon of Macedonian independence. By his denunciation of Tito, Zachariadis had cut the umbilical cord of the Democratic Army.

At the start of 1949 the Athens Government resolved to strike a decisive blow. Relying on US support, the Athens generals decided to roll back the Democratic Army towards the North. In January the US Greek steam-roller got under way in the Peloponnese. It would not stop until it reached the Albanian frontier in August. On 28th–29th December 1948 4,500 communists were arrested in the Peloponnese. Thus the 3,500 guerrillas were cut off from their infrastructure. The royalist offensive began. 50,000 troops overwhelmed the *maquis* of Messenia, Laconia and Arcadia. The Democratic Army fought with desperation, isolated from its infrastructure with the countryside and the villages under Greek Army control, it could not re-group. Out of 3,500, 2,000 died, the rest hid as best they could, hunted like wild beasts by the new elite army units. On 25th March the Greek National Day, prime minister Sofoulis announced that the Peloponnese had been cleared of 'bandits'. This final clearance had cost the government only 2,000 men. It was their first big victory after the lamentable failures of 1946, 1947 and 1948.

From 12th–15th February the Democratic Army launched its last grand offensive against a town; 3,500 partisans, led by Goussias, tried in vain to seize Florina. The operation ended in disaster: 700 were killed, that is 20% of those involved and 3% of total strength. These losses were irreplaceable. On 6th March 250 of the Democratic Army's cavalry perished, victims of the theory of liberation of Northern Greece. Guerrilla courage could no longer effectively oppose a modern army.

Parallel with 'monarcho-fascism's' military successes, repression was intensified. Communism must be rooted out and to that end all means were justified. On the night of 1st March 300 prisoners on Makronisos were beaten up with several deaths. The State Department indeed protested to Sofoulis about the executions of Jehovah's Witnesses (for refusing military service), but the communists could die. Paparigas, leader of the General Confederation of Labour 1945–46 was found hanging in his prison cell. Manolis Glezos was sentenced to death a second time despite the intervention of General de Gaulle (though this doubtless helped to save his life). The likes of Grady, Rankin and Van Fleet even rated SKELD, Tsouderos and Sofianopoulos as crypto-communists. On 25th March the *New York Times* headlined: 'Greece is our laboratory for policy towards other nations.' But their quarry was a tough one. At the beginning of April, the

Democratic Army succeeded in re-establishing its control over Grammos.

Having re-asserted his authority over the Democratic Army and over KKE by the demotion of Markos and his friends, Zachariadis re-shuffled his Provisional Democratic Government with Partsalidis as prime minister. As with its predecessor, this second edition had no sort of power.

In 1947–48 the Democratic Army had been led by Zachariadis, Markos and Bartziotas; in 1948–9 by Zachariadis, Bartziotas, Vlandas and Goussias. But this new army was completely different, not only from ELAS but also from the original Democratic Army. The 16,000 men and 7,000 women were organised in 8 divisions, 4 on Grammos-Vitsi, the 7th division in Thrace, the 6th in Eastern Macedonia, the 1st in Thessaly and the 2nd in Roumeli. There were also still a few detachments in Crete. In 1949 recruiting became less and less a voluntary issue and increasingly took on the character of conscription among the villagers of Free Greece. But it was not the strength of the enemy which discouraged the guerrillas. The loss of morale was due to the absence of Markos, Kikitsas and 5 other senior officers and the suicidal strategy of Zachariadis.

On 30th August, at 5 am, Kamenik, the last bastion fell. Grammos returned to its stony silence. 8,000 survivors had fled into Albania. The Democratic Army had lost 1,000 men and women on Grammos, the government army 2,000. Of the 16,000 guerrillas at the start 3,000 were dead, 1,000 prisoners and 11,000 had escaped the massacre, of whom more than a thousand were wandering about on the mountains. Papagos had lost about 5,000, about 2% of his force. But he was happy: he was again a victor. The civil war was at an end militarily and KKE had been defeated.

For KKE the end of 1949 signified defeat and exile. About 2,000 guerrillas were trying to reach the north in small groups. 600, under Giotis and Giouzelis, tried to keep the guerrilla war going in Roumeli and Thessaly. But within 4 months these 'laggards' had either been killed, made prisoner or had gone underground in the larger towns. Despite the broadcast programme 'the fighter's school' transmitted from Eastern Europe and calling for sabotage operations, all military activity had ceased. Only a band of intractables held out on the White Mountains of Crete. Of 25 in 1949, 14 were still holding out symbolically in the 60's. The two last, Spyros Blazakis and Giorgios Tzobanakis, came down only in autumn 1974 after 30 years in the *maquis*.

On the 1st October, the Soviet Union appealed for reconciliation. On 16th October the Provisional Democratic Government announced the cessation of hostilities in order to avoid 'the total destruction of Greece'. Radio Free Greece repeated this on the 20th. On the 27th the last British soldiers left Greece. On 21st December martial law was lifted. In the general melée, the Provisional Democratic Army went into liquidation. But KKE's life continued in exile and in the prisons.

In Albania, Bulgaria and Yugoslavia, the 16,000 guerrillas joined up with the fugitives of 1945-46. But they were not alone. Their families, especially those of activists, of the frontier villagers and a good proportion of the Slavo-Macedonians had followed the retreat. Thus, about 80,000 Greeks had fled their country.

The balance-sheet of the three years' fighting was a heavy one, even heavier if added to that of the Second World War. Greece had to wait till 1951-52 to regain its living standards of 1938 and the 60's to begin its economic take-off. Of the 33 who made the first symbolic attack on Litochoro (in March 1946) 29 were dead in 1949. The Democratic Army had attacked 2,000 villages and 1,500 army advance-posts. 855 acts of railway sabotage and 476 of road sabotage had been carried out. 50 planes had been destroyed.

The Athens Government had spent 8,600 dollars per guerrilla and in 5 years had received 2 billion dollars of aid, 75% from the US. The US had supplied 4,130 armoured cars and planes, 90,000 bombs and 160,000 items of personal arms. KKE had lost 26,000 (20,000 guerrillas and 6,000 who fell before firing squads after trial). 20,000 guerrillas had been taken prisoner. But the Democratic Army had killed 20,000 of its enemies (15,000 soldiers of whom 1,000 were officers, and 5,000 civilians). 30,000 soldiers, including 2,000 officers, had been wounded. 600,000 peasants had migrated to the shanty suburbs of Athens. It was the civil war that made Athens into a huge metropolis. The country had lost approximately 50,000 men and women (the Athens Government reckoned losses at 40,000 and the US at 75,000). To these must be added the 80,000 refugees in

Eastern Europe. The Left had been physically annihilated. The US had lost only 3 officers.

The Greek people were amongst the first victims of the Spheres of Influence policy. By refusing to recognise this reality, KKE had indeed played Russian roulette. Theoretical paralysis, the stifling of KKE's internal political life, the successive purges of 'rightists' and 'leftists', the attempt to adapt to the oscillations of Soviet internal and foreign policy had inevitably led the Party to lose touch with national reality and to isolate itself from the masses exhausted by their sufferings.

The civil war had created a 'lost generation'. The political, ideological and cultural cleavage was exactly that of Spain in 1939.

NOTES

1. Manolis Anagnostakis. Interview. *I Lexi*, 11 January 1982, pp. 55-7.
2. Winston S. Churchill, *The Second World War*, Vol. VI, p. 523.
3. Greek units raised by the collaborationist Rallis Government and armed by the Germans to fight the Resistance.
4. Colonel C.M. Woodhouse, 'History of the Allied Military Mission in Greece, September 1942 to December 1944'. *Rapport au G.H.Q. des forces britanniques en Méditerranée*, 1st semestre 1945, Archives E. Moatsou, Epilogue, p. 8. Since this source is not available in England the quotation has been translated from the French version.
5. Organisation for the Protection of the Popular Struggle. The left-wing Resistance police.
6. Sosialistiko Komma – Elliniki Laiki Dimokratia (Socialist Party – Greek Popular Democracy).
7. Sosialistiko Komma Elladas (Socialist Party of Greece).
8. For English text see EAM White Book, English ed., New York, 1945.
9. The 'percentage agreements' with Churchill at the Moscow Conference.
10. Memorandum of 13th May 1947 to the CPUSSR published in the Greek newspaper, *I Avghi*, 12-13-14 December 1979.
11. KKE's daily newspaper.
12. The last year in which parliamentary elections had been held in Greece.
13. Allied Mission for Observing Greek Elections.
14. Leader of the right-wing wartime Resistance organisation EDES.
15. Report of the Allied Mission for Observing Greek Elections, Athens, 1946, pp. 55 and 63.
16. Memorandum deposé par l' EAM a la Commission d'enquête en Grèce du Conseil de Securité de l'ONU, published February 1947 by French Committee for aid to democratic Greece.
17. *Le Monde*, 27th December 1947.
18. The author's source, *La Voix de la Grèce*, No. 11, 31st March 1949 appears to omit No. 3.
19. Lawrence S. Wittner, *American Intervention in Greece 1943-1949*, 1982, p. 162.
20. Ales Bebler, *La paix en Grèce*, 1948, p. 59.

21. *New York Herald Tribune*, 28th July 1948.
22. Dimitris Gousidis, *Markos Vafiadis – Martyries*, 1983, p. 25.
23. M.S. Handler, *New York Times* correspondent in Belgrade. On 27th October 1948 the Yugoslav delegate to the UN proposed, without success that the Assembly receive a Democratic Army representative.
24. A repetition of the disastrous error of 1924.
25. *Beloyannis: Le procès de la verité*, 1951, p. 99.
26. Article 1. NOF aims to defend the national rights of the Macedonian people within a democratic Greece.

THE EXPERIENCE OF CIVIL WAR IN THE MOUNTAIN VILLAGES OF CENTRAL GREECE

Anna Collard

1. *Introduction*

'I will tell about the time of the *andartiko* (i.e. civil war) when there were many of them in the villages and they burnt our houses. This story that (I) will tell is very sad...'

(village woman)

During a snow storm one day in March 1977 I boarded a converted truck in the town of Karpenisi bound for the village of Agios Vissarios.[1] The village shelters in the foothills of Mount Velouchi — from where the famous resistance leader Aris Velouchiotis took his name[2] — and is some 18 kilometres north-east of Karpenisi by a steeply rising footpath across the mountain. Throughout the winter months the only accessible route is now by vehicle, a tortuous 85 kilometres, and may take up to 5 hours.

A chance remark about the weather to a fellow passenger brought me fact to face with the Greek civil war of 1946–49. 'The weather in Karpenisi,' he remarked, 'is always the worst. I know from when we lived there. That's when I got my bad chest.'

'Living there' referred to the enforced evacuation of all the villages of the province to neighbouring towns during the civil war (1947–50), and the 'bad chest' was the result of a bullet wound.

During my stay in Agios Vissarios over the next two years I was daily reminded of the civil war. It cropped up in every conversation and was talked about as though it had only recently occurred. Mentioning the climate, the local terrain or travelling could mean the weather in 1947 or leaving the village at that time; opinions about other places or other customs might involve a description of how they were during the civil war; attitudes to different people, to friends, relations or to the state or nation, as well as a host of other judgments might be predicated on that period as naturally as on anything else or on anything more recent. Gradually the picture of a catastrophic and tragically formative past in the lives of these people emerged.

Agios Vissarios is one among a group of villages which lie deep in the very centre of mainland Greece in the province of Evritania. They are unknown to most foreign visitors who are more familiar with the Greece of the Aegean islands or that of a classical past. Equally unfamiliar to most tourists is their 'sad story' of civil war following the country's involvement in the Second World War and consequent German occupation (1941-44). Yet this history is shared in different ways by the whole of Greece, has had profound effects on its development and continues to find resonances in everyday, contemporary life.

Here I wish to describe the burden of this past on a small group of mountain villages. My intention is to illustrate what the civil war meant to a number of peasant men and women and how they remember it today, forty years later.[3] In doing so I hope to show why the civil war is so central to understanding such villages today and how, as a result, it underlies the identity of modern Greece as a whole.

2. 'Agrafa': A Spirit of Resistance

> I will not become a *raya*, I will not salute a Turk.
> I will not respect the *archons*, nor the *kocabases*.
> I will only wait for Spring, for the swallows to arrive,
> for the shepherds to appear on the mountains, for the
> shepherdesses to return...[4]
>
> (Greek demotic song 1804)

In so far as they remain outside the main tourist trail, the villages of Evritania are distinctive. They are also in many ways historically unique. In order to fully understand the impact of the civil war on these villages it is worth giving a brief outline of their history.

Throughout the Ottoman era (1453-1821),[5] and probably

before, the whole area of which these villages are part, was known as *Agrafa*, which literally means 'unwritten'. With its 'veritable labyrinth of peaks, ravines, valleys and forests'[6] it was difficult to penetrate and it remained uncharted territory. Even today access to some of its villages is limited. Many are only reached by footpath and others have only the crudest of dirt-tracks leading to them. Partly because of this inaccessibility and the traditional reputation of its inhabitants as being 'wild' and 'ungovernable' *Agrafa* was never successfully controlled by the Ottoman Turks.

As a result the area developed some form of semi-autonomy and self-government, including systems of local arbitration and its own militias, or armed bands.[7] These were finally formalised into privileges by Treaty with the Ottoman Turks in 1525.[8]

By the early 19th century the local economy which provided an important support to the administrative and military autonomy of the area was well developed and still thriving.[9] Under these conditions *Agrafa* also became a centre of learning and various Greek schools were set up with the help of the Orthodox Church. In general the area became a refuge for Greeks fleeing the Turks and as such was able to play an important role in the Greek War of Independence (1821–28), nurturing freedom fighters (*klephts*) and supporting their fighting formations.

Even after the War of Independence *Agrafa* retained some of its autonomy though it was increasingly incorporated into the developing nation-state. The hundred years following Greek independence eroded much of this autonomy and saw the collapse of the local economy. During this period Greece was involved in almost continuous internal and external conflicts and by the 1920s the nation was virtually bankrupt. Finally, in 1936 following further economic and political upheaval, General Metaxas established his dictatorship.[10] These conditions led, among other things, to widescale emigration and added to the deteriorating position of peasants all over Greece.

Agios Vissarios, like many other villages in the province of Evritania, held on to the vestiges of its traditional self-rule which had characterised it when it was part of *Agrafa*. Notably, and as late as the 1930s, some of these villages engaged in a final struggle with the state to retain some of their autonomy and overcome certain economic, political and even legal obstacles. In the broadest sense the activities which took place in Agios Vissarios and the surrounding communities during the 1930s, also reflect the search for new directions and the attempts to set up a different kind of relationship with the state as well as reflecting an earlier history of self-government. Peasants all over Greece were involved in similar struggles during this period which in particular revolved around demands for radical land reforms and the distribution of the old Ottoman estates.

On the 23rd July 1933 a society called FED (*Filoproödos Enosis Karoplesi*) — the 'Karoplesi Union of the Friends of Progress', was founded in a small village north-east of Agios Vissarios. The main aim of the society was to encourage its members and the community as a whole to protect and develop the forests in the area and to 'cultivate the green and the beautiful in general'.[11] Its programme, however, included a range of other schemes which touched on issues such as the development of the local economy. It concluded by suggesting that the whole legal system was unsatisfactory and rarely solved the many problems brought to the courts by the local peasantry.

This was the point of departure for a movement that spread throughout the province. Many villages began to set up local committees in an attempt to solve some of their more pressing problems. Mass meetings were held in different villages and petitions sent to the government demanding various rights. Societies formed themselves proposing schemes for the development of the province as a whole, and groups were elected to carry out various administrative tasks. All these finally came together in August 1936 when a 'Pan-Evritanian Congress' took place in Karpenisi.

By this time arbitration committees had been formed and local courts were functioning in many villages. Finally, in May 1936 a local paper, 'The Voice of Evritania' (*'I Foni tis Evritanias'*), was set up. It too addressed itself to the local problems, reported on the many activities described above, offered solutions and relentlessly petitioned the government — suffering various closures as a result. In April 1941 its press was given to the anti-German resistance organisation EAM (National Liberation Front).[12] These activities contributed to forming the basis for the 'institutions of self-government and popular justice' which emerged during the German occupation and were developed and applied by EAM, and its military wing ELAS (Greek National Liberation Army), in all the free or liberated areas of Greece.[13]

Again, partly because of its inaccessibility, Evritania was never actually occupied by the Germans who remained a relatively distant threat for many of the villages.[14] The area became an important centre for the anti-German resistance movement — especially for EAM-ELAS — though other smaller resistance groups were formed in and around it. As such it was not only important in military and tactical terms but the administrative policies of EAM were developed and put into practice here for the first time. Agios Vissarios itself was the seat of the first general headquarters of ELAS. Set up on 25th May 1943 its GHQ officially began to function and issued its first orders from here.[15] As one woman remembered,

> ... they appropriated my house, they took it for themselves to be their headquarters. Yes, I met them all, Sarafis the General, Aris, that boy from Lamia, all of them passed through this very house and the British too. I knew them all...

On 10th March 1944 the Political Committee of National Liberation (PEEA) was created by EAM and in the following May, this first 'government of the mountains' met in a small village just south of Karpenisi. It aimed to organise and direct the struggle for liberation on a national level, to administer the regions already freed and, importantly, to ensure that post-war Greece would be governed by a real Democracy.[16]

All these factors had far reaching consequences for the area. Firstly, the fact of being part of free Greece and largely under the control of EAM-ELAS had profound effects on rural life. Even those unsympathetic to the general aims of EAM are agreed that there were large-scale changes,

> The benefits of civilisation and culture trickled into the mountains for the first time. Schools, local government, law-courts and public utilities, which the war had ended, worked again. Theatres, factories, parliamentary assemblies began for the first time. Communal life was organised in place of the traditional individualism of the Greek peasant... EAM/ELAS set the pace in the creation of something that Governments of Greece had neglected: an organised state in the Greek mountains.[17]

Secondly, all the villagers – whether actively or passively, negatively or positively – were involved at least with the administrative policies of EAM if not recruited to its ranks or those of ELAS as fighting people. Finally, exactly because of this widescale involvement with the resistance forces of EAM-ELAS, the effects of the civil war were bitterly felt.

In February 1945, ELAS was demobilised (under the Varkiza Agreement), and by March fighting between left and right-wing armed groups, combined with raids on villages and vendetta killings were already common in these mountain parts. By the summer the 'white terror' had assumed enormous proportions and the Right in general had succeeded in wresting control of many villages with the aid of irregular right-wing bands who were often no more than outlawed brigands.

By and large the agents of the 'white terror' were drawn from the National Guard, different nationalist organisations (the most infamous of which was the 'X'), and bandit gangs.[18] By the end of 1945 these had been co-ordinated on a national level. They formed in effect a paramilitary state within a state (the *parakratos*) which under the ensuing post-war governments was in place to exercise unprecedented power over the whole of Greece.[19] Apart from these bands who now terrorised the villagers, Karpenisi also became the scene of bitter fighting between the National Army and the Democratic Army.[20] Later, with evacuated refugees in the middle, the Democratic Army held the town in 1948 and again for eighteen days in 1949. It was finally defeated there and disappeared into the mountains on 8th February 1949 leaving government forces holding Karpenisi.

By 1947 many villagers previously sympathetic to EAM were forced to serve in the National Regular Army, while others joined or, particularly women, were pressed into the Democratic Army. Yet others who had simply lived under EAM administration in their villages or had been involved in – or elected to serve in – the institutions of self-government, not only lived in terror of reprisals but found they were suddenly discredited or forbidden to mention their previous involvements. Similarly those who had served as popular magistrates – or especially those who had been tried – in the popular courts were encouraged to condemn them as illegal. Gradually the whole resistance organisation of EAM-ELAS was thrown open to doubt and discredited as being 'anti-Greek' and 'unpatriotic'.

In 1947 the Government evacuated the remaining inhabitants of the mountain villages. The action was explicitly aimed at denying possible recruits, supplies and information to the forces of the Left. The National Army continued to burn, loot and destroy houses and fields adding to the already existing devastation of the villages. One man remembered,

> I was doing my national service. I had been called up because I was of age. I remember we came near here to the village of S. . . . . We helped the families leave for fear of the *andartes* (i.e. partisans of the Democratic Army), those bandits. Then they (the officers in charge of the informant) made us set light to the fields, the fruit trees, the crops that were so high. . . my heart cried to see it, the trees of our grandfathers and the work that had gone into the fields. . . that's why afterwards I went far away from here (i.e. to America).

In this historical context, the name *Agrafa* has assumed wider connotations. It is still invoked as a source of pride to underline a sense of defiance to government, or a spirit of resistance to hostile forces. 'No-one sits on our heads for long up here!', people claim. At the same time, and as a direct result of the civil war which contributed to leaving the area undeveloped, the word is used as a term of defeat, a way of stressing a sense of isolation from the modern developing world. 'Ah! what do you expect in *Agrafa*? Here we are *agrafiotes*, nothing anymore – people have passed us by!', others lament.

3. *The Civil War: History Truncated*

> Why are the mountains black? Why are they filled with tears?
> Has the wind made war with them? Have the rains beaten them?. . .
> No, it is Charon who has passed through with the dead.
> Taking the young ones by the hair, the old ones by the hand,
> the little ones he grabs and hangs about his saddle. . .
>
> (Greek demotic song)

The civil war fractured the more or less continuous history of the mountain villages of Evritania. It put an end to the possibility of any such experimental forms of local self-government occurring for many years to come. The result, in Agios Vissarios and neighbouring communities was that none of the problems so vociferously tackled during the 1930s were again broached. At the same time, the civil war brought about a profound transformation of village life within a few years and for most people marked the abrupt end of an era. Thereafter these villages fell into rapid decline.

This break in continuity manifested itself at every level, demographically, topographically, in agriculture, politically and in social relations as a whole. The human death toll, evacuation from the villages (because many people never returned to them again afterwards) and increased migration from the area for direct political reasons, not to mention those imprisoned and in concentration camps, extensively depopulated the whole area. The widescale destruction of houses, fields and forests (as well as livestock), changed the villages physically. New houses — often temporary and unsuitable shacks — had to be built on different sites; nearly all the fields beyond the immediate periphery of the villages were abandoned forever. Some of the pre-war problems of land shortages were eased but this was matched by the loss of working hands.

Norms and expectations were fundamentally affected and as familiar categories of behaviour could no longer be used it became difficult to judge another's actions. The situation was expressed by an old woman describing her return to Agios Vissarios in 1950,

> Nothing was the same anymore, there were houses burnt and others without their roofs. . . There were grasses and weeds growing everywhere, out of the cracks in the walls, right up to the doors, from inside the windows. It was so high where there should have been paths, and all over the square. . . then I noticed them, wild cats. There were wild cats everywhere!. . . We saw people we knew, neighbours we'd come with but grew afraid of them. You could never tell anymore, who belonged to whom. Each family kept its secrets to itself. That was the worst, not knowing anymore.

There were numerous direct affects on the local economy. In Agios Vissarios the growing of chestnuts had to be intensified to become a cash crop after 1950. The production of cereals, pulses on a large scale, or fruit was abandoned, as were shepherding in general and its related activities such as cheese-making and weaving. The loss of labour and the increased production of a single crop undercut much of the self-sufficiency these villages might have had. Consequently there was an increased dependence on foreign remittances and on state subsidies of every kind. Such changes in production also meant the loss of co-operative agricultural practices and customs which in the past had contributed to creating a sense of community. Today the villages are, by any standards, desperately impoverished. They survive on foreign remittances (which are themselves subject to the vicissitudes of foreign markets), on subsistence agriculture and on their dreams of 'getting out of the village'. It is the old and the sick who are forced to remain.

The most notable change in political life after the civil war was the persecution and prohibition of any left-wing or progressive party in Greece. The way in which the civil war was subsequently interpreted by the dominant, right-wing Establishment which came to power in 1952, influenced all political life. In villages like Agios Vissarios there were corresponding changes in the power structure. The national formation of the paramilitary civil guard (TEA) with its locally appointed members played a role in this. Constituting a permanent barrier to the penetration of any non-conformist or even mildly critical thinking — let alone leftist views — they assisted in preventing the development of any alternate local power bases. Families who before the war had played little part in village politics now became more powerful under the auspices of the ever-watchful state. Field and forest guards were centrally appointed and assumed a direct political role in the villages as 'informers' and were no longer accountable in any way to the inhabitants whose fields they ostensibly guarded. To be counted as a 'Communist' — which was very broadly defined — meant, among other things, the forfeiting of agricultural insurance and pension rights or of government loans. It also meant that one could not obtain the 'certificate of national probity' which was necessary for state employment and higher education, for acquiring a passport or even a hunting permit.

The rights that had been fought for during the 1930s, many of which had been acquired under the later system of self-government of EAM during the occupation period, were again lost. The plans for land reforms in the province, for agricultural improvements, for the development of light industry and forestry, for a review of the legal system, all these were shelved and women returned to their homes again without the vote.[21]

The civil war put an end to the relative autonomy of these villages. Some benefits did come to them after the civil war: roads were built, electricity and the telephone were installed (though many of the villages in the province are still without any of these) and primary education was improved. With these benefits came an increasing dependence on the state or at least on securing the favours of acceptable 'patrons' who had some influence in the workings of the state.

Attitudes to 'government', therefore, which up to the civil war had been largely those of antagonism, anger and resistance, changed into those of dependence, resignation and fear. The new awareness and different ambitions fostered by the civil war undercut the sense of community as it led to the rejection of 'village life' and increased emigration.

4. *Evacuation 1947–50: The Break Up of the Community*

> I had an apple-tree in the yard, a roof as red as cherries on the house;
> a cypress by the gate and a silver lamp hanging in the doorway.
> And now the apple-tree has withered and the cypress lost its roots
> and the roof as red as cherries, it has blackened too,
> and the lamp of silver's darkened and the house no longer shines
>
> (Greek demotic song)

For villagers all over Greece, a major event of the civil war was the enforced evacuation from their homes. Today, in Agios Vissarios they return to this single event again and again,

> ... the *andartiko* (i.e. civil war), the bandit war, came upon us in 1947 and we left, we were exiled. I went to Lamia and spent three years there. 1950 we came back... everyone left. They collected in the centres, in the central cities...
>
> (village man)

> It was July when we left. Our men (National Army) were already in Karpenisi and had arranged with the Nomarch, who knows with whom else, to come and take us from our villages. And we went together women and children from place to place hiding from them (groups of Left and Right). I took the two girls and two goats, that's all. Not that we ate anything of the goats because they

(National Army) took our food from us in Karpenisi and whatever else they (National Army and Red Cross officials) could find in the shops.

(village woman)

Many had already left their villages by 1947, out of fear of the 'white terror' or reprisals from the forces of the Left.

I was a girl then and with two other girls I had to flee and we went as far as Epirus... we went from village to village to Karpenisi and then up north to Epirus. We tried to flee the Communists but they caught us and took us north. We managed to escape them and gave ourselves up to the soldiers for protection... I was so frightened when they (Democratic Army) took us because I had a photograph of my brother in my pocket who was a policeman in Lamia.

Others had left under instruction from their husbands or co-villagers,

I was hanging the washing on the line. There were clothes still soaking in the tub and they (partisans) passed. My two girls were in the house. It was the first days of October in the year 1946... I was washing the clothes in the yard... and my husband passed with the others on the path above the house. When he saw me washing he came down (and said), wife are you still here? you must go quickly, go to the town this very night, there is danger here the 'X's' are coming... and then he went as quickly as he had come. What was I to do with the washing still wet and even my shoes not dry? I didn't have another pair. Then some women passed and told me the same, their husbands had passed. Take the children and go to the town, but not through the valley they said.

(village woman)

Evacuation meant that the actual physical continuity of these villages was broken for the first time since their settlement hundreds of years before.

We left (Agios Vissarios) with nothing. In the village of D..... they ('X's') had even executed 40 people. And the maize and the corn a few feet high and soon ready to be cut and when we returned everything was overgrown and everything destroyed, no village anymore...

(village woman)

... we came back and found the bushes as tall as the houses. Other branches inside and others (i.e. houses) burnt and gutted and only cats everywhere... the end of the village. No-one to know anymore... (village woman)

The break up of the village had a variety of consequences. The social community was dispersed and all forms of social reckoning — a whole body of knowledge in one sense — were rendered meaningless. Thus, for example, commonly held values and criteria for judging everyday events and behaviour were made inappropriate when removed suddenly from the boundaries of the community to which they referred.

This sense of 'inappropriateness' was expressed in a more light-hearted way by a woman describing the attempts of the Democratic Army to recruit her daughters to its ranks. For her this contravened a moral code which went against her idea of how women should behave in the village.

> Some girls went, some even wanted to, whoever heard of such a thing! Not mine, I told them, you want to make whores of them? I told them straight. And tell me how will they sleep, cold under the trees at night when the wolves might come and who knows what other mischief? And them so far from their home and mother. What do they know of such things? I asked them, and they not married yet. . . But they got others from the village. . . they put pants on the women, the shame of it! like men they made them and gave them guns to hold and they not knowing to write their names even, and anyone could deceive them for their lack of cunning!

(This, despite the fact that her husband had been a partisan and the whole family sympathetic to the Democratic Army.)

As refugees the villagers had to forgo nearly everything they owned, and most importantly, their means of livelihood. This only added to an already critical economic situation as foreign remittances had come to an abrupt end in 1941 with Greece's entry into the war, and by 1945 there were also many unemployed ex-partisans back in the villages. The loss of property, of all one's possessions and the social implications of this as well as the economic ones, is a theme which is constantly repeated in the vivid descriptions of leaving the village,

> . . . so I left the washing there and even my shoes. . . and I took the children and a blanket for the little one. Nothing else. I left everything. All we had in the house as it was, not a single needle with me. Nothing. I carried the little one strapped to my back like a sack of corn, the other walked by my side. And I had no shoes even because they were wet and not ready to wear. (village woman)

... I had the girls' trousseaux in the chest behind the door, we had to leave it all, the embroidered sheets, the woven rugs, the silk my husband had brought back from America. Everything in its place and the girls not wed yet! The Relief (Red Cross) in the town gave us packets later: two sheets and a pillowcase for the girls still unmarried. What is the good of it? I told them, who will marry them now? Where will they get a dowry from?

(village woman)

In this situation one or two were able to be a little more enterprising,

I don't remember when it was — only I know it was then when the *andartiko* happened and we went to Karpenisi and they (partisans) killed my husband (in fact he was killed in the crossfire between the National and Democratic Armies)... we bundled everything up and we went. I even took my loom. All the trousseaux of the girls, and me and my loom. And I set it up there where we stayed for three years and I wove for the neighbourhood. They saw what I made and I couldn't escape: you'll make me one!, you'll make one for me! I made things for everyone. I wove for the people for as much as they had...

(village woman)

For most, however, evacuation meant the loss and destruction of a whole way of life.

The following woman, who was eighteen when she left the village, sums up the actual evacuation, the sense of dislocation as well as her own spirit of defiance,

They came in the morning and took me and my mule... and they (National Army) said to the other ones (also soldiers) tie this one up well she has many things in her house and she will try to escape. You can tie me up if you like, I said, but I won't go with the others. I want to go to my house, I have bread ready to bake. No, they said, no bread and the house is closed, there's nothing left. All right then, I said, and they took me to the square. And there was a little girl, 15 years old... they had all the things from her house, the goats, the mattresses, the radio, everything from her house had been brought there and the girl was crying saying, Mother help me!... I said to her, quiet! they'll kill us all but she was crying... Then a partisan (soldier in fact) came and threw us bread, my bread which I had left on the fire to bake. They threw me some too but I left it... At last they said to us, go now! you'll go to Karpenisi or Lamia, wherever, you must go from here. As we passed our houses we saw all our things thrown out. One granny took a coat as she passed and she was crying... Altogether we were three, my mother, myself and that granny, and about twenty families from here. We set off and they (soldiers) took us as far as the ridge. I didn't say a word but in the morning I said I'm not going to Karpenisi with the others, I'm going to Lamia... so we left without shoes... we left and the old women were crying.

For many of the villagers one of the worst aspects was how, during the civil war, disputes and social relations in general often assumed national political significance in which, however unwittingly, few could remain neutral.

> People used the civil war to fight out personal animosities and hostilities, that was the worst. People who didn't like each other before or had some long standing complaint or quarrel with one another, used this as a basis for killing and fighting each other.
>
> (village man)

At a funeral wake in October 1978, a group of older women started to recall such events, how families had been destroyed and how relationships with anyone could become politically dangerous.

One woman told in lurid detail of how the younger son of a family known to her had killed his sleeping brother because he was 'on the other side', but how they had also fought for years about the family inheritance. Another told about a girl who had joined the Democratic Army and fought her brothers serving in the National Army. They had refused to acknowledge her ever since. A third remembered a neighbour's son who had been called up to serve in the National Army but had school friends with the Democratic Army. He had met up with one, tried to help him and finally endangered both his own and his friend's life.

It was not surprising that the civil war had spontaneously become the topic of conversation at the funeral wake, it entered most discussions and any death in the community triggered the memory of those earlier losses. What was remarkable in this gathering of women was that their political backgrounds were very different and some had not spoken to each other for many years. Indeed, there was one woman present who had not been to the village since the civil war. The discussion was possible, partly because none of the men were present at this point.

One woman was the wife of an ex-member of the National Guard. After the civil war he had become the head of the TEA (a 'Home Guard' institutionalised by Karamanlis mainly from right-wing bands), owned the state monopoly shop selling matches, paraffin and salt, and was secretary to the village-born right wing MP of the Province. His son was the MP's chauffeur in Athens. Another was the wife of an ex-ELAS partisan who had fled to Hungary — badly wounded — during the civil war. He had left his daughter in the village with his wife but taken his 10 year old son with him and educated him in Hungary. He had returned to the village in 1974 and his son had settled in Athens. A third woman had fought with ELAS and then fled with her partisan husband to Poland where they had raised their two daughters. They had returned to Greece — but not to the village — for the first time in 1978.

The women were bitter, they remembered atrocities ('... we found an arm, just an arm when we were collecting firewood on the slopes of Karpenisi. We never found the body') but they all wanted to 'speak their story'. They agreed that village life had been devastated, that they had been 'fanaticised' by a situation that they could not well understand. They agreed on its legacy of fear and mutual suspicion which lay beneath the surface of everyday life,

> What are the things that have happened and now we fear to speak to one another? It wasn't like that at first, there was still an order, we helped ourselves. It wasn't so bad after all when they (EAM-ELAS) were in our villages and ran our affairs...

The civil war overturned the relative order of the occupation period when the different 'sides' (the Germans and 'us') were clearly defined and the resistance groups more distinct. By 1946, however — also as a result of anti-EAM–ELAS propaganda and the 'white terror' — it was no longer clear to many villagers which group stood for what and which to trust. Thus a woman fleeing the village illustrates her confusion,

> Before we reached the village of N. . . . . they (partisans) appeared and stopped me and said, where are you going? I'm going to Lamia, I said. Your identification, they said. I have none. If we let on about you here, they said, they (partisans) will kill you. All right, I said, if they kill me they kill me... I want to go on. So they let me go on and we left. Before we reached the village of P. . . . . an old man

from our village appeared. Who are these partisans or soldiers? I didn't know how to communicate with him. At last I took my life into my own hands. I said, come here old man, who is in the village partisans or soldiers? He said, don't worry it's soldiers. Go right round the village for if you go through it they will catch you, go to the village of A. . . . . and that's what we did. . . They (partisans and soldiers) left nothing: houses, fields all damaged and destroyed.

Another woman, whose husband had been in the National Army, expressed surprise that the partisans of the Democratic Army were human,

After we left the village in 1947 and found shelter in a sheep-pen on the mountain. In the night while we slept two of them (partisans) came. They banged on the door and shouted for us to come out one by one with our hands over our heads. Now we are finished, we thought, well and truly done for. . . Then one of us. . . took courage suddenly and shouted that we were only women and children without a gun between us. They made us come out all the same. We expected the worst. Then they said we could go back inside again and we would be all right, they would protect us. We told them where we were going but we didn't say about our husbands. You could never be sure, each (side) as bad as the other.

After sharing these experiences the women gathered at the funeral wake turned to other topics, such as the question of the king.[22] Here there was greater disagreement,

After that (i.e. September 1946) our king came back. We wanted him didn't we? Things would be better with a king to rule. Bah! what did we want with the king? What does he know of our comings and goings up here in the mountains? And anyway didn't he leave the town the minute the others (Germans) arrived instead of staying like a fighting man?. . . they (the official Greek Government) put us to fight and be killed and those government lot ran off to sun themselves in another country while the trouble lasts.

There was also not full agreement on what, after the civil war, was described as the 'theft of children'. This concerned thousands of children who were allegedly forcibly taken by partisans crossing the borders into Eastern Europe.[23] The cases of so-called 'stolen children' among the villagers I talked to involved partisans taking their own children — often an eldest son — with them. This in the belief that they were protecting them or giving them the chance of a better future. For the mothers of these children it was indeed often hard to bear. Many resented it but also acquiesced.

> ... then in the early summer of 1945 he had come and taken the eldest boy with him and I didn't see either of them for many, many years. Later, my brother-in-law had said they had finally crossed the border into safety. He said not to mind, the boy would get a better education. Maybe he would become a doctor. Then they would both come back when things were quieter. It was only to protect. All right the man, he had his business to do, he had fought, but the boy?...
> (village woman)

Yet, even among those who accepted the propaganda that there was an indiscriminate rounding up of children, there was a tacit agreement that those who had gone had had a better education and were better off than most of their village counterparts.[24]

When the government started to repopulate the villages of Evritania in 1950, many people did not return. Some because their horizons had broadened beyond what they thought of as the confines of the village and they had managed to find employment elsewhere.

> They didn't all return to the villages, many remained in the towns or they left Greece... They found a better life, or they went abroad.
> (village man)

Others could not face returning to their devastated homes or the memories of that period.

> My brother suffered a lot then, in those years, that's why he never returned, why he didn't come back. It was a better life elsewhere and he went to find his fortune and forget in America.
> (village man)

Of those who did return some found it hard to resettle in the changed conditions and subsequently moved back to a town or emigrated. For the few ex-partisans or EAM–ELAS sympathisers who found their way back, there were a variety of difficulties. Or, as one man put it when he returned to his village from Hungary in 1974,

... it is difficult seeing my enemies everyday, sitting there in the *kafenion* (café) as though nothing has happened.

These factors led to a massive depopulation of the area after the civil war.[25] Communities were broken up in a literal and in a social sense. This sense of loss is expressed in the many Demotic or folksongs still sung by the villagers, some of which I have quoted here. None are specifically about the civil war or the war years in general but they do seem to refer to it as well and it is not unusual to find the word German or *andarte* substituted for Turk or *klepht*.

The loss of the social community was expressed in a very different way by a woman describing the death of her partisan husband who went missing in the mountains during the civil war,

> ... they never found him. So he lies forgotten, thrown away somewhere. Not even his bones to honour and take back to the village in a cedar box. He didn't deserve such a fate. He didn't want to go again (i.e. join the partisans again during the civil war) and now they've thrown him away like a bit of apple-peel... my husband left his house alive, didn't he deserve to return to it even as a box of bones? He was a family man and now he's died a gipsy without family or house.

5. *The language of the Civil War*

> The truth is the British caused the civil war. They fanaticised people so if you said to one man 'Communist' he would go to kill you, or to another about the other side, the same. It wasn't like that before in the village. They fanaticised us. We were working in their hands but we didn't know the deeper reasons. They were decided in Yalta by the big powers.[26]
>
> (village man)

Recent historical works have ably documented and analysed most of the features of conflict, and the complex causes of civil war in Greece continue to be passionately debated as new evidence comes to light.[27] The exact role played by — and the questionable motivation of — the British and later the USA; the activities of the OSS (to become the CIA);[28] the secret agreements with the USSR and the role of the Greek government, the king and the *parakratos* on the one hand; on the other, the inconsistent policies of EAM and the changing demands of the PEEA; the arguments within the Greek Communist Party, its changing character and the growing rift between its Central Committee and the fighting people in the mountains; as well as the precipitative events of December 1944[29] are all essential components in this complex picture.

Within this general — and even detailed — knowledge however, there is one area which has remained less explicit and is only now beginning to find expression in the analyses of those concerned with the period.[30] This concerns the lived experiences of the many men and women who were involved with the events — actively and passively. How did they understand the politics of the time? What was their interpretation of the civil war? In what ways do they remember it today?

Part of the reason for the relative silence in this area is that many of these people have not been 'available' to give opinions. Many were obliged to leave Greece, put the past behind them and start new lives elsewhere. Others were imprisoned for long periods. Some preferred silence. It was the only way to begin re-creating village life, or it was safer. As one man put it,

> The village does not know me as leftist. I keep my mouth shut. If you open your mouth you are Left, if you keep it shut you are Right.[31]

The majority were forced into silence. Not only in the ways described above but because a major consequence of the civil war was to deprive them of a framework within which to interpret these events or of a language in which to discuss them beyond the strictures of what was officially sanctioned.

By 1950 Greece was nominally at peace. At least 600,000 people had died in the preceding ten years, a period which had included the German occupation and widescale resistance to it (1941–44) and two phases of civil strife (1944–46 and 1946–49). One and a half million Greeks were homeless and over 2,000 villages had been completely burnt down. All communication networks (telephones, roads, railways, bridges, harbours etc.) had been virtually destroyed. Approximately 100,000 refugees had fled across the borders while thousands were still in prison or exiled on remote islands. National production was almost at a standstill.[32]

The first elected post-war government fell within 8 months and the second within a year. There followed a chaotic period of coalition and cabinet realignments between Liberal factions and the Right — during which time American presence became more dominant both in terms of economic aid and behind-the-scene manipulations. Finally, on 16th November 1952, in the third general election in two years, Marshal Papagos[33] was elected (with American assistance) and the future of the Right in Greece was assured. With it an unprecedented anti-Communist and 'anti-progressive' ideology grew to dominance and permeated every aspect of social, cultural and political life.

This created an irreconcilable rift between what was labelled as the 'national attitude' on the one hand, and the remnants of the progressive forces on the other.[34] Attitudes and opinions about the civil war and its causes which did not accord with this ideology — as well as thinking about the past in general terms — were influenced and moulded by this single fact.

In the villages of Evritania very few of the Left, or former partisans, remained and those who ventured back even much later, were carefully watched. This, for example, was the case for Thanasis, the only openly avowed Communist in Agios Vissarios today.[35]

Thanasis joined the resistance forces of ELAS in 1942 at the age of sixteen and in 1947 enlisted in the Democratic Army. His father and two brothers, also ELAS partisans, were killed. He was captured almost immediately in the early stages of the civil war and sentenced to death on the evidence supplied by four co-villagers. His sentence was commuted at the last minute and he spent the next 16 years in prison. He was released in 1964 and decided to return home. In the face of almost total opposition this was a brave decision.

Because of his previous record it took him several years to acquire an Agricultural Pension, to which he was entitled. He did so only when he found someone, not from the village, 'to speak for him'. In 1966 the province was again devastated by earthquakes and landslides. Most villagers acquired a government grant to rebuild their houses. Thanasis was prevented from getting one. In 1967, with the coup which brought Papadopoulos and his dictatorship to power, he was again arrested and beaten up 'to keep him quiet' and he spent several months in hospital as a result.

Significantly, other villagers are frightened to be seen with him and he usually sits alone in the *kafenion*. This was still the case in 1977 when I arrived in the village. Although many villagers privately think him 'a good man' — he accords with village standards of being 'honourable' and hard-working and has many chestnut trees — publicly they will shun him for fear of being 'coloured', that is, for fear of jeopardizing their own political reputations. This is crucial in a situation where villagers depend on the local MP and other officials to get their children educated and jobs outside the village. Thanasis' enemies in the village, the extreme Right, 'warned' me about him, calling him 'a liar', or 'a bad man' or even 'a drunk' though never actually naming him a Communist.

The wariness of anyone on the Left arises directly from the civil war. In a village like Agios Vissarios this has grown into a general distrust which permeates all social relations and especially of people from outside the village. Still in the late 1970s, odd building workers contracted to do a job in the village, for example, might be obliged to show identity cards to the local police; were regularly questioned by other members of the village on political matters, or continuously forced — as in my case — to listen to 'the real story' about the civil war which is propounded by a handful of men who hold important positions in the village. Teachers, the occasional doctor and other professionals who are appointed to serve in the village are also carefully watched, to see what newspaper they order or whether they spend too much time in the company of 'the Communist'. In recent years appeals were made to the local MP to remove a teacher, a doctor and even a bulldozer driver on the grounds that they were 'dangerously Left', because of something they had said or because they kept company with the Communist. Newcomers to the village are 'observed' by the fieldguard whose job is also to inform on anything 'untoward' in the community.

These factors suggest how the 'national attitude' grew to dominance after the civil war and seeped into the thinking of many villagers. This does not mean, however, that there is either a consensus of opinion on these matters or a uniform political interpretation of the civil war. What it means is that most people reflect this ideology in the manner in which they talk about the civil war. It also means that the interpretation of events – history itself – has had to be reformulated in terms of the official version and a particular terminology.

One of the most striking features in the constant talk about the civil war is the terminology used. It soon became clear, for example, that only those who did or do sympathize with the Left, or with the resistance of EAM–ELAS, called the civil war *emfilios polemos* (lit. 'inter-tribal war'), the standard dictionary use of the term. The Right – and mostly those who hold key positions in the village – referred to it as the *simorito-polemos* (the 'bandit war') or that of the 'Russo-Bulgarians' or of 'a handful of foreigners'. Many, and especially the women, called it the *andartiko*, 'the time of the partisans'. The use of these terms might reveal to another Greek the political affiliations of the speaker but they are not so clear to an outsider.

The common use of vague terms in talking about the civil war, suggested to me at first that local memory was not much concerned with clarity or a chronological time-scheme. The use of the terms 'then', 'after', 'not like now', 'before', instead of spelling out exactly when was meant, emphasizes this point. Again, to those who share this history these terms are not necessarily as vague as they might at first appear. In fact, it was generally the case that the very use of 'then' indicated precisely the subject-matter: that is, the civil war.

This terminology seems to reveal a particular verbal style which indicates just how the past is conceptualised in relation to the present. The point being that the civil war represents above all a discontinuity of the past with the present. To most villagers the distinction between a remote period during the Ottoman era, a time when the Greek nation-state was emerging in the 19th century, or life in the 1930s is unimportant in this context. They are seen as a continuous period, 'before', when the order of things was known. The civil war, 'then', put an abrupt end to this sense of continuity and traditional village life. Modern history is, therefore, divided by the villagers into two main periods: 'before the civil war' up to 1947, and 'after it', 1950 onwards. Most events are referred to this single division. However, the use of 'then' to describe the civil war is also more neutral as it avoids the choice of a more politically significant term.

The civil war has now come to express not only very real but threatened disorder. As such it is used to represent other types of relationships. For instance, many current agrarian disputes are often couched in terms of the civil war – Georgos was on the other side to Jannis – when, it emerges, they involve contemporary issues. Disagreements among families may also be attributed to the civil war when more recent causes are at stake,

> ... it is because of then (i.e. civil war), one side of the family with them (the Left), her husband with the others (the Right) and I don't know what else besides. Now they can't agree where the boundary lies, so they are not talking and remembering only the past...
>
> (village woman)

Actually, the boundary disputed in this case had only been set in the 1960s when the land in question was divided.

Most remarkable in the talk of civil war is the common use of 'they', rather than specifying who is meant; or the general use of *andartes* (partisans) to describe anyone involved in the conflict. This accords with the post-war ideology as the overall effect is to lay the blame for everything that occurred in the villages on the partisans of EAM–ELAS. For almost a year I went along with this, assuming that Agios Vissarios and the neighbouring villages had been the victims of only EAM–ELAS reprisals and aggression; that it was the Democratic Army which had forced people from their homes and that they were responsible for most of the burning and looting.

One day I asked an old woman who was describing how the *'andartes'* had ransacked her trousseau to describe 'them' in more detail. It turned out that 'they' were soldiers of the National Army. After that I questioned people more carefully on who was meant by 'them' or *'andartes'*. The results were startling. 'They' in a single paragraph could refer to two or three different groups of people. 'They' could refer to soldiers of the National Army, partisans in ELAS or the Democratic Army, other resistance groups or even Red Cross officials. This forced me to reconsider everything I had been told. In all the quotations given I have attempted to specify who was meant at every point. Sometimes, however, this was difficult as the speakers themselves were no longer certain, they were repeating hearsay or use of the official terminology had finally obscured the real identity of 'them'. The result is that all the misfortunes of the period are laid at the feet of the *andartes*.

One effect of employing these vaguer terms, of course, is that they tend to minimize the implied antagonisms involved in discussing the period at all, as well as putting some distance between 'them' and the villagers' own responsibilities. To an outsider the use of 'they' or the generic *andartes* is not only misleading but gives the impression of a united front (albeit heavily weighted against the Left) whatever the personal beliefs of the speaker. Most importantly, these terms have become part of a political language whose significance lay in supporting the prevalent post-war 'national attitude'. To challenge it meant finding other means of expression.

Direct questioning about certain wartime events elicited only official responses, evasive answers, or at best silence. This was strikingly true about the occupation period when under the auspices of EAM these villages were administered by a system of local self-government and popular justice. No-one could be directly drawn on the subject of self-government beyond the official 'it was all bad', 'we were forced into it by them', 'how could we know how to run our affairs, we don't know how to write and read'.

In part it is the civil war which has made subsequent assessments of these earlier events impossible. The institutions of self-government were totally discredited as being 'Communist imposed' and 'unpatriotic activities'. Partly, it is because these events belong to the period 'before' and therefore to another kind of memory that makes them so difficult to discuss.

A major result of the civil war, and subsequent propaganda, is that many villagers today feel they were grossly deceived. For all the reasons outlined above this sense of deception is mainly aimed against the Left, but not just because it 'turned out to be unpatriotic' – as many have been led to believe – but because the progressive forces failed to hold onto the power they had 'to create the new Greece they had promised us'.

The feeling of having been deceived extends to others and especially to the British. The response of the village man quoted at the beginning of this section is typical. Another villager joined the right-wing resistance organization EDES (Greek Democratic National League) favoured by the British.

He felt the British played a double game throughout the resistance and civil war and quoted the apocryphal story usually cited by the Left,

> ... we needed supplies, we asked them (the British) for things, they parachuted them to us. We found a box of boots, but only right-footed ones. The left ones they had sent to the others.

Another man was a cook for British liaison officers. He greatly admired the British but still felt that his services had not been recognised after the war. There were many who felt the British 'allowed' the civil war for their own political ends and contributed to setting Greek against Greek. In general their voices have been lost under the weight of the official version.[36]

Beyond the official responses oblique references are made to certain events. Thus I found that self-rule under the Ottoman Turks was often cited as was the spirit of resistance among the freedom fighters of the War of Independence. Could these be different expressions for the later events?

In addition, obscured events are sometimes recalled in pinning down another kind of memory. On seeing a tall, bearded stranger in her village in 1983, an old woman suddenly remarked,

> ... they (partisans) looked wild. I found one on my balcony one day when I returned from the fields, and the girls inside too – ripe for the picking! But he hadn't harmed them, though he looked angry and rough with his beard and the gun propped against the door. Later, he even took out the tooth that hurt in my mouth. He gave me something to stop the pain and not a penny to pay!

Up to this moment the old woman had always evaded any questions about the presence of EAM in her village. The memory of a wedding, of a bad harvest or a funeral might be pinned down in passing by reference to a person's involvement in the system of self-government, of fighting with the partisans, but no-one would talk directly about such things when asked.

6. *Conclusions*

> On a high mountain, on a rocky crag
> sits an eagle, poor bird,
> with his wings all frozen through
> and asking the sun to rise,
> rise sun, sun rise and melt my frozen wings.
>
> (Demotic song)

There have been important changes among these villages since the late 1970s. The Papandreou Government which was first elected in 1981 has recognised the resistance and EAM-ELAS are no longer officially discredited. Many 'dissidents' have returned to Greece for the first time since the civil war. Memorable achievements of the resistance — such as its role in blowing up the Gorgopotamos bridge[37] — are now officially commemorated in a new spirit and the dead and missing of the Left are remembered together with the others. I recently learnt that even a questionnaire concerning the self-governing activities of the occupation period has been circulated in the province neighbouring Evritania. In 1985 the latter also elected its first left of centre MP (PASOK) for fifty years.

These are significant new factors in the overall situation described here and for the memories of the villagers. Such factors have undoubtedly had their effect although it is still too early to say in precisely what ways. With the recent General Election in June 1989, the 'demise' of Andreas Papandreou and the failure to elect a majority government, new elements must now be added to the overall picture.

In general — and subsequent visits to the area confirm this impression — there is today a greater willingness to reassess the period. Freed of official shackles and the fear of discrimination for the first time it is probable that more people will begin to remember more about the civil war. Those like Thanasis will be more confident in telling their story. The nation — and the law — is no longer against the Left in the same way and the repressive actions of the Right no longer have (in theory at least) legal sanction. Thus it will be possible to build a more accurate picture of what happened during the civil war, and even before it, as well as a clearer picture of the institutions of self-government and popular justice.

In the new atmosphere generated by PASOK, which at first at least attempted to encourage nation-wide agricultural co-operatives and other local initiatives and sought to promote a measure of decentralisation and the development of local government, a knowledge of the earlier events may, in turn, have provided valuable experience for future generations.

Those returning to their villages for the first time since the civil war face the difficult task of coming to terms with the development of Greece in the intervening period. For the many returning from the Eastern Bloc there is the additional problem of coming to terms with a still developing, peripheral Western nation. For the men and women who remained in their villages the task is that of confronting anew a hitherto obscured past.

One major problem has emerged with the return of political refugees to their villages to which there is no easy solution. This concerns the ownership of land. Already, unfortunate incidents have occurred in many villages and new feuds have broken out as those returning attempt to claim what they see as their rightful inheritance. Meanwhile, those who remained claim these lands by virtue of having worked them in the intervening years. It is difficult to see how this issue can be resolved both generally and in individual cases, all of which differ in detail. On one level a solution will depend on the strength of the Greek economy and employment possibilities, but this is not its only aspect.

The greater willingness to reassess the past cannot, of course, change the facts of needless devastation and loss but it has given the younger people at least — who did not live through this period — greater freedom to appraise the period in a more balanced way. They are already, in Agios Vissarios, asking more questions and seeking out people on both sides of the conflict for their opinions. Official recognition cannot eradicate the memory of forty years of enforced silence nor the bitterness and the mainly anti-Left prejudice which still exists in such areas as Evritania. The sad story, the fractured history of these villages during which communities were broken up will remain harsh facts. But in the changing atmosphere that old spirit of resistance might be reawakened enabling these villages to develop and take their place in the modern world on their own terms.

The civil war was fought out at different intensities in different parts of Greece, not everyone was affected in the same way. Here I have outlined what the civil war meant to a group of mountain villages in Central Greece. For others it is solely the experience of German occupation which remains indelibly written in their memories. The effects of the civil war, however, the consequent persecution, the return to an old system which hindered dynamic economic and cultural development, is often barely concealed beneath the surface of so many of the picturesque villages visited by hundreds of foreigners each year.

NOTES

1. This is a pseudonym for the chief (*kephalohori*) village among a group of six communities. The province of Evritania lies in Central Greece or Sterea Hellas, part of Roumeli. The total population of the six communities is today approximately 1,000. In 1940 it was 2,500. Between 1977-79 I was carrying out social anthropological research in the area based on Agios Vissarios. All the quotations cited are from interviews and discussions carried out between 1978-79.
2. Aris Velouchiotis was born Athanasis Klaras in 1906 in Lamia. He was a trained agronomist and became a Communist in the 1920s. He was imprisoned and sent into exile under the Metaxas dictatorship but released in 1939 when he signed a 'declaration' renouncing Communism. During the German occupation he became a renowned partisan leader and *Kapetanios* on the ELAS command. Despite his popular appeal among many people he remains a highly controversial figure. For a more balanced view of him see, for example, Sarafis, S., *ELAS: Greek Resistance Army*, English translation, Merlin Press, 1980.
3. My research began in 1977 which was, in fact, 30 years after the civil war. Subsequent visits to Agios Vissarios over the next ten years, however, suggest that though there have been important changes since 1977, the civil war is still generally remembered in the same way. But see Section 6 of this paper.
4. *Raya*: subject class of, mostly infidel, peasants under Ottoman rule; *Archons*: Greek or Turkish notables; *Kocabases*: Greek landlords. The song refers to the shepherds as *vlachs* — an ethnic group of transhumant shepherds with distinct language and culture — but as the term is also used generically to refer to any shepherd I have translated it as such.
5. Greeks date the beginning of Ottoman rule with the fall of Constantinople on Tuesday 13th May 1453. Tuesdays remain unlucky days in the popular imagination with 'upside down hours' as the villagers put it.
6. Vacalopoulos, A. E., *The Origins of the Greek Nation*, Rutgers University Press, 1970, p. 170.
7. Systems of self-government and local arbitration were also developed in other parts of Greece during this period: on the islands of Mytilini and Chios, for example, in parts of Epirus, Thessaly and in the Peloponese where armed bands recruited by Greek landlords were known as *kapi*.
8. Vasiliou, P. 'H Episkepi Litsas kai Agrafon epi Tourkokratia', Athens 1960. The Treaty was made between Bey Leberis of Thessaly and the people of *Agrafa* during the rule of Sultan Suleyman 1.
9. Leake, W. M., *Travels in Northern Greece*, London, 1835.
10. General Metaxas imposed a dictatorship on 4th August 1936. Leader of an

earlier, unsuccessful coup in 1923, he was known for his totalitarian ideas even before that. Despite his affinities with fascism and Nazi Germany – and the Greek monarchy's German connections – and largely because of British pressure, he entered the war on the side of the Allies after trying unsuccessfully to remain neutral. His refusal to come to an agreement with Mussolini – known as the 'great no' – marks Greece's entry into World War II.

11. Beikos, G., 'H Laiki Exousia stin Eleftheri Ellada', Themelio, 1979, Vol. 1.
12. EAM was the first resistance organisation founded on 27th September 1941. It was a coalition between the Greek Communist Party and various other smaller, republican parties, under whose political authority the creation of a people's liberation army was envisaged. The expressed aims of EAM were to resist the occupation and ensure that a new democratic regime should be established in post-war Greece. By 1944 EAM membership was somewhere between 500,000 and 2,000,000.
13. It is generally agreed that the first definitive steps for the development of self-government under EAM were taken on the 11th October 1942 when the partisan leader, Aris Velouchiotis reached the village of Fourna in Evritania. Once there he disbanded the regional magistrates court, the local police force and field and forest guards. Shortly afterwards, with the assistance of local EAM representatives, the surrounding villages summoned community assemblies and decided to elect general committees to direct village affairs. There is evidence, however, that some forms of self-government were already in operation among these villages.

ELAS: The Greek National Liberation Army was formally established by EAM in February 1942. See Sarafis, op. cit.
14. The Germans did in fact reach Karpenisi but were never able to hold it. Those who joined ELAS saw active service against the Germans in guerrilla actions, such as blowing up the Gorgapotamos bridge. A handful of people in Agios Vissarios also remember that three German hostages were brought to the village,

> ... They (ELAS) brought three of them hostage and took them to (the slope above the cemetery) and shot them. For a long time in the night we could hear their blood moaning... then after the war their families came and took away their bones. Afterwards we didn't hear them anymore... (village man)

For most villagers, however, the Germans seemed fairly distant though the occupation intruded into their lives through food shortages and the news of deaths and reprisals etc.

The Axis powers had agreed distinct zones of occupation in Greece. After Italy's capitulation in 1943 many Italian POWs were held in a camp outside Karpenisi and others distributed among the villages. These Italian hostages are more clearly remembered by the villagers, though as objects of pity rather than enemies.

15. See Sarafis, op. cit., p. 117.
16. To achieve this end, the PEEA insisted on its own democratic structure from the beginning and before assuming governmental functions organised free elections by secret ballot for both men and women. These took place throughout the country on 9th April 1944. The elected representatives, voted in by over a million votes (in a country still occupied by the Germans and out of a total population of little more than 7 million) constituted themselves into a National Assembly becoming the representative government of Greece and working within the country itself. The Official Greek Government went into exile to Cairo in the Spring of 1941. It was made up of mostly ineffectual, pro-Metaxas members of the political scene and had

the support of the king, George II. This government lived and functioned in its small world – the British manipulating various postings to it – until 1944. It elicited little but indifference in Greece and was completely cut off from the country. Because of the events following the liberation of Greece from the Germans, however, neither it nor the PEEA ever came to power.

For a fictionalised but comprehensive picture of events in the Middle East during this period see Tsirkas' Trilogy, 'Drifting Cities'. See also Papastratis, *British Policy towards Greece during the Second World War, 1941-1942*, CUP, 1984, and Woodhouse, *The Struggle for Greece, 1941-49*, Hart-Davis, MacGibbon, 1976.

17. Woodhouse, C. M., *The Apple of Discord*, Hutchinson, 1948, p. 147.
18. Up to December 1944 a few National Guard Battalions had been formed by call-up but these were dissolved when fighting broke out as many of the men turned out to be EAM sympathisers. After December 1944, 36 new Battalions were formed specially composed of strongly anti-Communist elements. New Battalions were then formed – the bulk of whom comprised the notorious Security Battalions who had collaborated with the Germans but which also included criminal elements – in the localities each occupied. By May 1945 they were in control of most of the country. Many right-wing, nationalist organisations also made their appearance at this time. The most important of these was the 'X' (*chi*) of Colonel Grivas which by the autumn of 1945 claimed 200,000 members.

These two groups formed the basic agents of the so-called 'white terror' which set out to literally annihilate Communists, the Left in general, their sympathisers and anything to do with them (offices, presses were ransacked and destroyed).

For fuller details see for example, Richter, H., *British Intervention in Greece – From Varkiza to the Civil War*, Merlin Press, 1986 and Alivizatos, N. C., 'The Emergency Regime and Civil Liberties 1946-49' in Iatrides, J.O. (ed.), *Greece in the 1940s – A Nation in Crisis*, University Press of New England, 1981, pp. 220-229, and Woodhouse, op. cit.
19. One of the Ministers responsible for general order during this period was General Zervas, the highly suspect right-wing leader of EDES (National Democratic Greek League). This resistance group was defeated by ELAS in 1944 when Zervas had to be ignominiously rescued by British submarine.
20. Under the Generalship of Markos Vafiadis, the Democratic Army was formed on 28th October 1946. It was comprised of former ELAS partisans and the remnants of the progressive forces but was controlled by the KKE. By August 1949 it had been pushed back into its last stronghold on the Grammos and Vitsi mountain ranges. Here, surrounded by the National Army, it was forced to fight a conventional battle against artillery and aircraft (including naplam). Defeated, the remnants of the Democratic Army were pushed over the border into Albania and the civil war was in effect ended.
21. Women were given the vote by EAM and they could also stand for election in the local organs of self-government and in the popular courts. They were not formally enfranchised in Greece, however, until 1952. In fact, they were not given the vote in time for the General Elections that took place that year but voted for the first time in the by-election held in Salonica in January 1953 when the first woman candidate was also elected.
22. The king, George II, had supported the fascist regime of Metaxas, suspending the Constitution. He then fled the country when the Germans occupied Greece. He went to various places ending up in London from where he was, in effect, forced back to Cairo to form the government. He was staunchly supported by Churchill who sought to reimpose the Monarchy as a means of

re-establishing British influence in post-war Greece. However, the republicans in Greece, the vast majority of the Greek people, were vehemently opposed to a Monarchy and especially to George II. Following the events in Athens in December 1944, the British were forced to concede a plebiscite.

23. See Wittner, L.S., *American Intervention in Greece 1943-49*, Columbia University Press, 1982, especially chapter 5.
24. It is also worth noting that the image of 'rounding up innocent children' touched on a collective memory of Ottoman Turks rounding up innocent Greek (Christian) children to form the *Janissaries* – the elite infantry and artillery arms of Ottoman power. This event was also greatly elaborated and emphasised by subsequent historical interpretation and in the building up of the Greek nation's image.
25. In 1940, for example, the total population of the province was 53,474 and in 1951, 39,678. Today it stands at roughly 20,000.
26. The Yalta Conference of February 1945 where Stalin made it clear he had no interest in Greece and he privately agreed with Churchill that Greece remain a British sphere of influence: an issue already settled at the Moscow Conference in October 1944.
27. The bibliography is lengthening. Indispensible in this respect is Fleischer, H. and Bowman, S., ed. Iatrides, J. O., *Greece in the 1940s – A Bibliographic Companion*, University Press of New England, 1981. But see also the following for example, Hondros, J. L., *Occupation and Resistance – The Greek Agony 1941-44*, Pella, 1983. Iatrides, J. O. (ed.), *Greece in the 1940s – A Nation in Crisis*, UPNE, 1981. Papastratis, P., op. cit. Richter, op. cit. Vukmanović ('Tempo'), *How and Why the People's Liberation Struggle of Greece Met with Defeat*, Merlin Press, 1985. Wittner, L.S., op. cit.
28. Office of Strategic Service. See Wittner, ibid.
29. On 3rd December 1944 a mass demonstration was called by EAM. Large unarmed crowds assembled in Athens' main square. Suddenly there was shooting and 28 were left dead and over a hundred wounded. EAM then called for a general strike and mass meeting on 4th December. While the demonstrators were dispersing they were attacked and the resulting conflict led to over a hundred deaths. There is much controversy about these events and who did the initial shooting. Nevertheless, this marked the beginning of armed confrontation between the forces of the Left and Right.
30. A recent example of this was the C4's trilogy, 'The Hidden War', made by Jane Gabriel which also sparked off a heated controversy both inside and outside the media and in other countries where the film has been seen. There are, however, different kinds of example in which the actual experience of men and women are made the focus. See for instance, Andrews, K., *The Flight of Ikaros – Travels in Greece During the Civil War*, Penguin, 1984 (reprint). Fourtouni, E., *Greek Women in Resistance*, Thelphini Press, 1980. (The journals of three women who were held in concentration camps in Greece.) And the novels of Haviaras, S., *When the Tree Sings*, Sidgwick & Jackson, 1979; *The Heroic Age*, Methuen, 1985.
31. Quoted by a Macedonian villager but much the same sentiments were expressed in Agios Vissarios. See Vermeulen, H., 'Repressive Aspects in the Process of Outmigration: the Case of a Greek Macedonian Tobacco Village', in *Mediterranean Studies*, 1977, Vol. 1, No. 2.
32. See, for example, Tsoucalas, C., *The Greek Tragedy*, Penguin Special, 1969.
33. Marshal Papagos: a royalist officer, Chief of Staff in the Albanian War (1941) and Commander-in-Chief of the National Army in the final battle with the Democratic Army in 1949.
34. Tsoucalas, C., 'The Ideological Impact of the Civil War', in Iatrides (ed.), op. cit., pp. 319-341.

35. There are in fact 13 regular communist votes in the village but apart from Thanasis (a pseudonym) no-one else admits to being a Communist.
36. It can be said that there are several 'official' versions of events. Firstly, the more or less uniform one propagated by post-war governments in Greece which, by and large, discredited the whole resistance movement, attributed the civil war entirely to a 'handful of fanatical thugs' variously described, and which kept thousands of patriotic resistance fighters in prison until the mid 1960s.

    The version propounded by the group of British Establishment and academic figures, usually themselves involved in undercover military missions in Greece during the German occupation, constitutes another official version (see, for example, Woodhouse, C. M., *The Apple of Discord*, op. cit., and *The Struggle for Greece*, Hart-Davis, MacGibbon, 1976). Both versions reflect in their way the beginnings of the pervasive Cold War ideology following World War Two. The first is more easily discredited for being both crude and so fanatically anti-Communist, though — as I have shown — it has entered the thinking of many ordinary people, and a variety of Greek laws reflected this version until very recently.

    The second version is now being hotly debated as a younger generation of historians and political scientists have access to a variety of archival material being released, according to the thirty year rule, and with the help of new insights from those involved at the time and now allowed back into Greece for the first time since the civil war.
37. The Gorgopotamos bridge was blown up on the night of 25-26 November 1942 and severed the main north-south railway line in Greece. This cut the Germans essential supply route for three months. The mission was carried out by a group of ELAS partisans headed by Aris Velouchiotis, a group of EDES men with General Zervas in command and a British contingent led by the head of the British Mission, Brigadier Myers. See Myers, E. C. W., *The Greek Entanglement*, Rupert Hart-Davis, 1955, p. 78 ff for a description of the actual operation.

THE COLONELS' DICTATORSHIP: 1967-1974

Robert McDonald

> It is a state of enforced torpor in which all the intellectual values... are being submerged in a swamp.... We all know that in dictatorial regimes the beginning may seem easy, yet tragedy waits at the end inescapably.
>
> George Serefis, March 28, 1969

I

The colonels' dictatorship had two objectives: eradication of communism and attainment of *enosis*, union of Cyprus with Greece. Its approach to the former was anachronistic and to the latter chauvinistic and, for the duration of the regime, the country was subjected to attitudes and policies that were at least a decade out of keeping with the tenor of thinking in the democratic states of Europe.

The Greek civil war (1947-49) ended with the communist insurgents in retreat in eastern bloc countries, where they became dependent upon fraternal parties for subsistence, and the victorious central government politically fragmented and heavily reliant on the United States for economic and military support. The Greek public was ready for reconciliation and, in the first elections after the fratricidal strife, cast a majority of votes for liberal, centrist and left-wing parties, which resulted in a succession of unstable coalition governments. As reconstruction mired in politicking and as American Cold War attitudes hardened because of Korea, Washington, coaxed by the king, came to believe that its interests would be better served by a strong conservative leadership. Thus, when Marshal Alexander Papagos, who had led the Greek armed forces during the latter part of the civil war, resigned his commission to form the Greek Rally, a conservative grouping which also attracted centrists, the US afforded his candidacy diplomatic endorsement of a kind that many felt constituted intervention in Greek internal affairs.[1] The US rationale was that Greece required a strong government to make efficient use of aid.

Papagos won the 1951 elections but with an insufficient majority to form a government, and a coalition of centrists and Liberals took office. Yet another poll, in 1952, under an electoral law which had been used twice before and favoured large parties, produced an overwhelming majority for the Rally. For eleven years thereafter the right held sway, Papagos died in 1955 and was succeeded by Constantine Karamanlis who re-organised the Greek Rally as the National Radical Union (ERE) which won the elections of 1956, 1958 and 1961. Much was achieved in terms of economic growth[2] and the replacement of infrastructure during the right's years in office but it was accomplished at the expense of political pluralism. The civil administration was filled with conservative placemen, the military establishment was identified with the monarchy,[3] centrists and leftists were excluded from public life as nationalism came to be equated with conservatism and monarchism.

The communist party had been outlawed in 1947[4] and former combattants who returned to Greece clandestinely to organize were treated as spies. Several were executed. Communists seeking to work within the political system formed the United Democratic Left (EDA) together with socialist and agrarian groups. Party members and their activities were closely monitored by the security services. The right portrayed EDA as a Trojan Horse for cadres plotting further insurrection. It became particularly anxious in 1958 when EDA, capitalising on anti-western sentiment engendered by the situation prevailing in Cyprus, won a quarter of the popular vote and became the official opposition.

Cyprus was a British colony in the 1950s. The Greek Cypriot community who comprised 80 per cent of the population, agitated for self determination which, in their minds meant *enosis*, union of the island with Greece. Their struggle evolved into a bloody four-year guerrilla campaign (1955–59) led by EOKA,[5] under the command of General George Grivas.[6] Greece supported the cause emotionally and diplomatically and to a limited extent materially. Turkey, intent that Cyprus which lies just 80 kilometres off its south coast, should not become an Hellenic island, nurtured the notion of segregation of the 18 per cent Turkish Cypriot community and *taksim*, partition of the island. Ankara gave succour to TMT,[7] a Turkish Cypriot separatist movement. The conflict between the three NATO partners strained relations within the Alliance and created in Greece, where it was perceived to favour Britain, a degree of disaffection.

In 1959, a compromise was struck between the governments of Britain, Greece and Turkey, and the following year Cyprus was given independence under a power-sharing constitution.[8] Britain retained two sovereign bases comprising some three per cent of the territory of the island. The remainder was ceded to the new Republic. The constitution provided for a complex consociational structure in government, the administration, the judiciary and the military.[9] The arrangement was supported by two tripartite treaties: of guarantee, which precluded union or partition and alliance which provided for the stationing of mainland forces on the island to help train a Cyprus Army.[10] Grivas, who opposed independence, retired in dudgeon to the mainland.

The power-sharing system proved unworkable and in late 1963 Archbishop Makarios, under pressure from disappointed unionists, sought to introduce constitutional amendments which would have reduced the Turkish Cypriots to the status of a minority protected by a charter of rights. This resulted in bloody inter-communal fighting which prompted Turkey to threaten to invade Cyprus. An attempt to introduce a NATO peacekeeping force was resisted by Makarios who was supported by the Soviet Union. A United Nations peacekeeping force, UNFICYP, arrived on the island in March 1964 and has remained since.

The Turkish Cypriots withdrew from the administration and many retreated into enclaves defended by irregular forces under the command of Turkish officers who took their orders from Ankara via the Turkish embassy.[11] The Turkish Cypriots maintained their own administration and security in these areas.

Makarios introduced conscription and established a National Guard consisting solely of Greek Cypriots commanded by seconded mainland officers. Greece infiltrated

10,000 regular troops onto the island to forestall a Turkish invasion. Grivas who returned to the island to head the Guard, eventually became *generalissimo* of all the Greek forces taking his orders from the general staff in Athens. Thus, Makarios, while heading the internationally recognised government of the Republic, did not exercise authority over the whole of its territory, nor did he have full control over the armed forces on the island.

* * *

Europe began to drift away from Cold War attitudes of confrontation towards communism in the 1960s, nearly a decade before its American allies. Politicians sought to deter it at home through social reform and to come to terms with it internationally by means of trade. In Greece, this more accommodating attitude found expression in the Centre Union (EK) party, a loose coalition of liberal, centrist and socialist interests, under the leadership of George Papandreou.

ERE was returned for a third term in the 1961 elections but only, it was alleged, by means of electoral fraud involving the military. The Centrists embarked upon a campaign of 'unyielding struggle' (*anendotos agonas*) and in the November 1963 elections were returned as the largest, though not the majority party. Karamanlis went into self-imposed exile in Paris bequeathing leadership of ERE to Panayotis Kanellopoulos, a politician of republican persuasion, who was happier in his scholarly pursuits than in the rough and tumble of politics. Papandreou, an acknowledged anti-communist, refused to form a minority government with EDA support. Conservatives nevertheless claimed that the Centre Union's 53 per cent, 171-seat landslide in February 1964 was only achieved by means of a popular front in which EDA stood down its candidates in more than 20 constituencies.[12]

The policies of the Centre Union infuriated and frightened the establishment. Of particular concern was its slogan the 'Army belongs to the Nation' which was seen as a direct challenge to the authority of the monarchy. The centrists' emphasis on an independent foreign policy stance was perceived as a drift away from the United States and NATO.

Papandreou's accession coincided with the crisis in Cyprus. Washington, concerned about the non-aligned policies of

Archbishop Makarios and about the strength of the communist party AKEL,[13] feared the creation of a Mediterranean Cuba on the southern flank of NATO. It proposed a Cyprus settlement which would have provided for *enosis* in exchange for a formal Turkish military presence on the island and substantial autonomy for the minority community.[14] The mainland governments initially were prepared to consider the arrangement but Papandreou demurred after Makarios rejected it. In March 1965, a UN mediator recommended that Cyprus should remain independent, the Greek Cypriots should renounce *enosis*, the island should be demilitarised and the crisis should be resolved through inter-communal talks. This was rejected by Ankara which sought further direct negotiations with Athens.

Greek conservatives, who believed that the American proposal should have been given greater consideration, were already working to discredit Papandreou. Grivas alleged that Papandreou's son, Andreas, was consorting with a cabal of socialist, neutralist officers in the army called Aspida (Shield).[15] When the elder Papandreou tried to sack his royalist defence minister to personally conduct the inquiry, King Constantine refused, causing the Prime Minister to tender his resignation. There was precipitate action on both sides but there is little doubt that the 22-year-old monarch, only 15 months on the throne, was poorly advised by conservative figures seeking to restore their lost authority.

The confrontation turned into a constitutional crisis when the king, instead of calling new elections, sought three times to form a government from among the ranks of the Centre Union. The party fragmented leaving in office a rump of centre-right politicians called the Liberal Democratic Centre[16] under the leadership of former Deputy Prime Minister Stefanos Stefanopoulos supported by ERE and the tiny Progressive Party of Spyros Markezinis.

During the two months in which the crisis unfolded, the streets of Athens were regularly filled with massive, often violent demonstrations. They were led by Centre Union supporters but also involved large numbers of militant EDA youths. Constantine was accused of reigning not ruling and the throne was openly called into question.

It was at this juncture that the colonels' junta began to form.[17] Col. George Papadopoulos and several key members, who were stationed together near the Thracian border with Turkey, concluded that the centrists were leading the country to a catastrophe. Major Dimitrios Ioannides and some others serving in Cyprus became convinced, that Makarios was insufficiently vigorous in the pursuit of *enosis*. Ioannides forged links with former EOKA extremists such as the assassin Nikos Sampson.[18]

The colonels were little men who had joined the army because it offered prospects of security and social advancement far beyond anything individuals of their status could hope to have achieved as civilians. They shared their superiors' visceral anti-communism but were contemptuous of them for currying establishment favour. With one exception the colonels were professional soldiers, graduates of the Military Academy. Three were from the class of 1940; the others from what would have been the class of 1943 had their studies not been interrupted by the German invasion. Evacuated to the Middle East,[19] they became members of a conservative officers' fraternity known as IDEA.[20]

During the civil war, as captains and majors, they were in the thick of the fighting. Their oath was the bond of men who had served together under fire.[21] They claimed to be a brotherhood of equals but Papadopoulos was their natural leader. An artillery colonel, he had been seconded to the Central Intelligence Service (KYP) in the early sixties and for a time acted as the liaison officer with the American Central Intelligence Agency (CIA). He always denied working as a CIA agent but there is little doubt that he was its creature.

The establishment was appalled by the seeming chaos of the summer of 1965. At a Crown Council of former prime ministers and eminent statesmen September 1-2, fears were expressed that a pre-revolutionary situation had been created.[22] Elections at that time would have forestalled the colonels' coup but at least some of those who participated in and supported the Stefanopoulos government believed they were acting to preserve democracy.

The Stefanopoulos administration was expected to last only for a few weeks but managed to muddle on for nearly 15 months. Because of the diverse interests it represented, little was accomplished; nepotism and corruption further undermned the credibility of the politicians.

The government entered into secret bilateral negotiations with Ankara over Cyprus. At a meeting in Paris in December 1966, Greece proposed *enosis* in exchange for an extensive system of minority rights for the Turkish Cypriots and the establishment of a Turkish sovereign base area at Dekelia.[23] The Stefanopoulos government fell the following day after George Papandreou agreed to a tripartite pact with Kanellopoulos and the palace for fresh elections.[24] The caretaker government appointed to conduct the elections foundered over plans to prosecute Andreas for his alleged role in Aspida. ERE was given the mandate to conduct the elections, a complete reversal of the popular mandate of 1964.

The staunchly royalist Hellenic Army General Staff (HAGS) feared that the political turmoil threatened the throne and made contingency plans to postpone the elections. Ironically, the Chief of Staff, Lieut. Gen. Grigoris Spantidakis, had used certain of the junta men to advance his scheme and had secured their appointment to key offices at headquarters. From these positions the conspirators were able to manoeuvre others of their number into vital commands. There were thirteen participants in what was styled the Revolutionary Committee.[25]

> Col. George Papadopoulos was deputy director of the Third Bureau HAGS responsible for operations, training and organisation.
> Lieut. Col. Dimitrios Stamatelopoulos headed the First Bureau dealing with assignments and promotions.
> Lieut. Col. Antonios Lekkas was in charge of the Fourth Bureau dealing with administration.
> Col. Nicholas Makarezos, another artillery officer, was seconded as security officer at KYP.
> Lieut. Col. Michael Roufougalis, also of artillery, was posted as Deputy Director of KYP.
> Brig. Gen. Stylianos Pattakos commanded the tank training school in the Athens suburb of Goudi.
> Lieut. Col. Dimitrios Ioannides was deputy commander of the Military Academy in central Athens.
> Col. Ioannis Ladas commanded the Military Police (ESA).
> Lieut. Col. Constantine Aslanides was the HAGS officer responsible for special forces.
> Lieut. Col. Antonios Mexis was commander of a heavy weapons training centre at Haidari northwest of Athens.
> Lieut. Col. Constantine Papadopoulos, brother of the junta leader, commanded a unit of Marines based at Dionyssos to the southeast of the capital.

Lieut. Col. Ioannis Anastassopoulos was in charge of communications for the high command for the whole of Attika.

Lieut. Col. Michael Balopoulos, an artilleryman who was also a trained pilot, was attached to HAGS.

Lieut. Gen. George Zoitakis, commander of the Third Army Corps with headquarters at Thessaloniki was Papadopoulos' liaison with the general staff. He knew about the colonels' intentions but was not deemed to be a member of the junta.

A month before the coup, Makarezos, in a move aimed at destabilising the political situation, presented a report to his superiors saying that a well-organised communist conspiracy was afoot with thousands of arms strategically cached about the country which the left planned to use to mount an insurrection.[26] The general staff dismissed it as wildly exaggerated. They were concerned, however, about Andreas Papandreou's election rhetoric to the effect that if there were interference to subvert the people's will at the polls, a popular government would be formed in Syntagma (Constitution) Square, outside the Parliament. The generals decided to demand that parliament give special authority to the government to postpone elections for three to six months in order to ensure security. April 20, 1967, they met to review the situation and agreed to put the proposition to the king. Lieut. Gen. Zoitakis apprised the colonels of the decision and the junior junta moved pre-emptively.

Article 91 of the 1952 constitution provided that in the event of a 'manifest threat to public order and to the security of the country from internal danger' the king could, on the recommendation of parliament, suspend 11 articles of the constitution governing civil and political liberties and implement a state of emergency. Among the army's contingency schemes was a NATO counter-insurgency plan codenamed Prometheus which called for the mobilisation of the army, the police, and some reserves: to secure all frontiers, including ports and airports; to occupy and protect from sabotage all public buildings, including ministries and communications centres; and to arrest several thousand people listed by security authorities as potential agitators.

In the small hours of the morning of April 21, the colonels initiated this process in reverse. They implemented Prometheus, arrested the politicians who were supposed to have recommended the emergency measures and presented the monarch with a *fait accompli*. When Constantine refused to sign the martial law proclamation which had been issued in his name, his signature was forged on the decree.

The young king was isolated. His personal diplomatic and military advisors were arrested by the putchists. Public Order Minister George Rallis, who was briefly able to make contact, counselled that, since the monarch could not communicate with loyal commanders in the field, he should offer such co-operation as was necessary to avoid bloodshed with a view to reaction later. Prime Minister Kanellopoulos, permitted contact about noon on April 21 while under detention at armed forces headquarters, urged Constantine to make a dramatic gesture to reassert his command warning that failure to do so would dissipate the authority of the crown and eventually lead to collapse of the monarchy. He recommended that Constantine, as commander in chief, should order the insurrectionists to surrender to his personal responsibility and instruct other officers to return to their posts without fear of repercussions. The king felt this impossible and the audience terminated after just five minutes.

The monarch instead negotiated with the colonels the formation of a 19-man government with non-political civilians in the majority and with the chief prosecutor of the Supreme Court, Constantine Kollias, as Prime Minister. A triumvirate of junta delegates was included in key ministries: Papadopoulos became Minister to the Prime Minister, responsible for KYP, the civil service and the media; Brig. Pattakos, Minister of the Interior, in charge of local government; and Col. Makarezos, Minister of Co-ordination, with control over all economic policy. Gen. Spantidakis, who, having been arrested by the putchists, was persuaded by them to issue the Prometheus orders to field officers, told the monarch that he had thrown in his lot in order to protect royal interests. He was named Deputy Prime Minister and Minister of Defence with Gen. Zoitakis as his number two at defence. Other members of the junta took up posts as secretaries-general, a position from which they could keep a low public profile but control government business.

The colonels' manifesto said that the old political world was corrupt beyond redemption and that a period of enforced stability was required while political institutions were refurbished and new parties forged. They styled their takeover a 'parenthesis' while this was accomplished. From the outset commentators were divided between those who believed that there would eventually be evolution towards a new political order and those who believed that the colonels sought power for its own sake.

Regarding Cyprus the new government said it aimed at *enosis* — 'without ignoring the rights of the minority'. Papadopoulos in the main pursued this goal through political and diplomatic means, however, others in, and affiliated with, the junta were prepared to use more drastic methods and it was an attempt by the extremist tendency finally to secure *enosis* by force which brought about the downfall of the dictatorship and the *de facto* partition of the island republic.

II

The state of emergency[27] subordinated police to military authority, allowed security forces to search homes without warrant, and provided for the establishment of courts-martial for all crimes deemed to be against the regime, security or public order. It permitted the abolition of political parties and other organisations considered to present a challenge to state security, the institution of prior censorship and the issue of regulations by military proclamation. The constitution required that parliament should ratify the royal decree imposing martial law within ten days and vote to terminate or extend it after two months. The colonels instead indefinitely extended the emergency powers by means of constituent acts.

In the security round-up, 8,270 people were arrested and temporarily incarcerated in sports stadia and at the Athens hippodrome. Civil war prison camps on the barren islands of Yiaros and Leros were re-opened and 6,188 of the detainees were interned. Many were former partisans or members of the Communist insurgent army who had been known to the security authorities for nearly thirty years. They were offered the opportunity to sign declarations undertaking to abstain from all political activity and within three months the number in custody had halved.

National and local elections were suspended. All party political activities were banned. Public gatherings and private meetings of more than five people required prior authorisation. EDA was outlawed and its property and archives seized. All youth organisations sponsored by political parties and some 260 trade unions, sporting and cultural organisations considered to have communist tendencies were dissolved and their property confiscated. The majority of the detained politicians were released within a matter of days but arrested EDA deputies continued to be held. So too did Andreas Papandreou who, on April 26, was charged with high treason for his alleged role in Aspida.

Press strictures were absolute and far exceeded the prior censorship authorised by the martial law. A Press Control Service was established headed by a colonel of the military justice department. It dictated news copy, editorials and pictures, together with their headlines, captions and placement on the page. Six of the thirteen national newspapers were either shut by the authorities or closed by protesting proprietors. The state-controlled broadcasting network (EIR) and the armed forces radio station (EDE) were placed under military control and broadcast blatant propaganda.[28]

Loyalty oaths were demanded of all civil servants, local government officials, public sector employees, judges, teachers, students and persons in state-licensed jobs. These had been required before the coup but the new document was more detailed and more coercively self-incriminating. Those who did not meet the required standards of 'national-mindedness' (*ethnikofrosini*) were dismissed and became the subject of police scrutiny. Greeks abroad who engaged in 'anti-national' activity were stripped of their citizenship and the ministry of the interior was empowered to confiscate their property.

Serving and retired military men loyal to the colonels were installed throughout the administration. The police and military security services established an extensive network of informers in all walks of life.

From time to time, proclamations were issued by the chief of the general staff banning 'subversive' activities such as the performance of the music of the popular communist composer Mikis Theodorakis. Lists of proscribed books and films were circulated. Most were works with a left-wing political bias but they included some classics of Greek and foreign literature. More ludicrous social strictures included bans on the then popular mini-skirt, beards and long hair.

The measures were indicative of the short-back-and-sides mentality of the military regime. During its first seven months in office, it attempted to regiment individuality out of the citizenry. Col. Papadopoulos epitomised the attitude with his infamous simile comparing the country to a patient strapped upon an operating table.

Though there was little overt support for the colonels, there was, in the early months, a larger than later acknowledged tacit acceptance. Some people fell prey to the disinformation about an imminent communist threat. Older conservatives agreed with many of the regime's enjoinders about the need for a return to traditional values. For others, the perpetual disarray of political life in recent years made the promise of refurbishment appealing.

The opposition of the political community was total but it remained fragmented and the extensive security made all but the most oblique contacts impossible. Politicians on the left-wing of the Centre Union were sent into internal exile together with several leading press figures. Several deputies were jailed for infractions of the martial law.

Resistance was limited. Communists, being the most practised from their years of enforced clandestine activity, were best placed. Mikis Theodorakis, who was also leader of a left-wing youth movement, went underground to found the Patriotic Front (PAM). By autumn a group of socialists had transformed an intellectual discussion group into the resistance organisation Democratic Defence (DA) and other groups had sprung up among trade unionists and left-wing supporters of the Papandreous. Early resistance consisted almost exclusively of distributing news bulletins, leafletting and painting graffiti, though later some groups planted protest bombs directed against property targets. The police with their wide-ranging network of informers rapidly cracked all but the cellular communist organisations and it soon became apparent that the security forces systematically used torture as a means of extracting confessions. Both police and military were involved in such maltreatment.

The colonels moved swiftly to consolidate their grip on the military. Within 48 hours of the coup, five members of the general staff were retired and the austere Lieut. Gen. Odysseus Angelis was nominated as head of the armed forces.[29] The king was presented with a list of 400 officers for retirement.

A law was enacted increasing the officer establishment by nearly 1,000, allowing promotions of junta supporters. The command of special forces units headquartered in the vicinity of the capital had been secured prior to the coup. In its wake, officers loyal to the junta were assigned as deputies to commanders in most active service units. Special emphasis was given to ensuring that adherents filled intelligence, security and communications posts.

Constantine surprised the military men in May with an announcement that he anticipated a draft constitution to be ready for a referendum by December. Later that month, a twenty-man revision committee was established under Harilaos Mitrelias, a former head of the State Council, though nothing was heard of its deliberations. The king publicly dissociated himself from the colonels during a visit to the United States in September.[30] The Greek embassy in Washington published a timetable, not made public within Greece for more than a week, which said that the revision committee would report on December 15, that preparation of a final constitutional draft would take a further six months, and that a referendum would follow two months thereafter. It concluded, elliptically, that 'parliamentary elections will follow according to the appropriate provisions of the new constitution' which some took to mean that the monarch was prepared to govern for a time without an elected government.

Domestic developments were overtaken, however, by events on Cyprus. The colonels, thinking they could take up the talks with the Turks where the Stefanopoulos government had left off, organised a prime ministerial summit September 9–10. They demanded *enosis* in exchange for Turkish bases in Cyprus, cession of territory in Thrace and a degree of Turkish Cypriot autonomy in local government.[31] The colonels repudiated the talks without consulting the Foreign Ministry and their arguments were ill-prepared. The meeting broke down in heated disarray.

In mid-November, Grivas inexplicably launched a major attack on two Turkish Cypriot villages killing 27 and taking captive 200 Turkish Cypriot irregulars.[32] Turkey reacted strongly and threatened to invade unless Greek troops were withdrawn, the National Guard was disbanded and the Turkish Cypriot community was allowed to maintain its own police force. To back up its demands, Turkey mobilised and massed substantial forces on the Thracian side of the Bosphorus. Greece responded by moving forward the bulk of the Third Army Corps together with the 200 tanks of the Twentieth Armoured Brigade.

US presidential envoy Cyrus Vance supported by UN Secretary-General U Thant and NATO Secretary-General Manlio Brosio embarked upon an intense round of diplomacy to defuse the confrontation. The junta, recognising that it could not be certain that the armed forces would fight on its behalf, recalled Grivas and withdrew the 10,000 Greek troops from Cyprus. It also agreed that the National Guard should be stood down. However, Makarios did not accede to this and by skillfully playing for time, managed to avoid its dissolution.

At the height of the crisis, on November 29, Constantine Karamanlis, who had till then remained silent in Paris, gave an extended interview to *Le Monde* in which he called for the departure of the putchists and the establishment of a strong government which would hold office for a reasonable time to resolve the Cyprus situation, reform the constitution, re-organise the administration, restore discipline in the army, then proceed to a referendum and elections. In a private message to Constantine he proposed that the king should dismiss the Kollias government and appoint him as prime minister. Karamanlis calculated that with the UN, NATO and the US government all involved in the endeavour to calm the Cyprus crisis Papadopoulos would step down.[33]

Constantine considered the time propitious for him to act though he says that the Karamanlis statements harmed, rather than helped, his cause by making the regime more vigilant. His calculation was that the colonels were unprotected because of the forward deployment of major army units. There was no evidence of any effort having been made to meet his mid-December deadline for presentation of a constitution and further delay would have deprived him of loyal officers as pressures for retirements intensified. On December 13, he launched a counter-coup.

It was a sketchily conceived action which had been well-signalled. The plan called for him to fly to Thessaloniki, secure Third Army headquarters, and broadcast a message — to the nation as monarch and to the army as commander in chief — calling for loyalty to the crown. Effectively he hoped to 'vote' the colonels out of office by securing more pledges from unit commanders than the junta could muster. He was, by his own admission, unprepared to fight for fear of provoking civil war.[34]

Two factors mitigated against success. Constantine had taken inadequate account of the degree of loyalty which the colonels commanded among the junior officers installed at strategic points in the hierarchy from where they were able to neutralise monarchist senior officers and the Third Army, commanded by his principal supporters, being in forward battle positions, was unable to secure Thessaloniki.

The head of the Air Force flew to the 28th Tactical Command at Larissa with a tape recording of the royal address to the nation. The monarch's broadcast went out on a low power transmitter which was so weak that it could not be heard in Athens. The junta meanwhile secured EIR and EDE and began broadcasting denunciations of a royal rising about which the majority of the population knew nothing.

Constantine travelled to the Macedonian town of Kavalla where he received an enthusiastic reception despite the area's reputation as a left-wing stronghold. The king's speech was broadcast locally and printed on leaflets to be scattered by air on Thessaloniki. Before this could be accomplished, however, the minister of northern Greece, Brig. Gen. Dimitrios Patilis,[35] claimed command of the Third Army and went on the national radio network calling for northern Greek troops to obey his orders. The counter-coup was effectively over before it began and in the small hours of December 14, Constantine fled to exile in Rome.

The junta convened as the Revolutionary Council (the only occasion on which the existence of this institution was ever formally acknowledged) to consider the way forward. One camp wished to declare a republic immediately but the majority argued that this could create difficulties with international recognition as ambassadors were accredited to the crown. A policy line was devised to the effect that disloyal officers, and not the king, were responsible for the counter-coup.

Lieut. Gen. Zoitakis was appointed regent. A new government was sworn in, the composition of which was largely unchanged, except that Papadopoulos stepped up to be prime minister and minister of defence in addition to his post as minister to the prime minister. Kollias fled with the king and

Spantidakis, who was abroad at the time, hesitated too long before deciding to which camp to pledge his loyalty. His duplicity and uncertainty were rewarded with retirement.

To assuage public opinion, the triumvirate resigned their commissions. A ceremony was staged to hand over a draft constitution and an amnesty was announced for offences prosecuted under the martial law. It did not apply, however, to those detained in the island prison camps.

III

The departure of the king fully exposed the unconstitutional nature of the regime. Increasingly it came under international scrutiny. In January 1968, Amnesty International published a damning report which revealed the terrible tortures inflicted by security interrogators and concluded that these were used 'deliberately' with official sanction. That same month the European Commission on Human Rights accepted to hear complaints concerning the elimination of civil and political liberties.

The colonels abandoned the pretext that their tenure was simply a parenthesis and declared that they constituted a National Revolution seeking to create a New Democracy of New Men and New Ideas. They said there would only be a return to representative government once 'the aims of the Revolution' were accomplished. These embraced an amorphous vision of a society imbued with 'Hellenic–Christian ideals' in which citizens subordinated their private interests to the greater good as conceived and sanctioned by the state. The colonels embarked upon a programme of 'political education' of the electorate with Papadopoulos stumping the country preaching 'a new democratic order' in which Greeks would 'socialise' their interests for the good of the nation. His speeches were collected as *To Pistevo Mas* (Our Credo). A civics reader, *Politiki Agogi* (Political Education), was disseminated widely among students, civil servants and opinion makers.

Papadopoulos was obsessive in his effort to regulate all aspects of public life by law and he constantly attempted to overlay the junta's usurpation of authority with a veneer of legality. What hallmarked the regime as a dictatorship, however, was its arbitrariness when its authority was challenged.

Papadopoulos cultivated the idea that he wished for an early return to elected rule but implied privately that he could not move quickly towards restoration of representative government because others within the ruling group were so disaffected with political life that they would not countenance elections. According to Col. Ladas, a leading figure in the hardline camp: 'The aims of the revolution could be achieved only by the present system.'[36] This division within the junta eventually led to open rupture.

To make the image of the regime more acceptable. Papadopoulos insisted that military supporters who wished to participate in the administration resign their commissions. It was indicative of just how secure the junta felt that as early as February 1968 the majority became civilians. Press controls were marginally relaxed but rigorous prior censorship remained. Constitutional guarantees of association and assembly were reinstated for trade unionists just days before the International Labour Organisation was to consider the Greek case. Andreas Papandreou was released from prison and allowed to go into exile in Canada.

The ameliorative effect of such measures was countered by purges of large numbers of professors (later retired generals were appointed as university commissioners) and by an unprecedented incursion into the independence of the judiciary with the dismissal, without appeal, of 30 senior judges.[37]

During the summer of 1968 great play was made of preparations for a new constitution. The colonels had known for some time what they wanted to incorporate in the charter[38] and, in seeking a method to impose their design, exploited the concept of public consultation. The draft prepared by the Mitrelias committee was published. Each day newspapers were required to carry cutout coupons containing articles from it alongside the comparable articles of the 1952 constitution. The public were then invited to write in to a special committee at the ministry to the prime minister which, it was implied, would collate the recommendations for consideration in preparation of a final draft. The committee claimed to have received five million comments but the junta's 'amended' draft appeared within weeks of completion of the process — scarcely time for the papers to have been sorted let alone for any significant consideration to have been given to them. The exercise was typical of the cynicism with which the regime approached any expression of the popular will.

The junta draft, published July 11, was in its general assumptions and definitions anti-communist and authoritarian. Its most significant changes were to make the monarchy a figurehead, stripping it of all its political and military prerogatives, and to remove the armed forces from political control by assigning promotions, retirements, assignments and transfers to the competence of military councils. The executive and legislative branches of government were to be strictly separated. To avoid parliamentary interference, the executive was in certain instances to be able to legislate by statutory decree subject to *post facto* ratification by the parliament. The size of the assembly was to be halved from 300 to 150 and deputies were to represent the nation not their constituency. A Constitutional Court was to be introduced whose members would be appointed for life by the regime. It would make irrevocable decisions on the powers of the king, parliament and government and on the constitutionality of laws. It would also adjudicate on the eligibility of candidates for parliament. In sum, it was a charter for a 'guided democracy'.

In the course of the 'debate' on the constitution, ground rules emerged for participation in the colonels' political life. Criticism was acceptable provided one first acknowledged the regime. Comment was to be confined to the acts of the government and not to its legitimacy or legality. Western diplomats urged the former politicians to seize on even this limited scope for criticism in order to try to re-introduce at least the forms, if not the substance, of political debate but the parliamentarians insisted that any comment would have been tantamount to recognition of an illegal regime. There were tentative contacts among some former deputies with a view to issuing a joint condemnation but these came to nothing, partly because inter-party feuds were still too fresh and partly because the Security curtailed proper consultation. Several MPs were sent into internal exile for making individual adverse statements while the two main party leaders, George Papandreou and Panayotis Kanellopoulos, were placed under strict house arrest for six months prior to the constitutional referendum as a precautionary measure.

An alternative to the boycott was proposed by the former Conservative foreign minister Evangelos Averoff. He believed that isolating the colonels could only entrench them in an absolutist mode. He adopted what he termed a bridge-building policy offering to provide a loyal opposition if only they would hold an election. He hoped by this means to beat them at their own game. He was under no illusions that the party he would form would be allowed to win but he felt one of two things would happen. Either the relaxation which would be required to conduct a simulacrum of fair elections would so erode the dictatorship that it would dissolve; or, the army, witnessing the inevitable corruption of the electoral process to secure the colonels' victory, would be so disgusted as to intervene to restore valid voting. He failed to appreciate the perversion of democratic principles wrought among the officer corps by the perquisites of power. Averoff was ostracised by other politicians for his policy. Coincidentally, he maintained contact with an underground organisation of dismissed royalist officers and indicated privately that he would be prepared to give political support to a military revolt provided it lasted no longer than two weeks. Prolonged fighting, he argued, would only benefit the communists.

The left, however, was riven with schism and in no condition to mount significant opposition. The communist camp had split into Moscow-line and Eurocommunist factions. The leadership in exile continued to try to control all left-wing activity by means of directives broadcast by its radio station, the *Voice of Truth*, and through the periodic despatch of functionaries to the country to enforce party discipline. During the early 1960s it had argued that the left should be campaigning for legalisation of KKE. The communist leadership of EDA, on the other hand, was more intent on mobilising the broad spectrum of the left to oust the conservative establishment and had concentrated nearly all its resources on its parliamentary activities to the exclusion of clandestine organisation.[39]

The differences came to a head in February 1968 at the 12th plenum of the central committee abroad when secretary general Kostas Koliyannis secured removal of members of the politbureau sympathetic to the leadership inside the country. Dissension became an open rupture after the Soviet invasion of Czechoslovakia in August 1968. The split led to duplication of all communist activities which meant almost as much time was spent on organisation as on resistance.[40]

In May, 1968 Andreas Papandreou announced the formation of the Panhellenic Liberation Movement (PAK). It was '. . . committed to the co-ordination of the activities of all resistance efforts in Greece, to the end that the junta be overthrown. . .' and it rejected 'any establishment-inspired "guided democracy" type of solution. . .'[41] This constituted a refusal to recognise any interim solution which might involve the King or Karamanlis ruling without benefit of parliament.

Patriotic Front and Democratic Defence had already established a working accord. In August, PAK agreed with representatives of PAM associated with the communist party of the interior to co-ordinate activities. Government propagandists characterised the agreement as 'a new popular front' and it was publicly denounced by some members of the Centre Union.

On August 13, an army deserter Alexander Panagoulis made an abortive attempt to assassinate Papadopoulos by blowing up his car as it travelled from his villa on the west coast of Attika to the capital. Panagoulis was acting for an organisation called Greek Resistance, however, the prosecution linked him with Papandreou and with other centrist political figures. More significantly, it named the Cyprus interior and defence minister, Polycarpos Georgatzis, as the source of funds, false documents and weaponry for Panagoulis and claimed that the explosives for the attempt had been sent to Greece via the Cypriot diplomatic bag. Georgatzis denied all responsibility but was forced to resign. In the wake of the attack there was a fresh security clampdown in which former politicians, party aides, senior journalists and retired officers were arrested and sent into internal exile. November 17, Panagoulis, who claimed to have been horribly tortured under interrogation, was condemned to death though, after an international outcry, the sentence was stayed indefinitely, albeit not commuted.

Papadopoulos abandoned any idea of an early election and, just two weeks before the September 29 referendum on the constitution announced amendments to the draft including a transitional clause empowering the 'National Revolutionary Government' to determine the dates for implementation of twelve clauses ensuring civil and political liberties.[42] Papadopoulos declared that the 'wounds' of the Greeks had not yet healed and that the Greek people would 'have to remain in a plaster even after the referendum...'

The result was that each vote in favour of the constitution became a vote for acceptance of the right of the colonels' regime to dictate the pace towards restoration of representative rule. The rigged referendum produced a 92 per cent yes vote. Papadopoulos hailed it as a mandate both for the regime and for the *status quo*. When this and the fact that the referendum had been held under martial law were legally challenged before the Supreme Court, the judges ruled that a revolution makes its own law, giving effective legal sanction to all future acts of the regime.

A better test of popular feeling was the funeral of George Papandreou on November 3. The centre of Athens was packed with half a million or more mourners shouting 'Greece votes today'. Police could only contain, not stop the crowd, but, though there was some fighting, there was no attempt at the popular rising which the colonels claimed to have seized power to avert. The occasion provided the opportunity for members of parliament to talk among themselves and during the obsequies EK and ERE made the first tentative commitments to political co-operation.

IV

Papadopoulos ostensibly was first among equals, though his pre-eminence in the government led gradually to the consolidation of power and personal dictatorship. In the wake of the referendum, his priority was to assert authority over the military. There was a substantial circle of junior officers — known as 'the pistoleros' — who secured the regime's interests within the armed forces but who themselves had become prone to the forming of cliques. They divided between those following Ioannis Ladas, who sought to establish a permanent authoritarian regime modelled on that of the fascist dictator of the Thirties, Gen. Ioannis Metaxas, and those siding with Lieut. Gen. Angelis who wanted to progress towards the restoration of elected government under the new, structured constitution. There were numerous reports of clashes, both verbal and physical, between the two camps.

Papadopoulos, appeared to prefer the evolutionary course, though his public statements were ambiguous and his actions contradictory. One moment, he would appear set to press on with the creation of new political institutions while the next he would be party to some repressive action which emphasised the authoritarian nature of the regime. If an underlying pattern could be discerned, it was towards creation of conditions in which he, and perhaps some of his junta colleagues, could get themselves elected to power as the representatives of the new political ethos which he propounded.

In November 1968, Papadopoulos transferred Ladas from the post of secretary-general at the ministry of public order, where he had control over internal security, to that of secretary-general at the ministry of the interior, where the loyal Pattakos was his immediate superior. It was several days before Ladas reluctantly assumed his new duties. Similarly it was proposed to transfer Dimitrios Stamatelopoulos from being secretary-general at the vital ministry of communications to the job of director-general of the National Tourist Organisation where he would report to Papadopoulos. Stamatelopoulos, however, refused and resigned to become a carping critic of the regime. He claimed that the original aim of refurbishing institutions for a return to political life was being corrupted and that 'a chapter was being turned into a tome'. It was the first public breach in the hitherto outwardly monolothic unity of the junta.

In December 1968, a law was introduced re-organising the armed forces. It created a Supreme National Defence Council empowered to name the commander of the armed forces and the three service chiefs who, in their turn, were to head councils responsible for all military appointments. The intention, it was claimed, was to limit political influence on the military, however, the composition of the cabinet of the day meant that the Supreme Council consisted of the junta triumvirate plus the loyal foreign minister, Panayotis Pipinellis. Angelis was named commander-in-chief, a title previously held by the monarch,[43] and Papadopoulos delegated to him all his administrative functions as minister of defence. It was a partnership which was to be sustained throughout Papadopoulos' tenure. He assumed, and got, absolute loyalty from

Angelis.

Lieut. Gen. Vassilios Tsoumbas, a careerist dedicated to discipline, was appointed chief of the army and, together with Angelis, moved to restore the chain of command. Junior officers loyal to the junta had assumed responsibilities greater than men of higher rank. The process of rationalisation required retirement of many seasoned senior officers in numbers[44] which caused concern among NATO planners. Officers who did not raise objections were compensated with places in the administration, ranging from seats on the board of public utilities to the directorship of the National Opera which was awarded to a brigadier of tanks. Scattered throughout the state apparatus, they provided stable points of contact for Papadopoulos.

Two junta men kept their military posts: Col. Michael Roufougalis, as deputy head of KYP, and Col. Dimitrios Ioannides, as commander of both the Military Police (ESA) and the Groups of National Security (OSA) responsible for internal regimental security. At the time it was argued that Papadopoulos had not been able to get rid of them[45] though, with hindsight, it would appear that he trusted both and kept them in place. Together with Dimitrios Karayannopoulos, a cousin, who served as head of Athens Security Police, they provided his personal eyes and ears against internal plots. In the case of Ioannides there was a delicate balance to be struck. He was an obdurate man and commanded loyalty among many hardline junior officers. He differed with Papadopoulos about the approach that should be taken to Cyprus. Ioannides was eventually relieved of his OSA title but continued to command ESA which became virtually an autonomous unit with its own transport, communications and other equipment.

A new constitution was drafted for the church, a press law was promised and, in April 1969, the gradual process of dismantling martial law began. In an address on the second anniversary of the coup, Papadopoulos announced that freedom of association and assembly were being fully restored together with the sanctity of the home. Appeal procedures were instituted against court-martial verdicts, internal exile orders, and dismissal from the public service. Eighteen committees were set up to draft institutional laws to flesh out the skeleton of the constitution. It was promised that priority would be given to the law on the constitutional court to help speed progress to elections.

These developments unfolded against a backdrop of foreign pressure for a return to elected government. NATO declined to comment on the dictatorship claiming it was not the role of a defensive alliance to interfere in domestic politics. But ministers of the Council of Europe, which included a majority of the NATO governments, voted to expel Greece by December 1969 unless, as British Foreign Secretary Michael Stewart put it, '. . . the evolutionary process towards democracy. . . has either been completed or is within striking distance of fulfilment'.[46] As part of secret negotiations that summer for a 'friendly settlement' of the complaints being heard by the Commission on Human Rights, the government offered a timetable for political developments: immediate limitation of the jurisdiction of courts-martial to cases against public order or security, a press law by November 1969, restoration of civilian courts by September 1970 and the implementation of the institutional laws by December 1970.[47] The regime refused, however, to be drawn on a date for a return to representative government. 'As regards elections, the Government is not able today to fix an exact date. . .'[48]

The regime produced a draft press law to take effect in 1970 and concluded a formal agreement with the International Committee of the Red Cross giving its representatives regular access to the interned communist detainees. It intimated that there might be a role in the new order for a number of politicians associated with the former Progressive Party leader Spyros Markezinis. Whether these tentative steps would have been sufficient to persuade the Council of Europe ministers to postpone judgment became academic, however, after the report of the Human Rights Commission was leaked to the press. It itemised 213 cases of heinous torture and concluded that maltreatment of political prisoners was routinely practised and officially sanctioned.[49] Greece withdrew from the Council before it could be expelled.

The United States government initially distanced itself from the colonels. The Democratic administration of Lyndon Johnson applied a heavy arms embargo as a sign of disapprobation.[50] Following the election of the Republican president Richard Nixon in November 1968, ambassador

Phillips Talbot resigned and no replacement was named for nearly a year. Washington continued to press discreetly for movement towards restoration of representative rule in exchange for lifting of the embargo.[51]

The colonels acquired an ally in the Nixon administration in vice-president Spyro Agnew. He was linked with Republican party financier Tom Pappas who spoke for a large part of the Greek-American business community in pressing for open US endorsement of the military regime.[52] Nixon, pre-occupied with Vietnam, seemed intent on doing only what was necessary to maintain such relations as would protect American military and business interests. Ultimately, as so often was the case with his foreign policy, he succumbed to pragmatic geostrategic considerations.

Colonel Khaddafi seized power in Libya in September 1969 and ordered the Americans out of the Wheelus airbase and Britain out of its naval station at Tobruk. Jordan was on the brink of war with Syria as King Hussein expelled the Palestinian guerrillas in the autumn of 1970. Egyptian President Abdul Gamal Nasser died and was replaced by Anwar Sadat who appeared in the beginning to be pro-Soviet. There was political upheaval in Turkey with students and workers staging demonstrations against visits by the US Sixth Fleet and American air bases and intelligence-gathering installations. In June 1971, Dom Mintoff was elected prime minister of Malta and made it clear that NATO vessels were not welcome in the harbour at Valletta. These events took place at a time when the Soviet Union was rapidly expanding its Mediterranean fleet, the Fifth Eskadra.

The apparent stability offered by the colonels, who also afforded the US extensive port and air facilities, caused Nixon to opt to lift the embargo. A new ambassador, Henry Tasca, was nominated to Athens within weeks of the Khaddafi coup and a decision taken by the National Security Council to restore arms aid without political concessions.[53] It was delayed for a year because of rearguard action in Congress but ultimately the administration prevailed. The improved relations were publicly acknowledged by the visit of vice-president Agnew to his ancestral village in October 1971.

Domestic tolerance of the colonels had by now evaporated but the former political leaders were unable to reconcile their party differences in order to offer a viable alternative which might have caused the army to withdraw its support for the regime. Attention focussed on Karamanlis who was widely held to be the only option acceptable to the Americans. In summer 1968, Constantine Mitsotakis, a leading Liberal Democrat who had escaped to Paris, publicly recommended an alliance of the former parties under Karamanlis' leadership. The idea was dismissed by the Centre Union who were still unprepared to countenance any co-operation with the Liberal Democrat defectors. George Papandreou left a political testament urging co-operation between Andreas, Karamanlis and the king — though not the communists. Andreas wrote to Karamanlis in February 1969 saying that he would accept a solution in which the former prime minister was leader,[54] however, neither Karamanlis nor Kanellopoulos trusted Andreas and Karamanlis was openly contemptuous of '[King] Paul's naughty little boy'.[55]

Moreover the leadership of the Centre Union was now at issue. Former parliamentary spokesman Nikos Bacopoulos briefly inherited Papandreou's mantle but when he died in April 1969 the several tendencies in the party each had their own representative. George Mavros eventually became titular head and, together with Kanellopoulos, agreed in summer 1969 to broad co-operation in any government which might follow the colonels, though they did not detail how such collaboration would work.

The colonels took their own political soundings. In August 1969, Pipinellis met with the king. Constantine reiterated that he would not return to Greece without the release of political prisoners, the restoration of freedom of the press and free elections under international supervision. Oblique approaches were also made to Karamanlis but he was insistent that he would not return as the head of any interim administration in which the colonels would be involved. The former military men would have to quit the scene entirely before he would consider returning. In October 1969, at the height of the crisis with the Council of Europe, Karamanlis issued another public denunciation describing the colonels as tyrannical and responsible for the disintegration of the armed forces and the economy. If they did not withdraw, he said, they would eventually be overthrown; it was the duty of their fellow officers to impress this fact upon them.

He wrote separately to retired Chief of Staff General Solon Ghikas asking him to use his influence to get the colonels to negotiate a handover of power and 'if the government chooses war. . . [to] examine with a group of your friends and colleagues what should be done next with my initiative, so that it does not fall into the void'.[56] It was an open invitation to rebellion and the colonels accused Karamanlis of 'terrorist activities'.

Efforts to promote disaffection had already been undertaken by a resistance group called Free Greeks (EE). It united retired conservative and centrist officers who sought to persuade active service colleagues to withdraw their support from the regime. The military police rapidly penetrated the organisation and, by the autumn of 1969, 37 former officers and 13 civilians had been detained. Sixty serving officers were reported disciplined. The arrested men were held for nearly a year in isolation in hotels on the outskirts of Athens and later, when it appeared that the relaxation of martial law would make it mandatory either to try or to release them, they were sent into internal exile. Most were amnestied by the end of 1971.

The other major resistance organisations – PAK, PAM and DA also suffered depredations at the hands of ESA which, having taken a single member of an organisation would methodically use torture to extract the identities of other members of the group. Democratic Defence was broken after a bomb misfired in the hands of professor Dionysios Karageorgas who was brutalised even as he convalesced. The 34 intellectuals who eventually went on trial in April 1970 testified not only to physical maltreatment but to fiendish psychological humiliations. Their sole consolation was that their court martial provided one of the first public platforms for joint political statements by Kanellopoulos and Mavros who testified in their defence.

Inroads were made into KKE ranks with the arrest in 1969 of Grigoris Farakos, a member of the central committee, and the following year of Nikos Kaloudis, a member of the politbureau. In October 1971, security forces detained two leading figures of the dissident communist leadership, Dimitrios Partsalidis, who had been prime minister in the insurgent government during the civil war, and Haralambos Drakopoulos, secretary general of the interior party. In each case large numbers of party workers were rounded up with the principals.

The security apparatus was so extensive that it was able to pick off resistance workers almost at will. The ineffectuality of the underground resistance was demonstrated by the proliferation of organisations. Literally dozens of small groups sprang up, usually of young people, and often they had not proceeded beyond the planning stage of their activities before being arrested. In late 1970 the police detained more than 100 prominent left-wing figures on suspicion of membership of PAK. They were interrogated over the course of a year, then quietly let go without charges ever having been pressed.

The painstaking process of political evolution continued in 1970 with application of the press law and further limitation of the scope of martial law. Papadopoulos now described it as 'a light walking cast'. Overnight the enforced press endorsement of the regime gave way to a semblance of hard news coverage, although commentary remained curtailed by the groundrule that the regime's legitimacy was not to be challenged.

A cabinet shuffle in June 1970 brought into government a one-time centrist mayor of Athens as minister of justice and a former ERE youth leader as minister of labour. This was not a drift back to the old political order, rather it was minor politicians acknowledging the new. The more significant appointment was that of George Georgalas as undersecretary to the prime minister. A former communist, Georgalas had been trained by Agitprop to work among Greek refugees in eastern Europe but, after the death of Stalin, he defected to work as an adviser and lecturer for Greek intelligence. For more than a year he served the colonels as ubiquitous spokesman and ideologue, perpetually projecting the 'revolutionary' image of the regime as a popular movement intent on establishing a new social, economic and political order. He was a particular exponent of the Papadopoulos thesis that the populace had to 'socialise' its individualism before political life could be restored.

This shuffle was accompanied by a re-organisation of government which transformed the cabinet into a presidential style executive with powers concentrated in the office of the prime minister. He acquired five special counsellors and a twenty-five man secretariat plus the power to appoint and to define the competence of an unspecified number of ministers without portfolio. In terms of Papadopoulos' authority, such consolidation was superfluous as he was already prime minister, defence minister, minister to the prime minister, minister of education, and soon to become, on the death of Pipinellis in July, foreign minister. Rather it was part of a process of grooming new figures to serve in his 'guided democracy'.

The Advisory Committee on Legislation which began operation in January 1971 served a similar function. It consisted of 56 individuals selected by the prime minister from a short list 'voted' by a college of 1,240 electors most of whom were regime nominees to local government, professional and union organisations. The committee, fallaciously dubbed a mini-parliament, met in the old assembly chamber to discuss draft laws presented to it by the government but its opinions were in no way binding and it had no powers to generate legislation. On more than one occasion its members were publicly rebuked by regime leaders for being too critical. Nevertheless six committee members were given senior posts in the administration and the pay was substantial, so that, when the second selection was declared the following December, more than 900 candidates put themselves forward. The 'electoral college' was increased to just over 10,000 – a quarter of one per cent of the Greek electorate.

The years 1971 and 1972 had an air of experimentation, as Papadopoulos sought to define the shape of his new political system and to give new men government experience. He embarked on a series of meetings with 24 members of the last parliament, who became known as 'the contractors', and a political line was enunciated that anyone, even the former politicians, could participate in the new order provided they accepted the 1968 constitution. Those who refused would be considered to have voluntarily withdrawn from political life. To reinforce the idea that all were welcome to participate in the new order, the contact group included a former MP detained for a time as a suspected member of Free Greeks and another who had been implicated in the Panagoulis affair.

In a sweeping government re-organisation in August 1971, Papadopoulos amalgamated several service ministries into two umbrella ministries dealing with economics and communications and reduced the size of his inner cabinet. Cabinet councils were re-organised to further concentrate policy-making power in his hands while a wide range of new under-secretariats were created without voting rights in government. Several of Papadopoulos' counsellors filled these posts. His fellow triumvirs were elevated to the rank of deputy prime minister and relieved of their responsibilities at the ministries of interior and co-ordination. Several members of the junta were brought into the government and appointed as heads of new regional departments based in the provinces. At the time, the move was viewed as an internal coup, an end to collegial rule, with Papadopoulos asserting his absolute authority.[57] Again it would appear that it was part of his process of gradual evolution to give junta colleagues cabinet experience and to cement the regime's interests in the countryside. At year end martial law was lifted throughout the country except in Athens and Thessaloniki.

Cyprus continued to be a destabilising factor. Following the withdrawal of Grivas and the Greek troops in December 1967, the Turkish Cypriots declared a Provisional Cyprus Turkish Administration in the enclaved areas adopting a Basic Law which provided the germ of a constitution for an autonomous Turkish Cypriot state. Hardliners sought to consolidate the Turkish Cypriot enclaves in order to establish a bizonal federation.

A majority of Greek Cypriots, while aspiring to *enosis*, did not relish the thought of union under the dictatorship. AKEL was particularly opposed because of the colonels' anti-communism. Cyprus became a haven for opponents of the regime of all political persuasions. Makarios adopted an ambiguous posture declaring that, while *enosis* was desirable, it was not feasible under present circumstances.[58] He accepted the UN recommendation for inter-communal talks as the means of finding a new constitutional order which would preserve the independence and unity of the island. At the presidential elections of February 1968 he secured 97 per cent of the vote giving him a mandate for this policy. Talks commenced in the summer of that year.

Extreme unionists were not prepared to abide by the wishes of the majority and an underground organisation called the National Front was formed. In the course of

1969, its members shot the chief of police and the government spokesman and bombed the homes of the Justice Minister and the leader of AKEL. The Front had the tacit support of Greek officers seconded to command the National Guard. These men, hand picked by the Greek military authorities for their loyalty, inculcated their recruits with propaganda against AKEL and communist fellow-travellers, among whom they included the Archbishop. Turkey and the Soviet Union accused Greece of conspiring to secure union by force. The commander of the National Guard had finally to be recalled after having told a public meeting that *enosis* would be imposed, forcibly if necessary.

March 8, 1970, Archbishop Makarios narrowly escaped assassination after a helicopter in which he was travelling was machine-gunned. Makarios implicated former Defence Minister Polycarpos Georgatzis. A week later, Georgatzis was murdered during a late night rendezvous. His bodyguard produced a document purporting to be a plan for the National Guard to seize power. The names of two Greek special forces officers intimately associated with the colonels were linked both with the attack on the Archbishop and the murder of Georgatzis[59] but investigators accepted their alibi and four Cypriots, including two policemen, were found guilty of the attempted murder of Makarios. The Georgatzis murder remained unsolved. The Archbishop declared the coup plan to be a forgery. Against this backdrop, the intercommunal talks deadlocked in the Spring of 1971 over the issue of the degree of autonomy to be afforded to the Turkish Cypriot community.

The Greek junta members fell broadly into two camps: those who saw Cyprus as purely a Greek affair and were prepared to confront Turkey if it attempted to intervene; and those who perceived that the issue had to be resolved without conflict and in a manner acceptable to Greece's western allies. Papadopoulos fell into the latter category. He seized upon the opportunity afforded by the March 1971 military *pronunciamento* in Turkey – which brought to power a non-political government under Nihat Erim, one of the drafters of the 1960 constitution – to broach with Ankara a bilateral approach to the Cyprus issue. In a private session at the NATO ministerial meeting in Lisbon in May 1971, Greek Foreign Undersecretary Christian Xanthopoulos-

Palamas and Turkish Foreign Minister Osman Olcay agreed that the best course would be resolution through continuation of the inter-communal talks but along lines agreed by Athens and Ankara. They acknowledged the validity of the London and Zurich accords and stressed the need for restoration of partnership in central government. They further agreed that there should be substantial autonomy for the Turkish Cypriots and that one of their number should be appointed to the Cypriot cabinet with extensive powers over local government. In exchange Turkey reiterated its adherence to the terms of the treaty of guarantee and agreed not to invade Cyprus without prior consultation with the Greek government.[60] Failing a successful outcome to the talks, the two sides said that they would act jointly to arrive at some 'definitive solution' though they differed about what form this should take.

Makarios rejected the proposal claiming it would create 'a state within a state', and be the first step along the road to partition. Tensions flared and UNFICYP was placed on high alert to prevent a fresh outbreak of inter-communal fighting. On October 18, following a further meeting between Xanthopoulos-Palamas and Olcay at the UN, Secretary General U Thant proposed that the negotiations should be expanded to include his special representative for Cyprus plus a Greek and a Turkish constitutional expert.

To confound matters, Grivas, who had been under house arrest since having been recalled from Cyprus in 1967, escaped and returned clandestinely to the island to regroup the underground unionist forces as EOKA-B. The background to his arrival remains obscure. It was assumed at the time that he had been despatched with the blessing of the junta in order to harry Makarios into compliance but, if Papadopoulos truly was seeking accommodation with Ankara, logic tells against this, for Grivas sought a form of unadulterated *enosis* which was anathema to the Turks. Instead, it is suggested that hardliners unleashed Grivas with the connivance of Zoitakis who was an old army friend of the general. Papadopoulos had to accept a situation not of his own making, hoping ultimately to manipulate Grivas to his own ends.

The former guerrilla leader began a campaign of terrorist attacks designed to destabilise Makarios. The president let it be known that he would be prepared to offer Grivas a ministerial post in government, possibly even defence, but only if he would commit himself to pursuing a common policy firmly based on independence.[61] Uncertain about the loyalty of the National Guard, Makarios increased the manpower of the police and created within it an anti-terrorist Tactical Reserve Unit which he planned to arm with weapons purchased from Czechoslovakia. These arrived in Cyprus in late January 1972. February 11, the furious Greek government issued a written ultimatum that Makarios should surrender the arms to the United Nations, form an anti-communist government of national unity and accept that Athens was the 'national centre' of Hellenism of which Cyprus was only a part. At a press conference the following day, the Greek ambassador declared ominously that 'the Cyprus government does not represent the whole of the national front in Cyprus. Governments in every country can be changed.'[62]

The colonels had anticipated that such a rebuke would force Makarios to resign, however, the Archbishop's supporters organised a massive public rally – said to be the largest in the island since his return from British-imposed exile in the Seychelles during the independence struggle – which he took as renewal of his popular mandate. The house of representatives voted for him to continue in office, though it did urge him to restore 'full relations' with Athens.

March 29, the Archbishop held a secret meeting with Grivas during which the guerrilla chief reiterated the demand for the president's resignation and the choice of a new candidate of 'mutual trust' who would contest elections on a platform of *enosis* through self-determination. Makarios' reaction in a letter dated May 4 was that *'enosis* is the compass of our national orientations but *enosis* cannot be realised unless the danger of another undesirable solution [forcible imposition of power-sharing leading to partition] is first removed'. In May the left-wing Foreign Minister, Spyros Kyprianou, resigned and in June Makarios changed seven of the ten members of his cabinet, but only to include less-left-leaning proponents of independence. He slyly commented that he had asked 'the nationalist camp' to join but that it had declined. The inter-communal talks resumed in June, with the inaugural session presided over by UN

Secretary-General Kurt Waldheim, thus reinforcing the image of Cypriot independence.

V

Zoitakis was made scapegoat for the crisis. He had backed the hardliners in allowing the 73-year-old ex-guerrilla leader to return to the island only to see Grivas fail to enforce Athens' ultimatum. Zoitakis was sacked and Papadopoulos assumed the title of Regent as well as that of prime minister, defence minister, foreign minister and minister of government policy.

Any revolutionary impetus the regime might once have had was now dissipated and it began to crack under the weight of its own inertia. April 21, 1972, the fifth anniversary of the coup, witnessed the first organised anti-junta demonstration. About a hundred students sat on the steps outside Athens university chanting 'Freedom' and 'Long Live Democracy'. When police charged, the students retreated, singing the national anthem. Five were arrested and later freed but the seed was sown of a protest movement that burgeoned so rapidly it precipitated Papadopoulos' downfall in just over a year and a half.

The youths were demanding free student union elections to get rid of regime appointees. They fought the issue in the courts and in campus demonstrations. Instead of toying with the students as it was doing with the politicians, the regime chose to confront them. On May 3, a decree was issued permitting the use of firearms in the dispersal of illegal demonstrations. Arrested students were expelled from university. Those attending court hearings had their identity cards taken and were told to collect them later at security headquarters where they were systematically 'processed' with beatings.

Student elections were allowed in the autumn but under conditions designed to ensure victory for regime nominees. The students responded with further strikes and sit-ins. A new decree was enacted empowering the ministry of defence to revoke the deferment of national service for students abstaining from classes or inciting others to do so. In nearly two months of continuous disturbances 130 students were called up and Papadopoulos intimated the fate that awaited them when he declared in a public speech that 'if I'd had the people behind this strike in my army unit, I'd have smashed their heads in with a revolver'.

The police, at the sharp end of the junta's repression and afraid of the reprisals that might await them should the regime fall, were maliciously brutal. When they stormed the occupied law faculty late in March, protestors and passersby alike were hammered senseless with flailing truncheons and boots and several students, including women, were hospitalised with severe internal injuries. Lawyers defending the students in court were manhandled and arrested. When the schools closed for summer recess, the violence abated but the pustule of unrest continued to fester.

The increasingly chaotic situation confirmed conservative fears that the colonels repression was spawning a drift to the left. Averoff made one last effort to build his bridge. It began in May 1972 when he approached the head of the political affairs section of the KYP and asked him to relay a proposal to Papadopoulos. He suggested that the junta leader should resign as prime minister; then, as regent, offer a mandate to a new government composed equally of his own and Averoff's nominees. This government would commit itself to conduct elections within one year. As a guarantee of the poll's fairness, no member of the government would stand for election. Papadopoulos could either remain aloof as head of state until restoration of the monarchy or he could come down and mingle in the political arena. Averoff had discussed the scheme with Tasca and understood it to be acceptable to the US government. He told the KYP man that if Papadopoulos concurred he would travel abroad to canvass support from the king and Karamanlis. The ambiguous response from Papadopoulos was simply *'Kalo taxidi'* (Good journey!).

According to Averoff, the king concurred, providing the monarchy was secure, but Karamanlis was dubious believing that no genuine political developments could take place without the colonels first standing aside. He believed Papadopoulos, with his hands on all the levers of power, could divert any such scheme to his own ends. Averoff's reaction was that if this happened he would resign and reveal all. The plan was said to have received a warm reception from the British foreign secretary and tentative approval from the French prime minister. In September, however, Averoff learned through an American intermediary that Papadopoulos had rejected the scheme as merely an elaborate ruse to restore Karamanlis.

Speculation was rife about a new constitutional order. It centred around two possible scenarios: the first a Franco model with Papadopoulos as *locum tenens* for the crown prince who would not be eligible to ascend the throne for another thirteen years; the second, abolition of the monarchy and formal installation of Papadopoulos as president. The idea that substantive changes were in the offing was reinforced when, in his August 1972 government shuffle, Papadopoulos elevated to ministerial rank the majority of the junta. This meant that most of the officers of the revolutionary committee who had agreed to the establishment of the regency were now members of the government and could approve any change by constituent act.

The cabinet included a number of the most trusted of the new men whom Papadopoulos had been cultivating for the past two years plus two under-secretaries from the group which had been associated with Averoff's bridge building scheme. In October 1972, a group of minor ERE and EK deputies made a tentative overture to Papadopoulos with a declaration that they would support a transitional government provided it was headed by Karamanlis. This was discouraged by the Kanellopoulos-Mavros alliance and Karamanlis issued a statement on November 7 dissociating himself from the initiative.[63]

There were hints that the king might be considering accommodation. In August, the monarch met Aslanides at an International Olympic Committee gathering in Munich. Then, in October, Constantine, who otherwise maintained rigorous public silence while in exile, addressed a university luncheon in Verona saying that 'as a modern king I shall neither have, nor do I want, executive power to impose my ideas on anyone'. It was tantamount to acceptance of the titular status laid down in the 1968 charter. On November 13, 1972 he had a meeting lasting several hours with Angelis. No details emerged though the king always maintained publicly that his minimum conditions for recognising the legality of any ballot were prior lifting of martial law, an amnesty for all political crimes and restoration of a free press.

In April 1973, the first of the new order parties appeared,

the Greek Cultural Movement (EPOK).[64] It was headed by Ioannis Xydopoulos, a lawyer who had briefly been minister of labour in the Kollias government which had been recognised by the king. Its membership included about a thousand individuals who were acknowledged adherents of the regime or who had been associated with the advisory committee on legislation. It was not clear whether it was meant to be the government party or the loyal opposition. The latter role might have been assigned to another grouping called the Social Union of Scientists created later by one-time press minister, Michael Sideratos.

On April 15, 1973, on the eve of the sixth anniversary of the coup, four retired generals — two former armed forces chiefs of staff and two former army chiefs of staff — issued a joint statement calling for the restoration of democratic rule. This was followed eight days later by yet another appeal from Paris by Karamanlis. He urged the colonels to recall Constantine and to hand over to an experienced government. He implied that if this were done now there would be no reprisals. To achieve this the government would rule for a time under emergency powers.[65] He accused Papadopoulos of attempting to perpetuate his structured regime through his programme of political evolution. Karamanlis pointed to the student unrest and said that any effort to hold rigged elections 'would be heading for bloodshed'. His appeal was acclaimed by all the senior political leaders within Greece while a further 34 retired senior officers endorsed the military men's initiative.

This joint military–political attack (the sort of action Karamanlis had first suggested four years earlier), far from shaking the regime, highlighted the impotency of the political opposition. The regime confiscated the three newspapers which printed the Karamanlis statement and continued with a round-up then in train of prominent centrist figures believed to be responsible for promoting the student disorder. The reaction confirmed the thinking of those who believed that the only way the regime would be unseated would be by violence.

Naval officers were already plotting a coup and had turned to Averoff for political guidance. He liaised with the king and Karamanlis. The degree of Constantine's complicity has never been made clear. Publicly, he categorically denied involvement though the regime produced evidence, which has proven correct in other details, that Constantine formally endorsed the revolt. Karamanlis on the other hand was of the opinion that the military was too thoroughly infiltrated for any plot to succeed, though he agreed that if the scheme came to fruition he would acknowledge it from Paris and make 'declarations for the purpose of finding a compromise solution'.

The plan involved some 20 warships including seven destroyers and two submarines. Some vessels were to sail to Syros in the Cyclades and take over the local garrison. From there the leaders of the rising would address a message to the nation outlining their political targets. The political programme was virtually identical to that which had already been advanced by Karamanlis.[66] Averoff and several other public figures would make the scheme known to the press and foreign embassies and attempt to start a run on banks and shops. If the regime failed to stand down as demanded, the naval vessels would blockade Piraeus and Thessaloniki. The action was scheduled for May 23.

The day prior to the action it became apparent to Averoff and his liaison, retired admiral Alexander Papadongonas, that they had probably been compromised. Averoff argued that, if they had been discovered, they would be arrested anyway. They should proceed even if it meant only the 'negative success' of demonstrating that the navy was not behind the regime.

When the first arrests were announced the regime tried to dismiss the plot as 'an operetta'. But it soon became apparent that a serious enterprise had been afoot. Some 200 people were detained for questioning and 74 referred for court-martial — 62 of them serving officers. The civilians included, as well as Averoff, former royalist defence minister Petros Garoufalias and several leading Athenian businessmen. One destroyer, the *Velos*, on manoeuvres off Sardinia at the time the rising was revealed, put into port near Rome where Constantine then resided. It may have been intended that this vessel should have taken the monarch on board, though its captain denied this. He and 30 members of his crew sought political asylum in Italy while the vessel and the remaining men on board returned to Greece.

The navy action provided Papadopoulos with a clear

justification for a republican solution. The speed with which he moved suggested that plans against such a contingency had long been prepared and needed only an excuse for implementation. June 1 a constituent act signed by the junta-dominated council of ministers declared Greece a republic and Papadopoulos its interim president. June 15, the regime published a 33-article constitutional revision document creating a form of government styled as a presidential parliamentary republic. The central feature was a reinforced executive which in theory would secure future political stability but which in practice would have meant continued control by the present rulers for at least 15 years and probably longer. Presidents were to hold office for only one term of seven years; however, the document specifically named Papadopoulos as the first president who would remain in place for eight years until June 1, 1981. His vice-president was to be Angelis who, it was assumed, would step up to the presidency when Papadopoulos' term ended.

The president was to be the commander of the armed forces and was empowered to name the chiefs of staff. He could re-invoke the state of emergency by decree. The only check on the presidential authority was a complicated procedure for impeachment for which the penalty was limited to removal from office and deprivation of political rights for life.

Papadopoulos was to retain the post of prime minister until the first elections but was given the right to delegate this function. After the poll, the Prime Minister had to be the leader of the largest party in parliament but the president retained the right to appoint the ministers and undersecretaries of national defence, public order and foreign affairs. Because of the 1968 constitution's division of ministers and members, these men would have to come from outside parliament. The president was constitutionally empowered to issue legislative decrees for the three ministries and to preside over cabinet when their business was being discussed. He was also to control their budgets.

Appointments to other ministries would be the responsibility of the prime minister but the president had to approve all laws and was given the right to put to a referendum any of which he disapproved. He could address the nation directly with no debate on the contents of his comments.

Parliament was to consist of 200 members, 20 appointed by the president and a further 30 to be elected indirectly in proportion to the parties' national standing. No individual could sit for more than four parliaments, in order to eliminate professional politicians; this was to apply retroactively.

The document promised establishment by December 31, 1973 of the constitutional court to vet candidates for political life and declaration of municipal and national elections within the course of 1974. The first and the second elections would be carried out according to a decree issued by Papadopoulos and the first elections would be carried out by a government authorised by him. The first parliament was to be a constituent assembly empowered to revise the constitution so that the electorate would be giving *carte blanche* for further changes to non-fundamental elements of the regime.

A referendum was set for July 29 but the regime made it clear that rejection would not mean restoration of the monarchy or the return of the military to their barracks. In the event of a 'no' vote Papadopoulos would simply essay another constitutional model 'always on the basis of the parliamentary presidential republic'. The revolution, a government spokesman said, 'will maintain all the initiatives'.

The proposals attracted universal condemnation from the king and from former members of parliament who banded together as the Committee for the Restoration of Democratic Legality which conducted a vigorous but, inevitably restricted, opposition campaign. For example, they applied for permission to hold gatherings in areas where martial law did not prevail but were refused and had to resort to subterfuges such as holding a press conference in Athens, advertised only by word of mouth.

Papadopoulos' intentions were challenged by former Colonel Stamatelopoulos who, in a newspaper article, offered himself as an alternative presidential candidate pledged to hold elections within 45 days. It was not a realistic proposition since there was no means by which his name could be written onto the ballot but it was a significant warning that not all the junta agreed with the way in which Papadopoulos was attempting to prolong the dictatorship by electoral means.

The extent and intensity of the opposition frightened the

regime and there was blatant polling fraud both in balloting practices and vote counting.[67] The official result was just over 78 per cent in favour though in Athens, despite the continuation in force of martial law, it was a mere 51.5 per cent. Constantine denounced the result as a fraud and declared himself the 'sole source of legality for Greece'.

Papadopoulos was sworn in as president on August 19, 1973 and immediately applied the amended 1968 constitution which lifted martial law throughout the country. His first act after investiture was to declare an amnesty for all political crimes. Some 250 convicted people and a 100 others still under investigation were released, among them Panagoulis and the naval mutineers.

Response to the return of civil rule was muted. The amnesty was greeted favourably and a part of the press implied that perhaps Papadopoulos was sincere in his intention to restore a form of representative government. But other newspapers, particularly the centrist publications of the Lambrakis group, insisted that the new arrangements could not bring about even a qualified return to democracy, only a continuation of authoritarian rule under the guise of electoral process. The conservative newspapers of the Botsis group endorsed the Papadopoulos formula, not, they would argue after the downfall of the dictatorship, because they believed it to be democratic but because it was known that Ioannides opposed such evolution and was lurking in the wings to re-impose full military rule.

While Tsoumbas and Angelis had remained on active service they had been able to neutralise instances of disloyalty among Ioannides' followers. Now, however, it was Ioannides himself who balked. Early in September, he was offered promotion and a transfer to head the Eighth Division in Ioannina. When he refused, he was put on two months compulsory leave. He continued to turn up each day at his ESA office.

Moving swiftly before Ioannides could marshal his forces, Papadopoulos pressed on with politicisation. On September 19, the constitutional court was appointed three and a half months before deadline. Then on October 1, despite six years vilification of the members of the former political world as corrupt has-beens, he gave the mandate as prime minister to Spyros Markezinis.[68]

There has been much debate over why Papadopoulos proceeded when he knew he no longer had full military backing. Reports at the time suggested that the Nixon administration had made recognition of the republic dependent on the exclusion from government of ex-officers and the holding of elections by a political cabinet. Certainly, in the course of the referendum, Ambassador Tasca had made it plain that he was in contact with, and approved of, the activities of the members of the Committee for the Restoration of Democratic Legality. Papadopoulos himself later claimed to have taken the extraordinary presidential powers simply to secure a peaceful transition to civilian rule. He said that he had done a secret deal with Markezinis to hold early elections and that the first parliament, as a constituent assembly, would have been able to revise the president's special powers.

Papadopoulos' junta colleagues were unhappy at the prospect of being excluded from the new government if his personal political proteges were to be included. On September 28, just days before Markezinis' long rumoured appointment was officially announced, three of them resigned: second deputy premier Makarezos, deputy minister for economy Balopoulos and deputy minister for education Aslanidis. Statements made by Makarezos at the time, were ambiguous but seemed to imply that if Papadopoulos were moving to a political regime then there should be a clean break with the past and Markezinis should be made wholly responsible for his policies. Aslanidis elaborated on the dissenters' position accusing Papadopoulos of seeking to impose a dictatorship 'under a parliamentary cloak'.

The Markezinis government sworn in on October 8 had a hybrid air. Eleven of its members — all of them with civilian backgrounds — had served in the last Papadopoulos government. The deputy premier was Harilaos Mitrelias, the man who had chaired the committee which prepared the royalist first draft of the 1968 constitution. Markezinis had managed to persuade Papadopoulos that foreign affairs should be the prime minister's responsibility and, having done so, nominated Xanthopoulos-Palamas to the post. The minister for co-ordination was Thanos Kapsalis who had been talked about for the job as long ago as 1969 when consideration of political evolution had first been mooted. Markezinis tried to persuade other former politicians to enter into the electoral process. He pledged 'impeccable elections' and said everyone would be eligible except those who refused to recognise the form of the regime — theoretically only royalists and communists. Throughout, the whole of October he made overtures to each political camp in turn but was universally rebuffed. He was scheduled to hold a press conference November 17 to announce that the date for the poll would be February 10, 1974, much earlier than anticipated, but he was overtaken by events.

VI

The Markezinis government sought to strike a delicate balance between the sort of liberalisation which might convince the population that restoration of democracy was in train and a degree of rigour sufficient to keep Ioannides and his ilk at bay. So, for example, on November 1, 1973, it announced that students who had been drafted into the armed forces would be allowed to return to classes but that the law under which their deferments had been lifted would remain on the statute books. Student activists immediately began agitation for repeal of the law and re-enrolment of students convicted of resistance activities, who had been freed in the amnesty. Fresh student union elections were demanded for December.

On Sunday, November 4, 1973, a memorial service was authorised to commemorate the fifth anniversary of the death of George Papandreou. Ten thousand people turned out in a noisy demonstration. Police panicked, ran amok firing shots in the air and furiously assaulted those who did not disperse. Seventeen demonstrators were sent for trial and five were eventually convicted. There were further angry clashes outside the court. Kanellopoulos and Mavros publicly denounced the police brutality.

Thus, when, on November 14, 2,000 students marched on Athens Polytechnic to demonstrate in favour of their demands, police, under a tight rein because of their recent behaviour, did not intervene for several hours. By the time they did seek permission to enter the campus, the students had barricaded the perimeter and begun to lay in supplies for a siege. The principal refused to allow the police to enter and they complied.

The student occupation began as a spontaneous local outburst of pent-up frustration against the years of martial law but it rapidly grew into a major confrontation with the regime. Thousands of curious Athenians poured into the streets to observe the students' protest and many joined them in chanting and distributing slogans. The communist underground spurred organisation of the amorphous crowds. The occupying students formed themselves into a co-ordinating committee to run the polytechnic precinct. On November 15 a trade union organisation calling itself the Workers' Convention held a joint press conference with them. A pirate radio station — Radio Polytechnic — went on the air broadcasting anti-junta slogans and calling for a general strike.

November 16 began with passive demonstrations. Groups of farmers, trades unionists and professionals paraded outside the polytechnic with banners denoting their work in order to demonstrate the breadth of opposition. By afternoon, violence had erupted. Construction workers, carrying staves and stones, briefly occupied the Attica nomarchy but were evicted by a strong police force. Demonstrators tried to march to the parliament building but were brutally dispersed. The ministry of public order was besieged by a chanting mob which, after darkness fell, attacked the building with stones and petrol bombs.

At dusk, the deputy military commander of Athens, Brigadier Nikolaos Dertilis,[69] arrived at the polytechnic to co-ordinate operations. Police used tear gas to try to disperse the crowd and, later, unidentified roof top snipers began to fire indiscriminately at anyone in the vicinity. Ambulances collecting the wounded frequently turned out to be manned by security personel. Taxis delivered escaping demonstrators to police units who administered severe beatings. Still the demonstrators continued to swarm round the campus and to besiege the ministry of public order. At 22.30, troops were ordered to move and tanks began to deploy in the city centre. By 01.30, they had secured the ministry of public order and by 02.00 three tanks were outside the polytechnic. A group of students sought to negotiate an evacuation but failed and a tank broke down the main gates. As the students rushed out of the compound, frenzied police and security men clubbed them to the ground. By 02.45 Radio Polytechnic was silent and within another three-quarters of an hour the immediate environs were cleared.[70]

The official account said that nine people had been killed and about 200 injured. A total of 866 arrests were said to have been made. The true figure of the casualties will never be known because many of the dead and injured were not reported to the authorities for fear of reprisals. The newspaper *Vima* in 1975 claimed 43 deaths and more than 1,100 injuries. A later official toll put the number of arrests at 2,473.

There was no legal basis for the military intervention. The police had not formally requested their assistance. Papadopoulos said at his trial that the decision to call in the army had been his responsibility but he claimed that he had given orders that weapons should not be used. Chief of the armed forces, Gen. Demetrios Zagorianakos, had asked the minister of defence for a written order to despatch troops but this had not been forthcoming by the time they moved. It was not until 09.42 the following morning that Athens Radio announced the reimposition of martial law together with a dusk to dawn curfew.

After the downfall of the dictatorship, an alleged plan was revealed according to which 150 *agents provocateur*, working under the command of Roufougalis, had helped foment the demonstrations at the polytechnic in order to create an atmosphere of anarchy such as to give Papadopoulos a rationale for the restoration of martial law which would then remain in force during the Markezinis elections. This is contrary to a statement broadcast by the government at the time which implied that the elections would be cancelled altogether: 'enemies of the nation have proved that they are unrepentant and do not want elections'.[71] Either way significant political evolution was now unlikely and the prospect was for a long sullen state of siege. Ioannides, who had been planning to take over ever since Papadopoulos elevated himself to the presidency,[72] had his justification to intervene.

In the small hours of Sunday, November 25, the tanks rolled again. Troops cut communications links and seized the radio stations. Papadopoulos was placed under house arrest in his seaside villa and Roufougalis was detained at Armed Forces Headquarters where he was closely interrogated over several days. The theory that Papadopoulos planned elections under martial law was given credence by the new group's takeover statement. It said that efforts were afoot to 'use the armed forces in a staged election which would humiliate the people'. The new ruling group said that its mission was the restoration of the revolutionary character of the April 21 regime and 'the creation of the suitable prerequisites for the country's return to parliamentary rule on a healthy basis'.

Lieut. Gen. Phaidon Gizikis, chief of the First Army Corps and a personal friend of Ioannides since they were posted together in Cyprus in the mid-1960s, was sworn in as president. The new prime minister was Adamantios Androutsopoulos, a Chicago-trained lawyer who was the only man apart from the triumvirate to have served in every government prior to Markezinis's.[73] His inaugural statement harked back to 1967 and spoke of the need to cleanse public life and to prepare the country for elections 'not among party clans but parties of principle'. The Markezinis government was dismissed as 'neither political, nor even a government, but rather a mixed and heterogeneous working group muddling along between the target to win the elections and to convince everybody that they will be carried out in an impeccable manner'.

Androutsopoulos promised a new constitution and rule in the interim by sparing use of constituent acts. (The first stripped the presidency of its extraordinary powers.) He said there would be tax and social reforms and a crackdown on the corruption of the former regime.[74]

The commanders of major military and police units were replaced.[75] Archbishop Hieronymos, who was closely identified with the former leadership and who had been sidestepped for the swearing in of President Gizikis, resigned. Papadopoulos' placemen in the administration were removed. Party leaders were released from house arrest as were a number of senior communist figures who had been re-arrested under martial law. Some of those detained following the polytechnic incidents were freed, though the pattern of releases was erratic. Initial reactions were favourable but cautious. Those with reservations quickly had them confirmed.

Ioannides was a zealot. He had a pathological hatred of communism and an abiding belief in the civilising mission of Hellenism.[76] An ascetic bachelor with few close friends, he was unused to compromise and expected absolute obedience to his dictates. Whereas Papadopoulos had attempted to sustain a veneer of legality for his administration, Ioannides tenure was characterised by its arbitrariness. He took no responsible position in the hierarchy but remained a shadowy presence in the background, ruling by fiat. For example, all Athenian newspaper publishers were convoked at armed forces headquarters and told that there would be no press censorship but that they would have to support the new regime or face closure. When two newspapers challenged the order they had their front doors padlocked by the military police. The prison island of Yiaros was re-opened and used to incarcerate scores of political opponents ranging from EDA parliamentarians through to Centre Union chief George Mavros. Reports proliferated of torture of regime opponents by ESA.

Ioannides' own position was not secure. Among the junior officers who supported him was a radical group which sought to corporatise the state by nationalising the banks, transport and heavy industry. Ioannides did not share their aspirations though he cultivated their allegiance. There were intimations of dissent among the senior ranks reflected in repeated rumours of yet another imminent coup by General Ioannis Davos, commander of the Third Army Corps.

The government was paralysed by uncertainty. Ministers did not know how to comport themselves for fear they might cross Ioannides and he, used only to barrack-room intriguing, could not articulate anything like a consistent policy even had he wished to do so. It was, as one foreign correspondent remarked at the time, like Beria trying to rule without Stalin.

The economy, which had grown rapidly under the stability enforced by Papadopoulos, stagnated under the confusion engendered by Ioannides. Inflation soared, fuelled by price increases caused by the oil embargo in the wake of the October 1973 Arab–Israeli war. There was real hardship among peasants and wage earners and deep-seated resentment of the regime but all dissent was ruthlessly quashed by the military police. Greece looked set for the sort of prolonged agony that Chile suffered under Pinochet.

Again, however, relations with Turkey were to provide the catalyst for change. In November 1973, Turkey issued oil exploration licences to the Turkish State Petroleum Corporation in areas of the Aegean sea which Greece considered constituted part of its continental shelf. Greece claimed that all its islands had their own continental shelf while Turkey counterclaimed that there was a natural prolongation of its mainland shelf which gave it seabed exploitation rights westwards of numerous Greek islands. Greece said that to recognise such rights would interrupt the political continuum of the country and threaten sovereignty over hundreds of thousands of inhabitants.[77] The Greek government threatened to attack any vessel which set about prospecting in contested waters. The situation was exacerbated by the discovery of oil in Greek territorial waters off the northern island of Thassos early in 1974.

With a law of the sea conference on territorial waters and economic management zones forthcoming that summer, Greece was also seeking to establish its prerogative to extend its territorial waters from six to 12 miles around each of the islands. The Turks claimed that this would cut off access through international waters to their west coast ports and said that if the Greeks were to proceed it would constitute a cause for war.

Tensions escalated between the two countries. There were demonstrations in Istanbul against the Greek Community. In March, Greece withdrew from joint NATO exercises with the Turks after Turkish military aircraft violated Greek airspace. Both sides moved armoured formations into forward positions along their Thracian border. In May the Turkish general staff announced that they were to create a military strike force which would not be assigned to NATO.

The Greco-Turkish accord to promote an inter-communal settlement in Cyprus had effectively collapsed. The internecine fighting within the Greek Cypriot community was escalating rather than diminishing and Archbishop Makarios could not have made the sorts of concessions demanded by the mainland governments even had he wished to. The elections which ended the period of military-backed, non-political rule in Turkey failed to produce a clear majority for any party. Bulent Ecevit, leader of the socialist Republican People's Party, managed to cobble together an unstable coalition with the Muslim-fundamentalist National Salvation Party and adopted the hard line that the only solution for

Cyprus was federation. Ioannides did nothing to assuage the tensions hoping to focus the attention of the Greek military away from internal dissension towards the external factor.

On January 27, 1974, just two months after Ioannides' accession to power, Grivas died of natural causes while still in the field. It was indicative of the gulf which had grown between the general and his one-time Athenian masters, that he named as his successor, ex-Greek army Major George Karousos. He had been jailed briefly for complicity in Free Greeks but later had fled to Cyprus to join the unionist forces. Karousos agreed to suspend EOKA-B guerrilla activities and to seek accommodation with Makarios. In March, however, he quit Cyprus in unexplained circumstances, surfacing on the island of Rhodes where he was arrested by ESA and transferred to Athens.[78]

In April, the mounting tension led to suspension of the inter-communal talks *sine die*. Diplomats worked feverishly to try to find an acceptable basis on which to restart them but Ioannides was already gearing up for a military solution. There was evidence of complicity by officers of the National Guard in the theft by EOKA-B of a substantial number of heavy machine guns. Officer trainees known to be sympathetic to the terrorist organisation were enrolled in the National Guard despite objections by the Cypriot government. In late June, the Cyprus government spokesman declared that recently captured EOKA-B documents 'confirmed that the terrorist movement was directed from Athens where it turned for instruction and guidance' and that the National Guard was 'a breeding ground of anti-government elements who also serve as a source of supply for the terrorist EOKA-B organisation'.

Makarios apparently thought Ioannides too uncertain of his grip on domestic power to risk overt military action against him. However, the chiefs of staff, confronting the possibility of a war on two fronts in Thrace and the Aegean were determined to secure Cyprus and open the prospect of a third on the Turkish southern flank. July 2 three senior Greek officers of the National Guard were called to Athens and ordered by Ioannides to organise a coup against Makarios. The Archbishop, apprised of the plot, pressed on with his dangerous brinksmanship, drafting a letter to president Gizikis in which he itemised all the instances in recent years of Athens' efforts to unseat him and openly accused the dictators of being behind the attempts at assassination. 'I have more than once,' he wrote, 'felt, and in some cases I have almost touched, a hand invisibly extending from Athens and seeking to liquidate my human existence.' On July 7 he made the letter public.

It failed to deter Athens. The National Guard staged its coup on July 15 and, after bitter fighting with the Tactical Reserve Force and paramilitaries loyal to the Archbishop, installed the former EOKA assassin, Nikos Sampson, as president. The coup failed, however, in its major objective. Makarios, who was supposed to have been murdered, survived and escaped abroad. Assisted by the British, he flew first to Malta and then to London and New York. On July 19, he addressed the United Nations Security Council as the legitimate leader of the state of Cyprus.

The appointment of the thuggish Sampson as president terrified the Turkish Cypriots. He was according to their leader Rauf Denktash as 'unacceptable as Adolf Hitler would be as President of Israel'.[79] The Turkish general staff, thwarted in their intentions to invade in 1964 and again in 1967, seized upon the opportunity to intervene under the treaty of guarantee. It is unlikely that Ecevit, could have restrained them, even had he presided over a more stable government. He did go through the motions of consultation required under the treaty, flying to London and demanding that Britain should allow Turkish troops to land via the sovereign bases. The Labour government declined and Ecevit refused to consider tripartite discussions with Greece which he said had invalidated its guarantor status by staging the coup.

US Assistant Secretary of State Joseph Sisco made two trips to each capital on July 19 in an effort to prevent the invasion but Ecevit, with troops mobilised and his grip on power in jeopardy if he failed to act decisively, gave the go-ahead in the small hours of July 20. The intervention was styled as a peacekeeping operation. Ioannides ordered mobilisation for retaliation but this revealed the chaotic state of organisation in the armed forces wrought by the years of politicking and plans for a counter attack were stood down. A ceasefire was obtained on July 22 through American mediation. The following day, the humiliated Greek service chiefs in consort with General Gizikis convened a conference of former political leaders to hand back power to civilian government.[80]

The conference after prolonged debate concluded that Panayotis Kanellopoulos and George Mavros should jointly form a government. It then adjourned while the men consulted their political colleagues. In the interim Averoff, who remained with the chiefs of staff, argued that this combination was not decisive enough to deal with the crisis. He convinced the military men that Karamanlis should be brought back from Paris. Kanellopoulos and Mavros returned to the president's office in the evening to find they had been superseded.

Karamanlis returned to Athens in a private jet provided by French President Giscard d'Estaing and was sworn in as Prime Minister at 04.15 on July 24. Kanellopoulos was offered the job of president but declined.[81] Constantine Tsatsos was eventually appointed instead. George Mavros joined the Karamanlis government of national unity as foreign minister, his first task being to try to negotiate a Cyprus settlement.

Britain convened a tripartite conference of the guarantor powers in Geneva July 25–30.[82] The meeting concluded with acknowledgement of a need for a degree of autonomy for the Turkish Cypriot communities and mutual undertakings that Greek forces would withdraw from Turkish Cypriot enclaves and the Turks would refrain from expansion of the territory that they then occupied. Prisoners were to be released.

A second conference to discuss new constitutional arrangements was convened on August 9, with the participation of Greek and Turkish Cypriot representatives. The Turks used the period between the two meetings to expand their bridgehead and to mass an invasion force of 40,000 men and 200 tanks. Britain, fearing 'the worst interpretation should be put on Turkish future intentions,'[83] offered to reinforce its troops on the island, assign the forces to the United Nations and have them stand astride potential Turkish lines of advance. It fell outside the mandate of UNFICYP but Secretary-General Kurt Waldheim felt he could get approval from the Security Council. US Secretary of State Henry Kissinger, then seeking to get Ecevit to accept a cantonal settlement, adamantly opposed the proposal saying that even to broach the idea could influence events to move onto a military plane. Britain, fearful of a repeat of the Suez fiasco when its invasion troops were frustrated by US intervention, refused to act unilaterally. Since, it has been a discredited player on the Cyprus stage.

The Turks provoked deadlock at the talks[84] and in a second major assault on Cyprus, on 14–16 August, seized contiguous territory in the north totalling 37 per cent of the island. The political government in Greece was no more able to mount a defence than the dictatorship had been. One hundred and eighty thousand Greek Cypriot refugees fled south during the fighting and, eventually some 40,000 Turkish Cypriots made their way north. Cyprus was partitioned *de facto*.[85]

Greece temporarily withdrew from the military command structure of NATO arguing that there was no value in membership of an alliance which could not protect it from aggression by an ally. Greek-Turkish relations have remained fragile ever since.

Afterword

The Karamanlis national unity government included individuals from the conservative right to the moderate socialist left, though it did not incorporate Andreas Papandreou who remained abroad for some weeks. Nor did it include any Communists for fear of provoking the military. The KKE was, however, legalised on September 23, 1974 allowing it to participate in the political process for the first time in 27 years. This was probably the sole virtue of the colonels dictatorship that by uniting politicians of all persuasions in opposition it taught them tolerance and brought ideological and political debate up from the underground and back from the streets into the parliamentary arena.

The national unity government abolished the colonels constitution and temporarily restored the 1952 charter. It also revoked much of the dictatorship's legislation. The transition from military to civilian rule was, of necessity, a tentative process. The generals, having ceded power voluntarily, expected no reprisals and it took several months before discipline and proper authority were restored to the military. A cabal of 37 supporters of Ioannides was arrested as late as February 1975 while allegedly plotting another coup. Eventually, the junta leaders were tried, convicted of treason and sentenced to death which was commuted to life imprisonment. Among their collaborators, only those who had committed demonstrably criminal offences were prosecuted. A small number of noted torturers were sentenced to up to 20 years imprisonment. Political collaborators went free.

Karamanlis' policy of reconciliation was highly unpopular with left-wing politicians and with the press, who demanded an extensive purge of all those who had been associated with the junta in any capacity. But it found favour with the public and in the first elections on November 17, 1974 Karamanlis' New Democracy party won 54 per cent of the popular vote and 220 of the 300 seats in parliament. A referendum on the monarchy on December 8, 1974 rejected the king by a vote of two to one. A new republican constitution was passed through parliament on June 9 1975 by 208 votes to nil, the opposition having walked out *en masse* over the extensive powers afforded to the president.

New Democracy's majority was sharply curtailed in elections in 1977 and Papandreou's PASOK became the official opposition. In the 1981 poll, it gained office with a majority of 174 seats, the sort of result which might have been expected in 1967 had the elections been allowed to proceed.

There has been intense debate over whether the colonels were a purely Greek phenomenon or whether they were agents of the United States seeking to secure division of Cyprus between two NATO nations. The Nixon administration countenanced the regime but principally for the apparent stability it afforded in a troubled region and for the facilities it provided the US Sixth Fleet and the US Air Force. Had the colonels been successful in producing in Cyprus a settlement which gave a similar impression of stability and offered comparable facilities, then no doubt the American administration would have accepted it. The US appeared to toy with the idea of recognising the government installed following the Greek-sponsored coup in Cyprus. The US ambassador to Nicosia, Rodger Davies,[86] met with Sampson's foreign minister. When Makarios flew to New York to plead his cause at the UN, Dr. Henry Kissinger indicated that he was being received as archbishop rather than as president.[87] The Americans sought to have a representative of the Sampson government address the Security Council on an equal basis with Makarios.[88] This, however, reflected antipathy to Makarios rather than support for Sampson whose continuation in office Kissinger considered 'the least desirable outcome'.[89] The attitude of the US administration thus could best be summed up as one of amoral pragmatism rather than active connivance.

The activities of the Central Intelligence Agency may, however, be another matter. It has been reported that the former CIA station chief in Cyprus, Eric Neff, met with Sampson and other EOKA-B figures in Athens on February 12, 1974.[90] Shortly before the coup against Makarios another CIA operative, Peter Koromilas, conferred with Ioannides.[91] Received wisdom in Athens is that the Agency assured Ioannides that were he to seize power from Makarios and allow a nominal landing by the Turks, then America would endorse a form of double *enosis* with Greece taking the lion's share of the island. Despite advance warning of the Turkish invasion plans, Athens did nothing to reinforce either the National Guard or the Greek national forces stationed on the island. Even after the National Guard reported sighting the Turkish landing fleet, Athens response was that it was probably on manoeuvres.[92] Perhaps the most telling evidence, however, comes from a western diplomatic source. On the night of July 20, Greek foreign ministry representatives canvassed allied embassies for support for an extraordinary session of the UN Security Council to secure a ceasefire. The western diplomat was told that the Greek military – including Ioannides – accepted that the 6,000 troops already landed at that time could be allowed to stay in Cyprus provided they withdrew to the Turkish enclaves.[93] This would have created a situation similar to that envisaged in 1964 with the island divided between two NATO partners and an end to the independent, non-aligned regime of Makarios.

Ioannides has said he was 'fooled' over Cyprus. The Karamanlis government's decision not to prosecute the officers who staged the coup in Cyprus in order to avoid 'possible disturbance of the country's international relations' fuelled speculation of a CIA plot. This in turn was compounded by the refusal of the Ford administration to release relevant classified documents to the House of Representatives

Select Committee on Intelligence. A Greek parliamentary inquiry reconsidered the existing evidence but came up with no new information that would constitute concrete proof.

NOTES

1. See, among others, Lawrence S. Wittner, *American Intervention in Greece, 1943–49* (New York: Columbia University Press, 1982), pp. 283–291; and, Richard Clogg, *Parties and Elections in Greece* (London: C. Hurst & Company, 1987), pp. 26–32.
2. The average rate of growth in gross national product during the 1950s and 1960s was 5.4 per cent.
3. The mentality was epitomised in a 1962 address to army officers by King Paul: 'God has united us – I belong to you and you belong to me.'
4. After the formation of an alternative government in northern Greece.
5. *Ethniki Organosis Kyprion Agoniston* (National Organisation of Cypriot Fighters).
6. Grivas, a Cypriot by birth, was formerly a Greek army officer, though he had retired before the EOKA campaign. He was an extreme anti-communist and led a white terror campaign on the mainland during 1945–46 which helped precipitate the civil war.
7. *Türk Mukavemet Teskilati (Turkish Resistance Organisation)*.
8. *Cyprus*, Command 1093, (London: HMSO, July 1960).
9. The Turkish Cypriots were guaranteed the office of vice president plus three of the ten ministries in government and thirty per cent of the seats in the House of Representatives. They were to have thirty per cent participation in the civil service and forty per cent in the security services. Electoral, communal and tax legislation required absolute majorities among the representatives of each community.
10. The Greek force, ELDYK, was to consist of 950 officers and men and the Turkish force, TURDYK, of 650.
11. See Richard Patrick, *Political Geography and the Cyprus Conflict: 1963–71*, Department of Geography Publication Series No. 4 (Waterloo, Ont.: University of Waterloo, 1976), pp. 83–86.
12. The EDA vote declined from 14.3 per cent in November 1963 to 11.8 per cent in February 1964.
13. *Anorthotikon Komma Ergazomenou Laou* (Progressive Party of the Working People).
14. The plan, evolved in negotiations with the former US Secretary of State Dean Acheson, provided for the creation of two sovereign Turkish military bases encompassing up to twenty per cent of the north of the island, cession of the Greek island of Kastellorizon to Turkey for the relocation of Turkish Cypriots who wished to emigrate, and creation of three Turkish Cypriot cantons exercising local autonomy for those who wished to remain on Cyprus.
15. It has been suggested that Aspida was intended to be a countervailing force to Grivas' influence in Cyprus. See Keith Legg, *Politics in Modern Greece* (Stanford, California: Stanford University Press, 1969), p. 223.
16. They were known to Centre Union loyalists as the *apostates*.
17. Evidence given at the trial of the dictators suggested that they had been plotting since 1951. This assertion that the genesis of the junta was during the troubled years of 1963–65 is based on conversations with one of its members, Colonel Constantine Aslanides. See also Robert McDonald, 'A Profile of the Greek Junta', *The World Today*, vol. 28, no. 5 (London:

Royal Institute of International Affairs, May 1972), pp. 229-234; and, George Zaharopoulos, 'Politics and the Army in Post-War Greece', *Greece Under Military Rule*, eds. Richard Clogg and George Yannopoulos (London: Secker & Warburg, 1972), pp. 17-35.
18. During the 1964 fighting, Ioannides and Sampson are reported to have approached Archbishop Makarios with a military plan to exterminate the Turkish Cypriot population. See Christopher Hitchens, *Cyprus* (London: Quartet Books, 1984), pp. 39-40.
19. There is evidence to suggest that Papadopoulos remained in Greece and fought in a Security Battalion, a local levy raised by the German occupiers to maintain public order.
20. *Ieros Desmos Ellinon Axiomatikon* (Holy Band of Greek Officers) was a fellowship of conservative and monarchist officers founded amongst Greek forces in the Middle East at a time when republicanism was rife. It was virulently anti-communist and thrived during the civil war. It survived into the 1950s when it was officially dissolved. Some of its members were involved in an attempt in May 1951 to install Marshal Papagos as Prime Minister. Dimitrios Ioannides and Antonios Skarmaliorakis, an air force officer involved in the 1967 coup, were party to that incident but, though their careers suffered for it, they were not dismissed from the services. See Nikolaos Stavrou, *Allied Politics and Military Interventions: The Political Role of the Greek Military* (Athens: Papazissis Publishers, 1976), pp. 136-144.
21. Aslanides said: 'We have all known one another and trust one another. For example, [Antonios] Lekkas in 1948 was stranded for 36-hours on the top of [a mountain] surrounded by 1,300 communists. I was able to breach the siege and relieve him. This is the kind of oath and trust we have.' Other sources say that the members of the junta belonged to the Union of Young Greek Officers (EENA) which was organised in 1965. The two accounts need not be mutually exclusive.
22. *Proceedings of the Crown Council* (Athens: Government Press Office, September 1-2, 1965), p. 46.
23. According to a Greek diplomat who was privy to the negotiations, the British government had let it be known that it was willing to promote a solution by 'putting one of the bases at the disposal of the two parties as an aid to settlement'. President Makarios put the matter in a different perspective claiming that the offer was to convert the British SBA at Dekelia into a NATO base at which Turkish troops would be stationed. In either case, he persuaded a Crown Council convened in Athens on February 2, 1967 to abandon the proposal!
24. The Turks were suspicious that it was the agreement which brought Stefanopoulos down.
25. This is a subject which is in dispute. The names given here were those acknowledged by Aslanides. Others who were prosecuted as members of the junta included Cols. Constantine Karydas (Armour) and Petros Kotselis (Infantry), Majors George Constandopoulos and Nicholas Dertilis (Special Forces, Attika), Major Evangelos Tsakas (KYP), Brig. Antonios Skarmaliorakis and Wing Commander Ioannis Paleologos (Royal Hellenic Air Force), Capt. Ioannis Lagonikis (Royal Hellenic Navy) and Cols. Nikolaos Gantonas and Stefanos Karaberis who helped effect the coup in Thessaloniki.
26. The junta was later to use this as its rationale for the takeover claiming that sixty thousand left-wing activists were to concentrate on the northern capital of Thessaloniki on April 23, 1967 for George Papandreou's inaugural election rally with a view to provoking a mass rising. It never produced evidence to support this claim.

27. Law 4069 Delta Chi Theta/October 1912 as modified by Legislative Decree 4234/1962.
28. For details see Robert McDonald, *Pillar & Tinderbox* (London: Marion Boyars, 1983).
29. He was a former member of IDEA. At his trial in August 1975, he claimed not to be of the revolutionary group but to have believed in its aims and to have wholeheartedly endorsed the takeover. Angelis committed suicide in prison in March 1987.
30. Asked by a member of the Senate Foreign Relations Committee what his government planned to do, he snapped: 'It is not my government!'
31. Miltiades Christodoulou, *The Progress of an Era* (Athens: Ioannis Floris, 1987), pp. 492–493. Christodoulou is a former Cypriot government official. Greek sources say no offer was made to cede Greek territory.
32. For details see Michael Harbottle, *The Impartial Soldier* (London: Oxford University Press, 1970), pp. 145-167. At the time, Grivas put it about that he had been acting on the orders of Gen. Spantidakis who had visited Cyprus late in October. Some years later Grivas claimed that the attacks had been ordered by Makarios with a view to destabilising the situation in order to get rid of the Greek troops on the island.
33. The message was supposed to have been relayed via Panayotis Pipinellis, a former ERE politician whom the colonels had brought into government as foreign minister in order to cope with the Cyprus crisis. Karamanlis says he does not know whether his advice was passed on but claims Papadopoulos later acknowledged that he would have been prepared to make way for such a solution at that time.
34. See C. L. Sulzberger, 'An Interview with King Constantine', *International Herald Tribune* (Paris, January 15, 1968). 'If we had taken Salonika. . . everything would have been finished. . . . I would have had a mass rally. I would have spoken on the Salonika radio and I would have called the ambassadors up there to meet with me. And all the generals who were hesitating would have stuck.'
35. Patilis, retired by the Papandreou government for political activism in 1964, was reinstated under the colonels, restored in rank and appointed to government in June 1967.
36. Max van der Stoel, *The Situation in Greece* (Strasbourg: Council for Europe, May 4, 1968), paragraph 125.
37. When, a year later, the State Council, defied the regime and upheld an appeal, its president was placed under house arrest.
38. Brigadier Pattakos had outlined in a private interview with the author several weeks before the Mitrelias committee was established many of the elements which eventually were incorporated in the colonels' constitution. These corresponded in some respects to a draft commissioned from Dr. D. George Kousoulas of Howard University, Washington but not made public.
39. To this extent, those who argued that there was a 'popular front' between the Centre Union and the Communists were correct but it was more an identity of certain political views than the revolutionary collaboration so many conservatives feared. This was amply demonstrated by the ease with which the police rounded up so many Communists during the takeover. A truly revolutionary party would have had a much better clandestine network in place.
40. For example, exterior loyalists began in March 1968 to publish an underground version of the party newspaper *Rizospastis*. Two months later, the interior group began producing *Rizospastis (Machitis)*, Radical (Fighter). For cadres not privy to the intricacies of the power struggle the situation conjured up memories of the Metaxas dictatorship of the Thirties when the

security chief had sowed havoc in Communist ranks by publishing a bogus *Rizospastis*.
41. Andreas Papandreou, *Objectives and Organizational scheme of the Panhellenic Liberation Movement (PAK)*, (Paris, May 1968). It is interesting in the light of the evolution of PAK into the Panhellenic Socialist Movement (PASOK) that the founding charter said 'PAK does not intend to eventually transform itself into a party organization'. It is also something which is overlooked by many European politicians who complain of the way PASOK comports itself: the party is successor to a resistance movement which, while it did not promote violence as one of its prime objectives, did not renounce it either. Many PASOK cabinet ministers were arrested, tortured and imprisoned for their underground activities during the dictatorship.
42. This may have been the regime's intention all along. It will be recalled that the timetable released the previous October had said only that elections would be held 'according' to the appropriate provisions of the new constitution'.
43. In March 1970, Angelis and Zoitakis were elevated to the rank of full general, the first Greek officers to hold the four-star post since Papagos.
44. In the five years after the coup just over three thousand officers were retired, a rate nearly three times that of the previous five years. See Thanos Veremis, *Greek Security: Issues and Politics*, Adelphi Paper 179 (London: IISS, 1982), pp. 28-29.
45. It was reported in June 1970 that they had been delivered an ultimatum, either to resign their commissions or accept transfers in keeping with the service regulations that no officer should serve longer than three years in one posting. Ioannides was said to have been offered the post of Military Attaché in Canada and Roufogalis a transfer to the War College in Thessaloniki. Both stayed on in their posts.
46. Max van der Stoel, *Introductory Report on the Situation in Greece*, Doc. 2637 (Strasbourg: Council of Europe, September 22, 1969), p. 3.
47. *The Greek Case before the Commission of Human Rights of the Council of Europe*, vol. I, Doc. 42 (Athens: Ministry of Foreign Affairs, 1970), pp. 138-140.
48. Ibid., p. 142.
49. *The Greek Case*, 2 vols (Strasbourg: Council of Europe, 1969).
50. It did not, however, cover small arms and other equipment which could be used to maintain internal security and, it was revealed subsequently, that more heavy equipment was provided to Greece during the course of the embargo than in the three years prior to the coup.
51. There was a running feud between the Congress and the administration about America's co-operation with the colonels. It is well documented in C. M. Woodhouse, *The Rise and Fall of the Greek Colonels* (London: Granada Publishing, 1985).
52. The colonels may have helped channel CIA funds to the Nixon election campaign via Pappas and Agnew. Democratic presidential candidate George McGovern made allusion to the connection in a letter to the Senate Select Committee on Intelligence in 1976 and the author Christopher Hitchens has implied a link with the Watergate affair. See Hitchens, *Cyprus* (London: Quartet Books, 1984), pp. 125-130.
53. See Seymour Hersh, *Kissinger: The Price of Power* (London: Faber and Faber, 1983), pp. 136-141.
54. C. M. Woodhouse, *Karamanlis* (Oxford: Clarendon Press, 1982), p. 191.
55. Ibid., p. 189.
56. Ibid., p. 193.
57. Woodhouse subscribes to this view saying that the dispersal of the junta

followed an internal attempt to unseat Papadopoulos from which the regime leader was saved by the support of Ioannides. See *The Rise and Fall of the Greek Colonels*, p. 98.
58. In a statement January 12, 1968, he declared, 'A solution, by necessity, must be sought with the limits of what is feasible, which does not always coincide with the limits of what is desirable.'
59. One of them was the son of a member of the junta the other a Ioannides loyalist who in February 1975 was arrested as part of a cabal said to have been plotting a coup against the Karamanlis government to restore the brigadier to power.
60. Polyvios Polyviou, *Cyprus, Conflict and Negotiation, 1960-1980* (London: Duckworth, 1980), p. 128. He says the accord was in large part due to 'NATO mediation'.
61. *The Times*, London, October 9, 1971.
62. According to some accounts the written ultimatum was backed up by oral demands that Makarios should retire to Greece where a villa and handsome pension would be provided.
63. Woodhouse, *Karamanlis*, pp. 196-197.
64. EPOK was alleged to have been funded by subsidies illegally channelled from the Secretariat for Sport with which Aslanides had long been associated.
65. 'Such a government would assume extraordinary powers for a specific time, so that, in an atmosphere free from passion and the desire for revenge, conditions should be created permitting democracy to function. . .'.
66. 'The people behind the coup d'etat would demand without any spirit of vindictiveness or enmity the return of the king as the legitimate representative of law and order to form a government headed by Constantine Karamanlis on the understanding that this government would carry out honest elections in a spirit of justice and within a predetermined time limit.' Testimony of Evangelos Averoff contained in the findings of the preliminary inquiry into the navy mutiny, released by the Undersecretariat for Press and Information, as appearing in the *Athens Daily Post*, July 21, 1973.
67. The author watched voters being given voting envelopes containing only the 'yes' ballot which would have required them to ask openly for a 'no' while their identity card was in the hands of regime-appointed scrutineers. In many instances unanimous 'yes' votes were recorded in villages where locals insisted that they had voted 'no'. In some cases, the 'yes' and 'no' tallies were reversed by the tellers. Nevertheless, the Supreme Court ratified the charter.
68. Markezinis who had worked as a British agent during WWII later served as legal advisor to King Paul. When he began his political career in the early 1950s, he was considered to have great potential but he was ambitious and did not work well to other people's discipline and soon found himself consigned to the sidelines. He viewed himself as a liberal, intellectual statesman — as early as the 1950s he had argued that the surest way of neutralising communist influence in Greek politics was to allow the party to participate in the electoral process. The popular perception of the man, however, was of an idiosyncratic conservative. He had kept out of politics throughout the dictatorship concentrating his impressive energies on writing a massive history of Greece. During the referendum, though, he had come out publicly in favour of the new regime saying he would be voting 'yes', not for the strengthened presidential powers but for 'the follow up to a positive outcome'. He argued in favour of a policy of reconciliation: 'forgive, forget and free elections'.
69. Dertilis, though not a member of the junta, was one of its closest collaborators. During the polytechnic incidents he shot a demonstrator in cold blood

for which he was sentenced in 1975 to life imprisonment.
70. Detailed accounts of the polytechnic rising are given in Woodhouse, *The Rise and Fall of the Greek Colonels*, pp. 126-141; Kevin Andrews, '1973. Blood', *Greece in the Dark* (Amsterdam: Adolf M. Hakkert, 1980), pp. 69-93; and, Taki Theodoracopoulos, *The Greek Upheaval* (London: Stacey International, 1976), pp. 232-235.
71. *Summary of World Broadcasts*, ME/4454/C (Caversham, Bucks: BBC, November 19, 1973), p. 1.
72. Woodhouse, *The Rise and Fall of the Greek Colonels*, p. 142.
73. Androutsopoulos was Minister of Finance until 1971 when he took over as Minister of Interior from Pattakos.
74. Junta member Michael Balopoulos was sentenced to four years imprisonment for taking bribes in connection with meat imports which broke sanctions against Rhodesia. A son-in-law of Constantine Papadopoulos was tried for obtaining loans from a state development bank by use of fraudulent documents. While there were numerous investigations of wrongdoing, there were few prosecutions.
75. By presidential decree of January 25, 1973 commander in chief of the armed forces Gen. Demetrios Zagorianakis was replaced by Gen. Grigorios Bonanos. (Gizikis subsequently promoted himself full general so as not to be outranked.) Commander of the army Lieut. Gen. Mikhail Mastrantonis was replaced by Lieut. Gen. Andreas Galatsanos and commander of the air force Air Vice-Marshal Thomas Mitsanas was replaced by Air Vice-Marshal Alexandros Papanikolaou. Vice-Admiral Petros Arapakis retained his position. The chiefs of police and gendarmerie were also replaced.
76. For complementary descriptions of the man's character from two individuals on opposite ends of the Greek political spectrum see Theodoracopoulos, *The Greek Upheaval*, pp. 18-19 and Panagoulis in Oriana Fallaci, *A Man* (New York: Pocket Books, 1981), p. 50.
77. For details of this and associated disputes between Greece and Turkey in the Aegean see Andrew Wilson, *The Aegean Dispute*, Adelphi Paper 155 (London: International Institute for Strategic Studies, 1979/80).
78. Woodhouse, *The Rise and Fall of the Greek Colonels*, p. 148. It is not clear whether he had fled to Greece to escape EOKA-B extremists or whether he was taken from Cyprus by a henchman of Ioannides.
79. Theodoracopoulos, *The Greek Upheaval*, p. 50.
80. There are detailed accounts of the invasion and the efforts to obtain a ceasefire in Theodoracopoulos, Woodhouse and Hitchens.
81. He said he was prepared to accept the Prime Minister's job as a national duty in a time of crisis but that with stronger, younger men available to tackle the crisis he preferred to retire from the political arena and concentrate on his academic pursuits.
82. For details of these and the subsequent round of talks see James Callaghan, *Time and Chance* (London: Collins, 1987) and Birand, *30 Hot Days* (Lefkosia: K. Rustem, 1985).
83. Callaghan, *Time and Chance*, p. 352.
84. Callaghan, *Time and Chance*, pp. 354-355.
85. The Turkish Cypriots entered into new inter-communal talks for establishment of a federation while at the same time creating all the elements of an indépendent state. In November 1983, Denktash declared the northern sector to be the independent Turkish Republic of Northern Cyprus. Turkey is the only country to recognise it. Subsequent efforts to negotiate a loose confederation have also proved fruitless.
86. Davies was assassinated two days after the second Turkish invasion.
87. Hitchens, *Cyprus*, p. 88.

88. Stavros Panteli, *A New History of Cyprus* (London: East-West Publications, 1984), p. 382.
89. James Callaghan, *Time and Chance*, p. 342.
90. Laurence Stern, *The Wrong Horse, The Politics of Intervention and the Failure of American Diplomacy* (New York: Times Books, 1977), p. 95.
91. Ibid.
92. Theodoracopoulos, *The Greek Upheaval*, pp. 61-62.
93. Carl Barkman, *Ambassador in Athens* (London: The Merlin Press, 1989), p. 183.

THE GREEK-TURKISH CONFLICT

Heinz Richter

To-day's conflict in the Aegean is both ancient history and highly contemporary. In the final resort the question is: who controls the two continental shores and the bridge of islands connecting them across the Aegean? The stages of this conflict start from the Persian Wars of 490 and 480 BC (perhaps even from the Trojan War) and evolve by way of the Fall of Constantinople (1452) to the Asia Minor Catastrophe of 1923. Whilst the historical significance of the events of 490–480 BC and 1452 must be clear to any Western European, familiarity with Aegean developments during the nearly four centuries of Ottoman occupation of Greece is probably confined to specialists.

These 400 years determined the relations between Turks and Greeks and close on 100 years of Greek Independence struggle – often conducted with great brutality on both sides – have created in the Greek mind the picture of an ancestral enemy against whom one must be on one's guard.

This fear has been strengthened by a collective perception of time wholly different from that of Western Europe. For Greeks the Fall of Constantinople is recent history, the Ottoman Occupation was the day before yesterday, the War of Independence yesterday whilst the Greek expansionist initiative of 1921–3 which ended in the Asia Minor Catastrophe and the expulsion of the Greeks of Asia Minor is still the living present.

Despite the Treaty of Lausanne (1923), which cleared up the main areas of conflict, settled the frontier issue[1] and the exchange of minority populations in Macedonia and Asia

Minor so that a superficial glance might suggest that no points of friction remained, the disaster had nevertheless left *trauma* and susceptibilities which could not be overcome in the short period of reconciliation under Venizelos until his fall in 1935. The presence of 1.5 million Asia Minor refugees amongst a population of at that time approximately 6 million (the comparative German figures are 5 million refugees in a population of 60 million post-1945) and the problem of their integration (without a West German 'Economic Miracle') occasioned a burden of memory, until recently still very much alive.

In addition, actions from the Turkish side have kept this mistrust alive. During the Second World War Turkey did indeed give humanitarian aid to Greece by food deliveries during the terrible famine winter of 1941–2, the first year of Axis Occupation, though these were largely financed by Greeks of the Diaspora; and she helped Greek fugitives on their way to exile in Egypt. But, at the same time, she began to take measures against the commercially prosperous Greek minority in Istanbul, an action overlooked in the turmoil of the war.[2]

In 1947 both countries became recipients of US aid under the Truman Doctrine and at the start of the 50s both joined NATO. The traditional enemies had become allies and the idea that allies could become involved in serious conflict which would, on several occasions, lead them to the brink of war seemed absurd. Franco–German co-operation had seemed to prove that it was possible to overcome traditional enmities.

But it was just the unexpected which happened. In the mid-fifties the Cyprus conflict flared up and both NATO allies were at once involved; and in the mid-seventies came the direct confrontation between Greece and Turkey in the Aegean. Each conflict influenced the other and each was only one aspect of the wider Greek–Turkish antagonism, so the following analysis must take account of both sources of conflict; whilst, at the same time, the international consequences for NATO will require comment.

Before we turn to the chronology of the conflict, it may be useful to summarise a few demographic, economic and military facts concerning the contending parties so that we may assess their relative potential.

At her last census in 1981 Greece had a population of

9.7 million of whom 65% lived in towns and 23% were under 15 years of age. In the last 30 years population had grown by less than 1% annually. The 1985 figure for illiteracy was 36%.

In 1982 Turkey had 46.9 million inhabitants (1978 census), 44% living in towns and 40% under 15 years of age. The annual population growth over the last 20 years was 2.5%. Illiteracy 38%.

In 1981 Greek personal income was rated at 4,420 US dollars per head and the Gross National Product in the same year at 42,890 million dollars. For the same date personal income in Turkey was 1,540 US dollars per head and Gross National Product at 72,100 million dollars. Inflation was rated at 20% in Greece in 1982-3 and at between 31% and 40% in Turkey.

The 4.1 million Greeks gainfully employed worked 35.7% in agriculture and 30.2% in industry. For Turkey the figures were 19.5 million gainfully employed of whom 51.5% in agriculture and 16.5% in industry.

Greece has the biggest merchant fleet in Europe and car ownership at 50 per 1,000 inhabitants, against 11 for Turkey. Greece's biggest foreign income is from tourism and Turkey's from the remittances sent home by 'guest-workers' abroad.

Greece's armed forces totalled 187,000 in 1984 of whom 137,000 conscripts doing their military service. Defence expenditure in Greece amounted to 1.7 billion US dollars in 1983.

The Turkish armed forces in 1984 amounted to 602,000 of whom 544,000 on military service. Defence expenditure 1.9 billion US dollars.

Both countries depend to a great degree on US military aid. Greece's numerical disadvantage is partly compensated for by better quality weaponry and a higher general level of technological expertise. Both countries' armed forces are incorporated in NATO except for their troops on Cyprus (in the Turkish case a much larger and more heavily-equipped contingent) and the Turkish 4th or 'Aegean' Army which does not come under NATO.

To look first at the Cyprus conflict: since Greece became a nation state, the majority of Greek Cypriots, under the leadership of the Orthodox Church, had demanded union (*enosis*) with Greece. Until the Congress of Berlin (1878) these efforts were directed against the Ottoman Empire and, after that date, against British rule — in 1925 Cyprus had acquired the status of a Crown Colony. Until the mid-fifties this demand for *enosis* had been little more than rhetoric. Great Britain would not hear of it and Greece, which until the Truman Doctrine had been a kind of British protectorate and after that a US protectorate, had felt obliged to conform.

In 1954, influenced by the newly-enthroned Archbishop of Cyprus, Makarios, Athens felt itself forced to take the Cyprus question to the UN. The British Foreign Secretary, Anthony Eden, declared: 'In geography and tactical considerations, the Turks have the stronger claim on Cyprus; in race and language the Greeks; in strategy the British, so long as their industrial life depends on oil supplies from the Persian Gulf.'[3] At the same time he told the House of Commons in so many words that the Cyprus question was also a matter for Turkey.

Eden's attitude was clear: Greek ambitions should be neutralised by Turkey. The right-wing Demirel Government took up the ball so conveniently thrown it. Its UN representative stated that, if the status of Cyprus were to change, the Treaty of Lausanne and the balance of power it had established in the Aegean would be invalidated; Turkey would advance her claim to Western Thrace and the islands bordering her Aegean coast; should Great Britain give up Cyprus, it must be returned to Turkey.[4]

Thus, Great Britain's tactical chess move, playing off Turkey against Greece, had serious consequences. From now on, in all issues concerning Cyprus, Turkey would be directly involved. At the same time the two future trouble-spots in the Aegean and in Thrace had come into view. Since no one contradicted Turkey's far-reaching demands — or took them seriously — this was interpreted from the Turkish side as a kind of silent consent and they became long-term goals of Turkish foreign policy, which might be realised given a suitable opportunity. Thus an anti-colonial struggle was transmuted into a focal point of international crisis, still with us at the present day.

Though Britain in tacit collusion with the US managed to prevent a Cyprus debate in the UN, George Grivas, encouraged by successful anti-colonial struggles in other countries, started the EOKA guerrilla campaign to which Britain riposted by inviting the Turkish and Greek governments to a conference on possible home-rule for Cyprus in London. Turkey was now recognised as an equal partner in the game.

During the following years all parties stepped up the conflict. Grivas, who was not only an ardent nationalist but also a militant anti-communist, launched his attacks in three directions. He fought the British and the Cypriot Turks but at the same time he struck at the Cypriot communists especially at their union basis. Thus he destroyed one of the few intercommunal links between the island's Turks and Greeks which might in the future have served to overcome the ethnic split.

To fight EOKA, the British raised a special unit recruited mainly from the Turkish Cypriot minority. Its use led almost immediately to an indigenous inter-communal conflict. When Ankara began to further the formation of a Turkish-Cypriot underground organisation, TMT, to fight EOKA, the conflict escalated to the proportions of civil war.

The TMT was as anti-communist and chauvinist as EOKA but not anti-British. Thus the colonial authorities watched it with a benevolent eye. TMT was created by the Menderes government and the Turkish general staff. Its leaders were Turkish officers and its political advisor was a former colonial civil servant Rauf Denktash. TMT's aims were identical with those of its masters.

As a first measure TMT attacked the Turkish Cypriot left, especially its union base. In contrast to Grivas who never had a chance to destroy the Cypriot CP (AKEL), TMT managed to wreck the Turkish Cypriot left. Thus for long years the only voice of the Turkish Cypriots was Denktash's. Only very recently has a new Turkish Cypriot left emerged. In 1958 *agents provocateurs* from TMT blew up the Turkish information centre in Nicosia. This provoked further intercommunal unrest.

London watched this development sympathetically. Apparently it proved the British and Turkish thesis that the two Cypriot communities were unable to live together peacefully. At the same time the British government encouraged Ankara to demand self-determination for the Turkish-Cypriot community and, as a result, Ankara launched a full-scale propaganda campaign for the division of the island (*Taksim*). In order to emphasise this policy Ankara introduced a new element into Greek-Turkish relations. It linked the Cyprus conflict to the Turkish minority policy. Whenever there was unrest between the two communities on Cyprus the Menderes government organised outbursts of 'popular anger' against Greek minorities in Istanbul and other Turkish cities. This in turn provoked tension between the two parent states which brought them more than once to the threshold of war. The British policy of 'divide and rule' had created a catastrophic focus of conflict between Greece and Turkey.

The independence of Cyprus, agreed between Great Britain, Greece and Turkey at the Zurich and London conferences of 1958-9 brought no real solution since the sovereignty of the new state was nullified by the three contracting parties' rights of intervention which even allowed them to station troops on the island. As long as Athens and Ankara were of one mind, Cyprus was an indirect NATO member; but if inter-communal strife were to be renewed, there would be immediate danger of a clash between Greece and Turkey.

Renewed inter-communal strife in the early '60s and ensuing tensions between the parent states brought in the US as decision-maker in response to British suggestion. President Johnson proposed to end the fighting on Cyprus by sending a NATO peace-keeping force to the island. Ankara and Athens agreed but Makarios considered this as an attack on the island's independence and appealed to the Soviet Union. Readily Moscow blocked the American plan and instead of a NATO force the UN peace-keeping force (UNFICYP) was sent to Cyrpus in spring 1964.[5]

Despite the arrival of UNFICYP on the scene the fighting still continued. Ankara responded to pressure by the Cyprus Government on the Turkish minority with repression against the Greek minority in Istanbul. By the end of May war between Greece and Turkey was threatening. By-passing the UN, Johnson again intervened directly. In a most uncivil letter he warned Premier Inönü that the US would not tolerate an invasion of Cyprus.[6] Then he summoned him and his Greek counterpart, George Papandreou, to Washington. The proferred solution was the now notorious Acheson Plan which provided for both *Taksim* and double *Enosis*, *i.e.* the division of the island between Greece and Turkey and its disappearance as an independent state. When Papandreou hesitated to accept this plan he, too, became the target of Johnson's rudeness.[7] Stern opposition from Makarios who again threatened to call in the Soviets convinced Papandreou to stick to his unyielding course. Thus for the time being the Acheson Plan was suspended but that did not mean that it had ceased to exist.

The right-wing Greek governments of 1965-7 were more dispossed to comply with US wishes and for that reason started to negotiate secretly with Turkey. In December 1966 the Greek and Turkish Foreign Ministers met on the fringes of the NATO Foreign Ministers' Conference in Paris and initialled a secret agreement on the basis of the Acheson Plan. But the US retained for itself the right to decide when the Plan should be applied.[8]

With the advent of the colonels in Greece in 1967 the interest of the Cypriots in *enosis* cooled since unification with Greece would have brought the dictatorship to the island as well. Accordingly Makarios strengthened his course of non-alignment and internally introduced a policy of intercommunal *rapprochement* aimed at overcoming the rift of the 1960s. A new round of inter-communal talks began which soon proved to be very promising. This provoked the Athens junta which in connivance with the US did everything possible to undermine Makarios' position.[9]

The Americans had become increasingly alarmed by Makarios' electoral victory in 1970 and by the increase in the Cyprus CP (AKEL) vote. There were sinister mutterings about Cyprus as the Cuba of the Eastern Mediterranean and Makarios as Castro in a cassock.[10] In 1971 inspired by the negative American attitude during a NATO Conference at Lisbon, the Foreign Ministers of Greece and Turkey agreed that the Cyprus conflict should be cleared up (in the sense of double *enosis*) and, if necessary, by force. Consequently Ankara torpedoed the inter-communal talks and the Athens junta multiplied its efforts to get rid of Makarios — it did not even shrink from putsch-plans and attempts on Makarios' life. In November 1973, at a working meeting organised by the US in Rome Cyrus Vance let it be understood that, in the event of a further Cyprus crisis, the US would no longer oppose a Turkish invasion.[11]

What followed is well-known. On 15th July 1974, the

Second Junta leader, Ioannidis, let loose a *putsch* against Makarios. The Turkish Prime Minister, Ecevit, went carefully to work. He addressed himself to London and suggested discussions, held there on 17th–18th July in the presence of the Assistant US Secretary of State, Sisco. But neither in London, nor in the subsequent discussions in Athens and Ankara does Sisco seem to have counselled restraint. The result was the Turkish landing at Kyrenia on 20th July 1974. Meanwhile the UN Security Council had taken note of the *putsch* and on the 18th Makarios appeared in New York to make his own complaint against the *putschists*. When, on 20th July, news of the Turkish landing reached New York, the Security Council met at once and ordered an armistice. This was accepted and on the 22nd July the armistice became effective.

On 23rd July the Athens Junta fell and, on the 24th, Karamanlis returned to Athens from his Paris exile and formed a democratic government. On the 25th, as a result of a British initiative, talks began between the Turkish and Greek Foreign Ministers. But over the next days Ankara sent in more troops and they went on 'rounding off' their bridgehead. The second round of talks began, as agreed, on 8th August in Geneva but ended on the 14th because, despite Greek readiness to compromise, the Turkish side demanded partition with 34 per cent of Cyprus territory to be accounted Turkish.

Two hours after the talks broke down the Turkish forces went over to the offensive. Despite UN intervention and apparent British readiness to oppose any further advance with force in the name of the UN,[12] the US Secretary of State 'permitted' a Turkish advance to the so-called Attila Line. During this advance the Turkish army which is renowned for its discipline made a planned use of terrorism to drive approximately 150,000 Greek Cypriots — roughly a quarter of the population, in panic flight towards the south, thus exculpating themselves from the charge of forced expulsion and at the same time achieving the goal of demographic change. This, in turn provoked the National Guard and EOKA B to terrorist acts against the Turkish minority in the south so that they thereupon fled north. The result was the ethnic partition of the island according to the Acheson Plan. But the second part of the Plan, 'double *Enosis*' — the union of each of the two Cypriot rump-states with its respective motherland — was, for various reasons, frustrated.

First, Makarios had survived the *putsch* and addressed himself to the UN. Secondly, on 24th July, the Athens Military Junta fell. Had Makarios been killed, 'double *Enosis*' could have been achieved under Ioannidis by a cynical act of *realpolitik*. But with the takeover by a democratic regime under Karamanlis, this was no longer on the cards. On 14th August the new Greek Government, appalled by US and NATO passivity, made the tactical mistake of withdrawing from the military section of NATO so as to have complete control of its own armed forces in the event of a Turkish attack on the Greek mainland. Thus Athens lost all possibility of influencing the NATO Council during subsequent developments. As has already been said, Turkey now held Cyprus territory up to the Attila Line and was deaf to UN appeals. The first stage in the expansion programme formulated in 1954 had been completed. North Cyprus was under Turkish control.

But Greece's over-hasty NATO withdrawal had further consequences. It reinforced Ankara's claims in the Aegean.

To re-capitulate: in 1954 the Turkish UN representative had stated that, if there were any change in the status of Cyprus, this would invalidate the Treaty of Lausanne and the balance of power in the Aegean and Ankara would lay claims to the Greek islands of the Eastern Aegean and to Western Thrace. But, until 1973, this had remained in the domain of rhetoric.[13]

In 1958, the first UN Law of the Sea conference had decided for the extension of the limits of each state's territorial waters from 6 to 12 sea miles. In 1972 Greece — in contrast to Turkey — had ratified this agreement but took no steps to carry it into action. At present, Greece controls 35% and Turkey 8.8%. The figure for international waters is therefore approximately 56%. Were Greece and Turkey each to extend their territorial waters to 12 sea miles, this would raise Greece's share to 63.9% but Turkey's to only 10%; whilst international waters would be reduced to 26%. Thus, the Aegean would become virtually a Greek lake. As remarked above, Turkey had not ratified the Geneva Convention and quickly gave Athens to understand that she would regard a Greek extension to 12 sea miles as a *casus belli*. Upon this,

Greece declared that she had no intention of extending her limits but reserved the right to do so. Curiously enough, Turkey did extend her own territorial waters in the Black Sea and on her South coast to 12 sea miles.

However, the Geneva Convention contained a number of further provisions regarding the continental shelf.[14] Article 1 (a) defined this as the sea bottom and its underground in underwater zones adjacent to the coasts, but outside territorial waters, up to a depth of 200 metres, or beyond this frontier to a depth in which exploitation of the zone's natural resources would be possible.

Article 1 (b) ratified the same provisions for islands. Since the depth of the Aegean beyond Greek territorial waters only at a few points exceeds 500 metres, the Aegean continental shelf can be said to form a single unit.

The frontier between the Greek and Turkish continental shelf derives from Article 6 of the Geneva Convention.[15] This frontier lies centrally between the Turkish coast and the Greek islands.

Until 1973 these definitions were matters of theoretical jurisprudence without material consequences for Greek-Turkish relations. But in 1973 oil was located near the North Aegean island of Thasos. In view of the world energy crisis, Ankara reacted at once. On 1st November it licensed the State Oil Company TPAO for exploration and exploitation of the Aegean continental shelf. At the same time the Turkish Government Gazette (Resmi Gazette, 14, iv, 199) published a map showing the boundary of the putative Turkish shelf in the North Aegean running west of the Greek island of Samothrace and over Limnos, Ayios Efstratios and Chios to Psara and Andipsara. Thus the Turkish Government claimed the shelf beyond the 6 mile zone of the islands, an area regarded by Greece as her own and for which she had already distributed a number of exploration licences.

On 7th February 1974 Greece formally rejected these claims, referring specifically to Articles 1 and 6 of the Geneva Convention. On 27th February Ankara replied to the effect that the Geneva Convention had no application here since Ankara had not signed it: the Greek islands had no continental shelf but were excrescences of the East Aegean shelf which was simply an extension of Anatolia: the frontier between the Greek and the Turkish shelf was the central line between the two mainland coasts. At the same time Ankara summoned Athens to negotiate.

In March 1974 NATO manoeuvres brought about an escalation. Turkish airforce planes invaded the Aegean airspace without informing Greek Military Flight Control, though NATO practice at this time regarded the Aegean as under Greek air control. Greek interceptor planes drove the Turkish bombers away and the NATO exercise was broken off.

On 25th May 1974 Athens declared herself ready for negotiation on the shelf, on the basis of the Geneva Convention. On 29th May the Turkish Foreign Minister Günes announced the despatch of a research vessel to the 'Turkish' section of the shelf waters: this vessel would be accompanied by naval craft but the intention was purely peaceful. The research vessel, the *Candarli*, accompanied by 32 naval craft, headed for the controversial area and remained there until 4th June taking magnetic soundings. Greece put her navy on the alert.

On the same day (4th June 1974) the Turkish Government informed Athens that it was ready for negotiations but without pre-conditions, that is without regard to the Geneva Convention; but on the 6th June it accorded the TPAO new drilling licenses. Athens replied on the 14th, protesting against the voyage of the *Candarli* and the expansionist statements of some Turkish politicians. On the 20th, at the NATO conference in Ottawa, the two foreign ministers discussed the situation, but without result. On the 25th the two prime ministers had an equally fruitless discussion in Brussels. On 10th July Ankara stated that it rejected the Greek reply of the 14th June and that it would continue to explore its continental shelf. In the official Gazette of 17th July, the Turkish Government published a further map which extended the so-called central line of demarcation to the whole of the Aegean.

At this point developments were overtaken by the Cyprus events.

From now on Ankara, encouraged by its successful invasion of Cyprus, could pursue its second expansionist goal in the Aegean from a position of strength, both by extending the previous conflict and by developing new aspects. As opportunity offered, first one and then another aspect was stressed but without ever losing sight of the real goal of Aegean expansion. Thus the conflict became so complicated that even the experts could no longer keep track of it. Under these circumstances it is not surprising that some part of West European public opinion swallowed the Turkish propaganda which appeared convincing — partly by force of repetition — and either did not take Greek feelings of threat from Turkey seriously or dismissed them as Athens propaganda. This was reinforced by the fact that the Greek counter-arguments were of a legalistic character and, at least until the early 80s, were not well promoted.

We must now look at these new aspects in chronological order and see how they developed.

After the landing on Cyprus, on 20th, 23rd and 29th July, the Turkish civil aviation officials informed the regional office of the International Civil Aviation Organisation (ICAO) that parts of the Eastern Aegean airspace should be declared danger zones and closed to civilian air traffic. When Athens protested, Ankara withdrew this Notice to Airmen (NOTAM), only to issue a renewed warning on 6th August as NOTAM 714. This demanded that all aircraft crossing a line in approximately the centre of the Aegean report to Turkish Flight Control in Istanbul with a statement of their position and itinerary: only thus could the Turkish military radar distinguish between peaceful civilian aircraft and potential attackers. Athens could not accept this NOTAM: it was in contravention of the ICAO statutes since Ankara was trying to extend her control-zone unilaterally; moreover the line indicated by Ankara corresponded remarkably closely with the 'central demarcation line' published in relation to the continental shelf. On 14th August, by NOTAM 1066 and 1152, Athens declared the whole Aegean a danger zone for which it could no longer undertake co-ordination and direction of air traffice. On the same day Athens announced its withdrawal from the military section of NATO.

Here, we must take a brief but closer look at the problem of Aegean flight control in general.

Already at the end of 1944 the growth of air traffic had made necessary the calling of an international conference 'on international civilian air traffic' in Chicago. The 37 participating states signed an agreement regulating in outline the problems of international air traffic. In 1947, after ratification of this agreement by 26 states, the ICAO was founded and the world was divided into regional organisations. The one which concerns us here is the European Mediterranean Regional Air Navigation Organisation. At two conferences, 1952 in Paris and 1958 in Geneva, in which both Greece and Turkey participated, this organisation drew the boundaries of its subdivisions FIR (Flight Information Regions) in the European Mediterranean.

For the Aegean airspace, the following rules were laid down: The Athens FIR would control the whole airspace up to the limit of the Turkish airspace. Thus, Athens controlled not only its *national* airspace over the Greek islands but also the *international* Aegean airspace. In this context, control meant that all civilian and military aircraft flying west from Turkey had to report to Athens Flight Control a couple of minutes after crossing the Turkish coast, and to declare their position and itinerary. Thenceforward Athens Flight Control took over direction of their flight. Aircraft flying east reported to Istanbul Flight Control on leaving Athens FIR.

Control within a FIR applies only to technical flight safety and should not be confused with air sovereignty above national territory. A FIR often extends far beyond national air sovereignty.

The Turkish demand (NOTAM 714) of 4th August 1974 required that all aircraft flying east should, after crossing the central demarcation line, report to Flight Control in Istanbul. This would apply to Greek domestic flights from Athens to the eastern Aegean islands as well as to the Greek Airforce using the same airspace. However, Ankara's demand contradicted not only ICAO rules but also the NATO air-safety and control system. According to NATO practice, the military air-control areas were congruent with the FIRs of the respective states, *i.e.* Greek military air-control extended as far as Athens FIR. The task of early warning, air defence and tactical operations in this airspace was the business of the 28th Tactical Flight of the Greek Airforce. Ankara's NOTAM 714 therefore called the NATO structure in question.

Athens' withdrawal from the military wing of NATO was to have serious consequences for the FIR problem. On 13th September 1974 Athens informed the ICAO that it disclaimed any responsibility for flights over the Aegean. As a result the international airlines suspended all flights between Greece and Turkey and made no further use of routes crossing the Aegean. These measures hit first at Turkey's air contact with Europe since she now had to use the Bulgarian or Lebanese FIRs.

ICAO's attempts to mediate in October 1974 failed owing to Turkish intransigence. In spring 1975 Greek initiative restored direct air traffic between Greece and Turkey but NOTAM 714 remained in force. Only in February 1980 did Turkey rescind this NOTAM on account of the economic damage suffered from the closure of Aegean air routes. But meanwhile Ankara had found another lever to advance its claim to air-control over the Aegean — NATO.

Until the Greek military withdrawal there had been two NATO HQs in Izmir (Smyrna), the LANDSOUTHEAST and the 6th Allied Tactical Airforce (ATAF), both under US command. The Greek and Turkish air-forces both came within the 6th ATAF. After the Greek withdrawal — apparently with NATO's blessing — the Turkish Airforce control zone was extended westwards over the Aegean. And Turkey put a very generous interpretation on this extension of her area of control.

In 1931 Greece had demarcated her national airspace 10 sea miles beyond her mainland coast and the island coasts.[16] Until 1975 Ankara had raised no objection since this demarcation conformed with international regulations. Under these rules, each state has the right to extend its airspace to a maximum of 12 sea miles, that is to the limits of its national waters.[17] Ankara now demanded that Greek airspace should be reduced to 6 sea miles in accordance with its national waters. To reinforce this demand Turkish military aircraft regularly over-flew the controversial airspace. Athens protested whenever its national airspace was violated and for this reason has, in recent years, frustrated several NATO exercises.

The fact of this unilateral change in the military air-control regions became apparent when, at the end of 1977, Athens declared its readiness to re-integrate in NATO. It soon became obvious that, in view of the continuing conflict between Greece and Turkey, it would be impossible to re-establish the two united NATO commands. The NATO High Command therefore decided to establish two separate commands in Izmir and Larissa. But demarcation of the operational zones assigned to the 6th ATAF in Izmir and the 7th ATAF in Larissa remained a point of controversy. Ankara wanted the maintenance of the *status quo* and Athens wanted a return to the *status quo ante*.

Athens feared that, if the extension of the Turkish military air-control was sanctioned, this would prejudice the FIR and continental shelf problem. In 1980, when General Haig, as NATO C-in-C, produced a plan envisaging a return to the *status quo ante*, it was vetoed by Turkey. Then, when Haig produced a modification which met Turkish wishes, Greece did the same. Later in 1980 the new NATO C-in-C, General Rogers, produced a fresh suggestion which Greece again rejected because it favoured Turkey.

Only when, in the same year, Foreign Minister Mitsotakis threatened to take Greece right out of NATO and close down the US bases, did the US apply pressure on Ankara. The result was the so-called Rogers Agreement which prescribed a return to the *status quo ante* for peacetime. Now the Athens FIR and the NATO flight-safety areas were again co-terminous. It would appear however that Rogers must have made the concession to Ankara that, after Greece's return to NATO, the demarcation of aerial defence regions *in wartime* would be a subject for bilateral negotiation. This would mean that, even during NATO manoeuvres, parts of the eastern Aegean, including Greek islands, would come under Turkish operational control. Since Athens saw this as possibly prejudicing her case on other controversial issues, she roundly rejected it and declared herself unwilling to establish the Larissa HQ before the problem was settled by a definitive return to the *status quo ante*. Since Ankara has rejected this, NATO will obviously have to get on for some time without the new HQ.

On the other hand, Ankara has continued with its policy of systematically violating Greek airspace right up to the present day. The object is clearly to leave the question of military control of the airspace open and let Athens appear, by reason of her regular justified protests to NATO HQ, as a querulous complainant.

The continuing invasion of Cyprus throughout the second half of August 1974 gave Athens cause to fear further Turkish landings on the East Aegean islands. A hasty start was therefore made with fortifying those islands adjacent to the

Turkish coast and large troop contingents were posted there. Against the background of the Cyprus invasion, expansionist statements by Turkish politicians of all political colourings gave rise to the worst fears.

For example, on 17th January 1975, the Turkish Prime Minister, Sirmak, declared that half the Aegean belonged to Turkey. On 20th January, Defence Minister Sancar put forward a claim to the Greek islands of the Eastern Aegean. Two days later Foreign Minister Esenbel added that Cyprus had been the first step in the Aegean direction. In April the new Foreign Minister, Caglayangil, reiterated that half the Aegean belonged to Turkey and other sources suggested that Rhodes could be the next Cyprus. Sentiments of this type can be cited from almost all prominent Turkish politicians up to the recent past.

No wonder the Greek Government hastened defence measures for the East Aegean islands by all means available. News of this had hardly broken when Ankara raised a storm of protest by diplomatic *démarches*, Government statements and a press campaign: by fortifying the islands, Greece was contravening international treaties and preparing a military attack on the Turkish mainland. The treaties in question here are the Treaty of Lausanne (1923) and the Paris Peace Treaty of 1947 between the Allies and Italy by which the Dodecanese was handed over to Greece.

The Treaty of Lausanne had divided the East Aegean islands into two groups. Para. 3 of Article 4 laid down that the Greek islands of Limnos and Samothrace and the Turkish islands of Gökçada (Imbros) and Bózaada (Tenedos), at the entrance to the Dardanelles, should be demilitarised.

The Montreux Conference (June–July 1936) restored to Turkey full sovereignty over the Dardanelles and, at the same time, abrogated the demilitarised status of the four islands. Interestingly, Greece was among the signatories. The then Turkish ambassador in Athens gave an official written assurance to the Greek Government that Ankara agreed to the re-militarisation of Samothrace and Limnos and, during the ratification debate in the Turkish parliament, the then Foreign Minister, Rüstü Aras, confirmed that the Treaty of Lausanne was abrogated and the demilitarisation provisions cancelled by the Montreux Convention.[18] Directly after the signing of the Convention, Ankara herself began to fortify her islands and Greece followed suit in December 1936.

The islands of Lesvos, Chios, Samos and Ikaria were covered by Article 13 of the Treaty of Lausanne, stipulating that no naval bases or fortifications should be established there and that armed forces should be restricted to the equivalent of the number of local conscripts and a modest *gendarmerie* unit.[19] In other words the treaty did permit basic defence measures.

This had become very clear during the discussions in Lausanne. Ankara had demanded total demilitarisation of the islands. Against this it was maintained that, in such a case, the islands would be totally dependent on Turkey's good graces. One way of avoiding this would be to have corresponding demilitarised zones on the Anatolian coast. As this was impracticable, partial militarisation was permitted.

Article 14 of the Paris Treaty stipulated demilitarised status for the Dodecanese but a police presence would be permitted.[20] However, Turkey was not a signatory to the Paris Treaty and therefore has no right in international law to make demands relative to the re-militarisation of these islands. Up to now Athens has refrained from posting regular army units to the Dodecanese but has so far augmented the *gendarmerie* forces that they differed little from military detachments.

But Greece can appeal to a higher law to justify her defence measures: the right of every country to self-defence as defined in Article 51 of the UN Charter.

If until the 20th July 1975 there could have subsisted some doubt whether the aggressive statements of Turkish politicians were merely verbal radicalism, the establishment of a 4th Turkish Army with HQ at Izmir, announced on that date, dispelled all uncertainty. This so-called Aegean Army did not come under NATO Command and has since been systematically strengthened. On US statistics, it now comprises 35,000 troops, two Infantry divisions, one regiment of 'leathernecks' and commando and parachutist units of unknown strength. In addition there is a considerable fleet of transport helicopters and about 50–60 landing craft out of an approximate Turkish total of 80.

The exercises carried out by the 4th Army in recent years have all been landing operations. Since operations of this type are a very minor element in NATO's defence plans for the area, it was natural that Greece interpreted them as a preparation for landings on the Greek islands adjacent to the Turkish coast and therefore, on her part, pressed ahead with the fortification of these islands. Another disturbing factor was the equipment of the 4th Army with a larger number of inflatable landing-craft which could serve for short-distance landings, for example on Samos or islands in the Dodecanese. However, Athens did not content herself with the military defence of the islands but endeavoured to secure her rear and win support from her allies through diplomatic channels.

Thus, when in April 1976 negotiations started for prolonging the agreement on US bases in Greece, Foreign Minister Bitsios demanded a US guarantee for Greece's frontiers against Turkish attack and support for the settlement of the Cyprus problem as conditions for prolonging the agreement. Secretary of State Kissinger was not prepared to accept this *quid pro quo* but he did write a letter assuring Greece of active assistance in the case of Turkish provocations or use of force; and the US would likewise contribute to a just solution for Cyprus. This letter had no status in International Law and was soon forgotten but it served to illustrate the new orientation of Greek foreign policy: the US and NATO were to be held responsible.

This was clearly demonstrated during negotiations over Greece's re-integration in NATO. In 1977 Karamanlis demanded that NATO undertake to collaborate in solving the Cyprus problem. In 1980, after re-integration in NATO, Athens demanded a fixed ratio of 7:10 for US military aid to Greece and Turkey, without which the bases' agreement would not be prolonged. In 1981, after his electoral victory, Andreas Papandreou demanded a NATO guarantee — since the US had refused this — as well as a confirmation of the 7:10 ratio. When, during the course of negotiations, he had realised that a guarantee would not be forthcoming, he insisted on the retention of the 7:10 ratio and got it written into the new Bases' Agreement of September 1983: the US undertook to maintain the existing balance of forces in the Aegean. Moreover, during these negotiations, Papandreou had succeeded in mobilising Greek–American opinion in the US and in welding its representatives into a Congressional pressure group which could not be ignored. Attempts by the Reagan Administration to tinker with the 7:10 ratio in 1984 and

1985 were promptly thrown out by Congress.

At NATO level too, Athens manoeuvred with dexterity. In 1979 Ankara had demanded that the islands of Limnos, Agios Efstratios and Samothrace be excluded from NATO's defence plan. NATO's Supreme Allied Commander Europe rejected this demand but, at the suggestion of NATO General-Secretary Luns a political decision was taken to exclude Limnos henceforward from NATO exercises since its military status was unclear. This decision prompted Athens to state that it would boycott NATO exercises in the Aegean until the Alliance recognised Greek sovereignty over Limnos.

In September 1984, when Athens announced her own manoeuvres in the North Aegean which included Limnos, Ankara protested strongly and questioned Greece's rights. Athens responded in November 1984 by bringing the Greek army and airforce units on Limnos (an infantry brigade and two fighter detachments) under NATO command. On 3rd December Ankara vetoed this at the NATO Defence Ministers' conference in Brussels. Athens riposted by vetoing the bringing of Turkish units under NATO command. Thus, in 1985, the grotesque situation was reached in which NATO had neither Greek nor Turkish units officially under its command.

In January 1985 Papandreou promulgated a new defence doctrine directing Greece's defence effort towards the East since Greece was more threatened from this direction than from the North. After his re-election in June 1985 Papandreou opened a diplomatic offensive on all fronts. In 1986 high-ranking Greek politicians and diplomats tried to explain the Greek position in the Aegean conflict to Washington, London and NATO. In June during the EC-summit Papandreou presented the case in such a sober and objective way that EC Commissioner, President Jacques Delors, confirmed that the problems were understood. At the same time Athens let it be understood that prior to a revival of the Turkish association agreement with the EC Ankara would have to respect human rights in Cyprus and must give up its occupation. Otherwise Greece would veto the revival. Turkey reacted with military provocations during naval manoeuvres in the Aegean.

Let us return now to the problem of the continental shelf. On 27th January 1975 Greece proposed to Ankara to submit the shelf problem to the International Court at The Hague. On 6th February Ankara agreed and suggested bilateral negotiations at high level to prepare the ground. Despite this, next day the Turkish Prime Minister announced on the radio that explorations would continue.

Though this soon failed because the Norwegian firm from which Ankara had chartered a research vessel refused to undertake seismic measuring in a controversial zone, statements by members of the Turkish Government showed that Ankara had not given up the project. On 6th April 1975 Demirel stated that the shelf must be demarcated by bilateral negotiation. On 16th April Foreign Minister Caglayangil announced Ankara's future theme-song: 'Let's negotiate — perhaps we'll reach an agreement. But don't let's go to The Hague' — in other words a political instead of a juridical solution.

Nevertheless, at their first talks in Rome on 19th May, Caglayangil and Bitsios agreed on a joint approach to the Hague Court. On 31st May Karamanlis and Demirel met at the NATO summit in Brussels and agreed that the legal work should be speeded up so as to bring the case before the International Court as soon as possible. They signed a joint communiqué in which they also stressed that the controversial problem should find a peaceful solution.

During the following months, on the one hand the legal experts continued to meet, whilst, on the other, Ankara built up the 4th Army. In September Demirel announced a temporary suspension of the legal work. Evidently Ankara wanted to avoid the joint approach to the Hague.

The Aegean problem was now in process of becoming a cause of internal strife in Turkey. The Opposition leader, Ecevit, accused Demirel of gambling with Turkey's prospects; Greece would only negotiate seriously under threat. Thereupon, in February 1976, Demirel announced the forthcoming despatch of a hydrographic research-craft (the *Sizmik 1*) to the waters around Thasos where Greece had found oil three years earlier. Athens reacted by offering Turkey a Nonaggression Pact. This was welcomed by Demirel but, in the face of a massive attack from the Opposition, he rejected the proposed pact.

During the next weeks Athens repeatedly warned Ankara that, if the *Sizmik* entered Greek continental shelf waters, a dangerous situation would arise. Ankara replied that, if Athens hindered the *Sizmik* in its voyage, measures would be taken. Eventually, on 6th August, the *Sizmik*, escorted by one Turkish minesweeper, entered the waters west of Lesvos, withdrawing on 9th August. Both sides were obviously anxious to avoid direct confrontation and restrained themselves accordingly. Nevertheless, on 10th August Athens applied to the UN Security Council for a special session. Here, both sides put forward their established positions. The Security Council passed Resolution 395/1976 calling on both parties to reduce tension, to open negotiations and to bring the whole matter before the International Court. Athens welcomed the Resolution; Ankara agreed to bilateral negotiations but was not ready to go to the Hague.

Athens thereupon made two requests to the International Court: 1) that the Court issue a temporary instruction forbidding both countries from undertaking further research in controversial Aegean waters and prohibiting military measures which could threaten peace; 2) that the Court clear up the continental shelf issue in principle.

The Court rejected the first request on the grounds that Turkey's actions had not seriously prejudiced the case. Athens in reply declared herself ready to resume bilateral negotiations until the Court had reached a conclusion on the second request. On 14th October the International Court called on both parties to put their case. Athens welcomed this, but Ankara refused and called the competence of the Court into question. In January 1979 the International Court eventually reached its decision, declaring itself incompetent to deal with the matter. This road to a solution was now closed, and there was nothing for it but to continue bilateral negotiations.

These had already been resumed in New York in September 1976 between Caglayangil and Bitsios and in Berne confidential discussions had been set up between experts with a view to determining the continental shelf frontiers of the two countries. These began on 2nd November and on the 11th the delegations signed the so-called Berne Declaration: the negotiations should be pursued seriously with the object of obtaining a result; strict confidentiality would be observed; during the negotiations neither side would undertake any action which could prejudice the negotiations; and both would abstain from polemics against the other; the negotiations would be based on international law and would be conducted by a committee of experts.

There would be little sense in recounting these discussions since they have, as yet, produced no concrete result. Ankara repeated over again her well-known theory of the shelf and Athens based herself on her secure case in international law which has received additional support from the decisions of the Second International Conference on Law of the Sea in 1982. Even this conclusion failed to move Ankara who interpreted it as giving further rights to the Aegean shelf.

In regard to Cyprus Ankara took an equally intransigent stand. In November 1974 the UN General Assembly had unanimously recommended Turkey to respect the sovereignty, independence and territorial integrity of Cyprus and to withdraw her troops; negotiations between the two communities should be resumed. These talks were in fact re-started but Ankara ignored the other far-reaching UN demands.

In February 1975 the Cyprus Government produced a plan which met practically all the Turkish demands of August 1974. There would be an independent sovereign Republic in the form of a bi-communal, multi-regional Federation with a strong central government. Some purely Turkish administrative units would function in the North over a territorial extent of about 18%. Turkey rejected this and proclaimed the North an independent federated state. When the Cyprus Government protested to the UN, Ankara let it be understood that any Resolution contrary to her interests would be rejected.

Despite the considerable readiness for concessions shown by the Cyprus Government during the subsequent intercommunal negotiations the first substantial results were achieved as late as February 1977 when Makarios and Denktash signed a document outlining certain basic principles: Cyprus was to become an independent, non-aligned, bi-communal Federal Republic. The territory of each federal state should be discussed in the light of economic viability or productivity and land-ownership. With certain restrictions, the three basic freedoms (movement, settlement, right of property) should be safeguarded. The powers and functions of the federal government would be such as to safeguard the unity of the country. By his signature Makarios had implicitly accepted the ethnic and administrative division of the island provided Cyprus as a whole would have a federal structure. But precisely this Denktash did not want. In the subsequent discussions it became obvious that he aimed at a loose confederation. Even in foreign policy the two states should be able to steer their own course. Obviously Turkey held fast to her plans for partition.

Despite this the new Cyprus President Kyprianou (Makarios having died in 1977) and UN Secretary-General Waldheim took pains to find a compromise solution. Inter-communal talks were resumed but they apparently had no more than an alibi character. In May 1981 there were general elections in unoccupied Cyprus. Denktash used this opportunity to hold elections in his part in June. Obviously he wanted to prove the statehood of the North. The situation during the following two years may be characterised as stalemate.

In May 1983 on Greek instigation the UN released another Resolution (37/253) asking Turkey to withdraw her occupation troops from Cyprus. Ankara refuted the resolution as legally not binding and Denktash considered it as an aggressive act against the Turkish Cypriots. He terminated the inter-communal talks and threatened to proclaim the North an independent state. Despite another effort by UN Secretary-General de Cuéllar who submitted new compromise proposals which were accepted by the Cypriot Government Denktash in November 1983 proclaimed the 'Turkish Republic of Northern Cyprus'.

There are doubts whether Denktash acted in connivance with Ankara. Most probably he used the governmental crisis in Turkey to take this step, knowing that Ankara could not let him down afterwards. In the parliamentary assembly of the North he ensured an unanimous vote for his step by blackmailing and threatening the opposition who considered this policy as disastrous for Cyprus.

Though the UN, the Commonwealth Conference, the EEC, the European Parliament, the Council of Europe and many governments condemned Denktash's action, Turkey officially acknowledged the new state. The hope that other Islamic countries would follow was frustrated. The secession, however, was not repealed.

In 1984 Kyprianou took the initiative. In January he presented the text of a framework agreement containing all elements the two sides had agreed to before. Moreover it contained concrete proposals for the structure of the future federal republic. Despite the fact that the document contained substantial concessions, Denktash rejected it and took further secessionist measures. In May 1984 UN Resolution 550/84 criticised Denktash's actions and asked the Secretary-General to make another effort. Though the inter-communal talks were resumed in September they bore no fruit.

In April 1985 de Cuéllar made another attempt for a solution. He submitted to both sides a document which became known as the 'single consolidated draft agreement'. In it de Cuéllar had merged all elements of the previous documents which had found the *placet* of both sides. Kyprianou accepted this as a basis for discussion. Denktash rejected it and stated that the bi-zonality in Cyprus should be radical according to the model of the two German states.

During the ensuing months the inter-communal talks continued and in March 1986 de Cuéllar believed the time ripe for a third effort at solution. He submitted the so-called 'draft framework agreement'. Its main features did not differ much from the earlier documents, the difference was in the chronological sequence of its realisation. During the first phase territorial and constitutional problems were to be solved and only after their solution were the Turkish troops to be withdrawn. Denktash, who knew that this sequence would be refused by the Greek Cypriot side, announced that he was ready to sign this document without any discussion. Kyprianou, who was not ready to take any risk, after consultations with Athens rejected the document. The Turkish side considered his refusal as a heaven-sent opportunity for a propaganda campaign denouncing Kyprianou's intransigence: *They* were ready for a compromise but Kyprianou's stubbornness prevented it.

Ankara's true intentions, however, were stated by Özal: If the Cyprus problem was not solved soon Ankara might be forced to re-evaluate the situation. Denktash added he would not take part in any international conference unless his state had been officially recognised. An official 'state visit' by Özal in the North showed that Ankara had decided to steer a tougher course. It is true that the indirect contacts via the Un Secretary-General went on but these negotiations brought no results. In fact they came to look like an alibi, with Ankara playing for time in the hope that this might bury the problem and lead world public opinion to accept the *status quo*.

Other facts deepened the division of the island even further. Shortly after the Occupation of Cyprus Ankara began to change the demographic balance of the population in favour of the Turkish element. Up to 1986 more than 40,000 settlers from Anatolia were brought to Cyprus augmenting the Turkish community by 38 per cent. The aim is clear: the Turkish part of the population would be increased to such a degree that in future negotiations the higher number must be taken as a basis and thus the occupied areas could be retained — justifiably — by the North.

When this colonizing policy was criticised internationally, the new settlers were declared re-migrants of Turkish Cypriot origin. Later settlers came as agricultural workers who, however, were soon equipped with the necessary papers. In contrast to the Turkish Cypriot refugees from the South, these settlers received accommodation and land from former Greek property. This naturally led to tensions between the Cypriot Turks and the settlers, the more so since the Turkish army helped the settlers.

The situation worsened when the settlers were organised politically. They founded the right-wing YDP/NBP-Party (Yeni Dogus Partisi — New Birth Party) which is closely linked with Denktash's National Unity Party. It was with the settlers votes that Denktash became 'President' in 1985. No wonder that he tries to augment their numbers. As this is accompanied by a mass exodus of Cypriot Turks, the population balance is slowly changing.

In the beginning the Turkish Cypriots had welcomed the presence of Turkish troops. In view of the preferential treatment of the settlers, this originally cordial relationship cooled down. The leader of the opposition in the North, the socialist Özker Özgür, expressed the grievances of the Turkish Cypriots if this trend continued: 'We fear that the Turkish Cypriots will be outnumbered and their identity as a more cultured and advanced political entity completely destroyed.'

Thus towards the end of 1986 the Cyprus conflict had reached a state of immobility which continued throughout 1987. Though Kyprianou succeeded in getting international verbal support, there was a stalemate. A feeling of frustration and helplessness spread in the South. Ruling circles were afraid of taking steps by which Makarios' heritage could be lost. The consequences were immobility and an anxious clinging to proven procedures. But there were also encouraging signs. People bgan to think and talk about the reasons for the present situation and about political and personal alternatives and were thus preparing the way for a generation-change in the political leadership and a fresh start.

At the end of this analysis of the Greek-Turkish conflict one must not forget the third aspect of the Greek-Turkish conflict, which has hardly been noticed in Europe, the minority problem of West Thrace.

To re-capitulate: in 1923 the Treaty of Lausanne had provided for an extensive exchange of populations between Greece and Turkey. The only communities excluded from this exchange were the Greek minority in Istanbul, the inhabitants of the islands of Imbros and Tenedos and the Moslem minority in West Thrace. The treaty specified full minority rights for both communities and, in addition for the islanders of Imbros and Tenedos extensive local autonomy. The treaty provided for the maintenance of a numerical balance between the minorities.

In 1934 the Greek minority in Istanbul numbered approximately 110,000 and there were about 10,000 Greeks living on Imbros and Tenedos. The Moslem minority consisting of Turks, Pomaks and Gypsies numbered approximately 106,000. To-day's figures give less than 5,000 Greeks in Istanbul and considerably less than 1,000 on the two islands. The Moslems in Western Thrace are reckoned at between 100,000 and 130,000. The balance has therefore altered to the disadvantage of the Greek minority. As has already been observed, the exodus of Greeks from Turkey began during the Second World War and increased rapidly in the 50s and 60s under the pressure of the escalating Cyprus conflict accompanied by pogroms sufficient to justify the use of the term 'expulsion' and to suggest a breach of the Treaty of Lausanne.[21] The Moslem minority in Greece which, as noted above, included three separate ethnic groups was — until the advent of the Colonels' Junta — well treated and not victimised by reprisals.[22] It was only under the Junta that reprisals began in the form of a government-sponsored attack on the social and economic circumstances of the Turkish minority on the principle of 'an eye for an eye and a tooth for a tooth'. After the return of democracy, Athens' policy towards minorities became more liberal but the reciprocity principle has not been wholly abandoned.

The Turkish minority in West Thrace is mainly agrarian but with insufficient land so that many are unemployed and industry is only gradually reaching the area. There are also language problems which, in the past, often led to discrimination. The resulting social and ethnic tensions have, of course, been exploited by Ankara and high-lighted as systematic oppression of the Turkish minority. But one gets the impression that Ankara is using this simply as a diversionary issue. Nevertheless the problem should be borne in mind.

Update

Since the completion of this study in autumn 1986 events have nourished the hope that there can be a solution to the Greek–Turkish conflict.[23] This new positive development rose from the crisis of March 1987 when Greece and Turkey almost clashed militarily.

In autumn 1986 the main aim of Greek diplomacy was maintenance of the *status quo*. On 20th November, however, there occurred a diplomatic clash between Greece and Turkey which seems noteworthy. On that date Turkey took over the presidency of the foreign ministers of the Council of Europe for the following six months. The topics of the meeting were human rights and refugee issues. Greece's Foreign Undersecretary used the opportunity to point to the differing conceptions within the member states of the Council of Europe. According to him a harmonisation of the legislation of the member states was necessary. Though Kapsis had not mentioned Turkey by name the Turkish foreign minister Halefoglou objected violently that it was Greece's policy constantly to launch attacks against Turkey. Kapsis replied that he had not mentioned Turkey in his statement but by his reaction Halefoglou admitted that his country was one of the cases of human rights violations. Replying to Halefoglou's statement that Greek–Turkish problems could not be solved without dialogue Kapsis confirmed that Greece did accept dialogue under one condition, that Turkey formally declared and committed itself to respect the *status quo* in the Aegean. The dialogue had begun at ambassadors' level but had been disrupted by the proclamation of the Turkish Cypriot pseudo-state. If Turkey had the intention to re-define Greece's borders the answer was: Greece did not lay claim to one inch of Turkish territory but would not concede an inch of Greek land, sea or air space. 'Let us begin dialogue here, right now, in the next room, beginning from the critical issue of the withdrawal of the Turkish troops from Cyprus', Kapsis ended. Halefoglou, who was then given the floor, stated that he had nothing to say.[24]

Similar arguments were heard from Papandreou during the EEC summit in London and defence minister Haralambopoulos during the NATO Defence Ministers' meeting in Brussels: a dialogue with Turkey could only be initiated if Turkey withdrew her troops from Cyprus and acknowledged the *status quo* in the Aegean.[25] From further statements by Papandreou it could be deduced that he was steering a conciliatory course towards Turkey.

This became evident when the international oil consortium NAPC (North Aegean Petroleum Company) which was mainly controlled by the Canadian Denison Mines Corporation (70%) let it be known that it planned to prospect east of the island of Thasos in the near future as the deposits in the 'Prinos'-field were dwindling. The Greek government wishing to avoid any confrontation with Turkey thereupon announced a forthcoming bill by which the NAPC and its plans for prospecting would be brought under Greek government control. On 25th February 1987 NAPC counter-attacked. They would begin prospecting 10 miles east of Thasos on 28th March. They did not need any permit from the Greek government. Their licence agreement entitled them to prospect wherever they wanted. The only legal way for the Greek government to stop them was to declare *force majeure* in this area for national security reasons. The price for the shares offered by the Greek government was an insult.[26]

The Minister of Industry, Athanassios Peponis retaliated that the government decision was not connected with its economic policy but was based on purely political and national criteria. It was Greece's right to refuse any prospecting in such a delicate area, in other words Greece forbade any prospecting east of Thasos.

So far the matter had been a conflict between the Greek government and the international consortium. But on 27th February it gained political momentum when the Turkish Ambassador in Athens raised formal protest against the envisaged prospecting: he hoped that Greece would respect the Berne Declaration. In Ankara acting Prime Minister Erdem (Özal was in Houston, Texas, for open-heart surgery) stated that drilling 10 miles east of Thasos violated the Berne Protocol. On 1st March it became known that the Turkish oceanographic vessel *Piri Reis*, had left Izmir for the Aegean.

Athens rejected Ankara's accusations and invited the Turkish government to put the case to the International Court in The Hague. According to Athens the Berne Protocol had become inoperative from the moment when Turkey broke off negotiations in 1981.[27] During the following days the *Piri Reis* left Turkish territorial waters but remained in international waters and soon returned. During the whole time it was monitored by planes of the Greek air force. Athens seemed not to be disturbed.

The following days saw two parallel developments. A diplomatic quarrel between the US and Greece about pro-Turkish statements by US Ministry of Defense officials including Secretary Weinberger and an exchange of vitriolic and bellicose statements between the Greek and Turkish government spokesmen.[28] A crisis was building up.

By 21st March the Greek government felt so alarmed that they informed US Secretary of State Shultz and NATO Secretary-General Lord Carrington that Greece could no longer tolerate actions such as that of the *Piri Reis* and would take measures to defend its sovereignty. Ankara let it be known that it would continue to carry out any activity it liked in any region it wanted, in the international waters and the Aegean air space. In a televised interview from Houston Özal stated that Turkey did not want trouble but he recommended particular care on the part of the Greeks. Further fuel was added to the fire when on the same day there appeared an interview with ex-Assistant Secretary of Defense Richard Perle in a Turkish newspaper. In this interview Perle claimed that Özal had tried to thaw the ice but Papandreou had not responded. Athens had prevented the creation of an atmosphere of *rapprochement* with Ankara and it was responsible for the lack of an agreement on the Cyprus issue. He did not think a war could be declared between the two countries nor would the Greeks undertake such a foolish action as extending their territorial waters. There might be incidents at the border, in the air or on the sea and these would be dangerous, but he did not believe in a war.[29]

Athens reaction was stern. Government spokesman Roubatis repeated the warnings of 21st March and charged Perle with acting as Ankara's paid clerk who had always endorsed Turkish views, no matter how absurd they were. He ought to show restraint at least as long as he was still in his present position. Despite several violations of Greek air space by Turkish planes on 25th March Papandreou in his National Independence Day speech showed moderation and did not go beyond his previous statements: Greece was not prepared to give up her national sovereign rights and, although she did not wish it, she was ready to fight for them.

On the same day (25th March) the Turkish National Security Council met, examined the situation in Greek–Turkish relations and called on the government to take necessary measures. These measures fatally resembled those of 1976 which had almost led to war.

On 27th March it became known that the Turkish *Government Gazette* had published a map of the Aegean, delineating regions outside Turkish territorial waters west of Lesvos, east and south of Limnos, around Samothrace and north of Imbros for which the Turkish Cabinet had granted oil exploration and exploitation licences to the state petroleum company TPAO. The map was almost an exact copy of that map of 1974: 95% of the area belonged to the shelf claimed by Greece. Later, the Turkish Minister of State Hasan Celal Güzel announced that the seismographic vessel *Sizmik 1* (the *Piri Reis* in need of repair had sailed to a harbour in the Straits) had left the Turkish port of Tuza in Istanbul and was heading towards the Aegean where it would remain until Turkish economic and political needs had been met. He hoped that the Greeks would not hinder the *Sizmik*. If that did occur, it was certain that Turkey would take all possible measures. He did not even rule out actions by the Turkish navy.[30]

In Athens the National Defence Council (KYSEA) decided that Greece would take all necessary measures if the *Sizmik 1* carried out seismic research. At the same time Athens invited Ankara to refer the shelf issue to The Hague. On 27th March Papandreou informed the full cabinet about the new KYSEA decisions: the *Sizmik* would not be permitted to carry out seismic research in the Aegean. 'Since Turkey stresses continuously that it seeks a dialogue, I would like to emphasise that the only legal issue which exists is the continental shelf issue. In other words, its delimiting and not its distribution. There is a big difference between distribution, which is carried out on the basis of a political–military correlation of forces and delimiting, which is clearly a legal action. We have called on Turkey, and I repeat this now, to accept our proposal to take the matter to The Hague. This requires a joint pledge, signed by both sides. And in this sense, a dialogue on a joint pledge is logical and we have never had nor do we now have any objection to such a dialogue taking place. A political dialogue with Turkey on other issues is not possible because all the other issues are political and would concern exclusively which sovereign rights Greece would concede to Turkey. That would not be a dialogue; it would be a message to the defeated. And such messages are not acceptable. Greece is neither defeated, nor will it be defeated. . . It must be made clear that in the event of a war over the entrance of the *Sizmik* into the Aegean, there would be a catalytic change in the Balkan region, and I believe even in the defence system of the West. In other words, NATO. . .'[31]

Papandreou then referred to the presence of Weinberger and Perle in Turkey and of Özal and Helefoglou in the US. Without going into this he stated: 'I would like to stress that if this constitutes an attempt, either by NATO or by the US, to force us, by means of the dynamic presence of Turkey in the Aegean, to go to the negotiating table with Turkey to discuss all issues, this government will not accept it. . . We are proceeding in a sober manner. The military preparedness of our country is presently capable of teaching a very severe lesson if our neighbours go ahead with their hostile actions.'[32] During the ensuing press conference Papandreou added that should there be an armed clash the American bases in Greece would be shut down.

Later in the day Foreign Minister Papoulias flew to Sofia to inform the Bulgarian government according to the stipulations of the Greek–Bulgarian treaty of friendship of autumn

1986. Foreign Under-Secretary Kapsis asked US Ambassador Robert Keeley for the suspension of operations at the Nea Makri naval communications bases. After his return from his lightning visit Papoulias briefed the ambassadors of the Warsaw Pact and the Islamic countries and only afterwards did Foreign Under-Secretary Kapsis instruct the western ambassadors which led to considerable embarrassment in NATO circles.

In New York the Greek Ambassador to the UN, Dountas, informed Un Secretary de Cuellar, refuting at the same time earlier Turkish accusations. De Cuellar was very concerned. In Ankara a high military spokesman said that the *Sizmik 1*, accompanied by an unspecified number of Turkish warships, would head into the Aegean the following morning. If the *Sizmik* was hindered the Turkish Armed Forces, which were in a state of alert, would respond without any hesitation. Turkish politicians reacted in different ways. Former Turkish Prime Minister Demirel advised both sides to keep cool: the differences could be solved through negotiations. The leader of the Socialist Democratic Populist Party Erdal İnönü recommended a tough course. Deputy Prime Minister Kaya Erdem opined that until a demarcation agreement was signed both countries had equal rights and interests: Turkey was compelled to resort to the same means as Greece to defend its rights.[33]

In Brussels NATO General-Secretary Lord Carrington offered to mediate. In the afternoon of the same day Foreign Minister Papoulias arrived in Washington. He met with Assistant Secretary of State for European Affairs Rozanne Ridgway and the entire staff of her department.

In this situation, when things were obviously moving towards war, Özal took the initiative. Flying home from Houston he stopped in London. After talks with Foreign Minister Sir Geoffrey Howe he told a press conference that he had ordered the *Sizmik 1* to stay in Turkish territorial waters. He saw no reason to escalate the crisis. If the Greeks did not move into the disputed waters Turkey would not either.[34] Ankara accepted Özal's decision and the *Sizmik* remained in Turkish waters. According to information from Reuters NATO members had exerted considerable pressure on Ankara.

On 28th March the crisis de-escalated. The NAPC

announced that it had abandoned its prospecting plans. The Greek government lifted its ban on the US communications base Nea Makri. In Washington George Shultz and Rozanne Ridgway appeared at the official opening of the Center of Hellenic Studies in the University of New York. Reuter was under the impression that the State Department was trying to regain the initiative in the question of Greek-American relations from the Pentagon.[35]

On 29th March Papandreou received the Turkish Ambassador in Athens, Akiman, who brought him a message from Özal. Papandreou in turn gave him a message to Özal which Akiman delivered on 30th March. In a press conference on the same day Özal stated that the differences with Greece should be solved by peaceful means and that he was satisfied by Papandreou's message.

Thus at the brink of war the two statesmen decided to begin a dialogue by letter. During the following months the exchange of messages intensified but almost nothing of their content leaked to the public. In the beginning the topics under discussion were limited to an argument (*compromissum*) for a joint appeal to The Hague but later on the exchange of opinions seems to have broadened.[36] Every now and then shrill voices were heard from Ankara but they were due to the pre-election campaign and Athens reacted accordingly. On 2nd October 1987 Özal informed Papandreou that their dialogue would be continued after the elections scheduled for the end of November.

In comparison with the Greek-Turkish storms, the Cyprus issue was passing through calm waters. The Cypriot government successfully tried to obtain international support but there was not the slightest substantial progress towards a solution. When in March 1987 de Cuéllar tried to start a new initiative the Cypriot government agreed to cooperate. Denktash on the other hand announced that negotiations could only begin if the Cypriot government accepted the Draft Framework Agreement of March 1986. Obviously Denktash was not interested in any solution. In September de Cuéllar stated that the Cyprus issue had reached a deadlock. The only positive development which might contribute to a solution was the association of Cyprus with the EEC which was established in December 1987. By the end of 1987 it became clear that there would not be any movement to overcome the stalemate prior to the Cypriot elections scheduled for February 1988.

In his last letter to Papandreou before the Turkish elections Özal had suggested a personal meeting. This took place on 31st January 1988 in the Swiss mountain resort Davos. In so short a perspective of time an evaluation of the Davos meeting is difficult. Apparently in view of the shock of the March 1987 crisis both sides moved away from their dangerous and barren pre-conditions for negotiations though they did not forsake their aims. Decisive is that both sides agreed on a policy of 'no war'. Moreover the two Prime Ministers changed their priorities: the primary aim is no longer the 'grand solution' which implies a defeat of the other side but a policy of small steps on the basis of *do ut des* towards each other, i.e. an effort to find solutions where they can be found easily and where the respective opposition in both countries cannot brand them as 'national treason'. On the basis of the confidence built up by these small steps the mutually acceptable 'grand solution' may be found in the future. Thus the Davos summit constitutes a radical change in the foreign policies of Greece and Turkey.

In the meantime the world has witnessed a process of *rapprochement* between Greece and Turkey. Many small steps have been taken in order to build up confidence and trust between the two countries. One of the more important was the withdrawal of the 1964 law against the Greek minority in Istanbul. Özal and Papandreou met twice more: in March within the framework of the NATO summit in Brussels and in June Özal's historic visit to Athens took place. The Foreign Ministers and certain committees agreed upon in Davos had productive meetings. Apparently the process of solving the Greek–Turkish conflict had been initiated.

Though the initial euphoria was soon replaced by a more wanted to continue the process of *rapprochement*. Subsequent developments have proved this; though from late summer 1988 Greece's internal policy was almost paralysed by Papandreou's ailing health and his personal problems, as well as the Koskotas scandal, the contacts at committee level continued and produced small but substantial results.

The reasons for this change of attitudes are of a complex nature. On the Greek side the main motive certainly is the sincere wish to live in peace with her neighbours. Greece has no longer any expansionist dreams and since 1974 has given up the idea of *enosis*. Her policy towards Cyprus is confined to contributing to the Cypriots' efforts to reunite their country and to re-establish its independence. The motives underlying Özal's new policy are more complicated. The desire to live in peace with Greece appears to have less weight than other elements of Turkish policy. Since the downfall of the Shah's regime in Iran, Turkish politicians have been dreaming of playing the rôle of the regional hegemonic power and this not only militarily but also economically. The first can only be achieved by foreign *i.e.* US help. American aid, however, is frozen to the 7:10 ratio. Any attempt to alter this has so far been successfully blocked by the Greco-American lobby in Congress. The only way for Özal to overcome this obstacle is to convince this pressure-group that his intentions towards Greece and Cyprus are peaceful. And his economic dreams can only be realised with the help of the Europeans.

On the other hand he seems to be afraid of Islamic fundamentalism which might engulf Turkey as well and thus ruin the secular state created by Kemal Atatürk. This fear is shared by the Turkish army which considers itself as the guardian of Kemalism. In this respect, to repulse fundamentalism, Özal can reckon with the assistance of the military.

In the last analysis, Özal's recipe against fundamentalism is the same as that of Kemal: make Turkey a European country. Özal knows that the European Community is more than sceptical as regards the entry of Turkey. He further knows that prior to a solution of the Greek-Turkish conflict he cannot even think of normalising European-Turkish relations. He is moreover aware that the key to the European door is held by Athens, and Greece has repeatedly stated and shown that it will allow Turkey's approach to the Community only on the basis of the *do ut des* principle. Thus Turkey can become a member of the EEC only *after* a solution of the conflict satisfying not only Athens but the EEC as well. Occasional efforts of Turkish politicians to change the time sequence (first entry and then solution) have met European resistance: The EEC is not ready to burden itself with this conflict. And Athens would certainly never be prepared to lay down its only trump-card.

The main obstacle in Özal's way towards a solution is the Turkish army which regards itself not only as the guardian of Kemalism but also as the only element of stability and continuity in Turkish internal politics. If Özal succeeds in winning the support of the military for his policy the solution of the conflict can become a reality. But this will require a fundamental change in their thinking. They will have to give up their attitude of disregard and contempt for international and supra-national institutions and their resolutions, cultivated since the time of Kemal. Moreover they must accept that the application of force in European politics has become anathema since the Second World War. The other Turkish *élites*, the political and diplomatic establishment, will have to learn this lesson as well. Conflicts with neighbouring states must no longer be issues of internal politics.

Turkey's wish to enter the EEC on the other hand offers a so far unique chance to the Europeans. Wise back-stage diplomacy by the European governments might convince the Turkish leadership that a solution of the Greek–Turkish conflict is in their own interest. If the military were won over, the chances for a solution in Cyprus would be enormously increased since the main impediment to a break-through, Denktash, has been their henchman from the beginning of the conflict. If the military let it be understood that they really want a solution, he would doubtlessly give up his intransigent position, provided of course that the Cypriot government offered him a face-saving way out.

That these considerations are not mere theory has been proved in recent months. When Athens' policy became increasingly paralysed during the second half of 1988 and was thus no longer able to play its traditional rôle as the international advocate of Cyprus the EEC stepped in. To the great astonishment of the Cypriots the Europeans offered their help – formerly the Cypriots had been obliged to beg for European assistance – and made it clear to Ankara among other things that until there was a solution of the Cyprus conflict even an approach to Europe was excluded. It remains to be seen whether the European politicians mean it or whether they are playing a Macchiavellian game, using Cyprus or Greece's possible veto as a kind of alibi to cover up their true intention of keeping the Turks out of the community.

Various facts, however, create the impression that the European initiative is serious.

Recent developments in Cyprus proper corroborate the view that there is a real chance for a solution. The overwhelming majority of the Greek Cypriots have given up the idea of *enosis*. Their aim today is a truly independent state where Greek and Turkish Cypriots can live and work together peacefully as equal partners. The tragic past has induced people to think about its reasons and they have discovered that terrible mistakes in the treatment of the Turkish minority had been committed in the early years of the republic. Even former EOKA-members admit this. To-day many Greek Cypriots comprehend how their Turkish neighbours must have felt then. The generational change in the Southern leadership represented by George Vassiliou may be considered as a symbol of this change.

A similar development can be noted in the North. The opposition around the socialist Özker Özgür went through a parallel process. They regard Denktash's policy with growing distrust. They fear that their Turkish Cypriot identity will be destroyed by the influx of Anatolian Turks and they demand their repatriation. The idea of becoming a Turkish province horrifies them. Özgür wants to overcome the vicious circle of mutual distrust. A kind of schedule for re-unification ought to be put forward. After the establishment of a federal government, all foreign troops should leave the island.

Denktash, on the other hand, stubbornly clings to his old concepts. He rules the North autocratically and enjoys his 'presidency'. There are voices who call him a pasha. He tries hard to avoid any concrete step towards reconciliation and re-unification. He condescended to the new round of intercommunal talks with Vassiliou only when Ankara pressured him. And so far he has constantly hampered any progress by making excessive demands, despite the fact that the Greek Cypriot side has followed a very accommodating course. Though he paid lip-service to reconciliation and re-unification, the closer analysis of his course shows that he refutes it. His aim at the moment is the perpetuation of the *status quo*. When Ankara's pressure on him lessened, he even dared to torpedo the mediation efforts of de Cuéllar and re-started the campaign for international acknowledgement of his secessionist state.

However, the chance for the opposition to gain the upperhand in the North is remote. It is split into various parties and Denktash can always count on the votes of the Anatolian settlers' party which will ensure his majority. Thus an endogenous Cypriot solution of the conflict appears almost excluded as long as Denktash is in power. Unless — as we stated above — the Turkish military change their mind and coerce Denktash to steer a more conciliatory course. But such a change of mind can only be induced if the military understand that their traditional policy towards Cyprus is more disadvantageous for Turkey than a compromise solution. The essentials of such a compromise can be listed: the future Republic of Cyprus should have a new constitution based on the existence of two equal peoples united in a federal system. The Northern federal state will have a Turkish and its Southern equivalent a Greek character. The federal government will have the same powers as other federal governments. The legislative body will be bi-cameral, consisting of a House of Representatives whose strength will mirror the relative strength of the two peoples and a Senate which will safeguard the special interests of the federal states. The often-mentioned three freedoms (property, movement, settlement) must be safeguarded after a certain transition period. In foreign policy the future Cypriot state, also, will follow a non-aligned course.

The critical point of any solution is the question of security guarantees. The Turkish Cypriot side wants the Turkish Army as a guarantor. The Greek Cypriots are afraid precisely of this. A feasible solution which is under discussion in the North and the South appears to be the sending of a European Peace Force under UN control into which a Greek and a Turkish unit could be integrated and thus both mother countries' faces would be saved. Prior to the sending of this force, both sides would disband their respective defence forces. President Vassiliou has already stated that he is ready to demilitarise the South, provided of course the North would follow suit. There remains the question whether the Europeans will be ready for such an effort.

The paralysis of Athens has had serious consequences in this context. As we stated before Greece's rôle as international promoter of Cyprus has been weakened. Thereby the position of President Vassiliou was weakened. He is obliged to fight the diplomatic battle almost alone. But at the same time the linkage of the Cyprus conflict with the bilateral Greek-Turkish conflict, where so much prestige is at stake, became looser. Paradoxically enough, by this Vassiliou might more easily succeed in winning European and international support, since the Europeans have at least not been very keen in getting involved in the bilateral Greek-Turkish conflict. Thus the character of the Cyprus conflict has changed fundamentally. The formerly tri-lateral conflict has become more international than before. Unfortunately it has so far not been included in the list of those conflicts where the global detente between East and West has led or is leading to a solution. Let us hope that President Vassiliou's wish that Cyprus, too, become infected by the peace epidemic which is endemic around the world will be fulfilled soon.

The galling problem of the Aegean conflict is that it is not only a problem of the two countries' foreign policies but that it is deeply rooted in their internal policies as well. The respective oppositions are watching their governments with Argus eyes always ready to cry 'treason'. Thus any major unilateral concessions from either side are excluded. A joint appeal to The Hague would probably end with a decision in favour of Greece. This, however, Özal would not survive politically. Neither could a Greek government survive unilateral concessions by Greece. Therefore this solution seems inopportune.

Thus there remains only a compromise solution enabling both governments to save their faces. Unofficially Athens has been ready for years to accept a solution according to the *façade maritime* principle and joint ventures in the exploitation of Aegean resources. The precondition for such a solution is that Turkey officially changes her Aegean policy in all respects and most importantly dissolves her Aegean Army. Such a step might swing public opinion in Greece so that it would accept the above-mentioned solution. Turkey on the other hand would not only gain access to the wealth of the Aegean shelf but would also lessen Greece's opposition to her entry into the European Community. However, as neither government is presently strong enough to sell this scheme to their voters, the 'grand solution' of the Aegean conflict will be postponed and the policy of small steps will continue for the time being.

In the last analysis the solution will depend on the EEC. Global detente is already weakening the traditional influence of the US and NATO on Turkey. Thus the chances for a solution via NATO channels are dwindling rapidly. The whole matter now boils down to two questions: Are the Europeans really ready to accept Turkey as a new member? And, when are they prepared to let the Turks in? The answer to these questions will constitute the solution to the whole complex of the Greek-Turkish conflict and simultaneously will provide the time-table, especially since Greece has expressed a not unnatural fear that, at some future time, Turkey might suggest an exchange between the Greek population of Cyprus and the Turks from West Thrace.

NOTES

1. *Article 16* of the Lausanne Treaty ruled: 'Turkey declares that it renounces all rights and titles, of any nature, concerning the territories situated beyond the boundaries provided for by the present Treaty as well as the islands (except those the sovereignty of which are recognised to her by the same Treaty), while the future of the said territories and islands has been or will be settled by the interested parties. The provisions of the present Article do not prejudice the particular arrangements agreed to or to be agreed between Turkey and its neighbouring countries on account of this vicinity.' *The Status Quo in the Aegean*, ed. Institute for Political Studies, Athens, n.d., p. 16.
2. Emmanouil Tsouderos, *Diplomatika paraskinia 1941-1944*, Athens, pp. 203 ff. Tsouderos was prime minister of the Greek Government-in-Exile 1941-4; and more recently Faik Ökte. *The Tragedy of the Turkish Capital Tax*, London, 1987.
3. Anthony Eden, *Full Circle*, London, 1960, p. 315.
4. Ludwig Dischler, *Die Zypernfrage*, Frankfurt, 1960, p. 31.
5. Niels Kadritzke and Wolf Wagner, *In Fadenkreuz der Nato; Ermittlungen am Beispiel Cypern*, Berlin, 1976, pp. 45 ff.; Van Coufoudakis, 'United States Foreign Policy', in US *Foreign Policy toward Greece and Cyprus: The Clash of Principle and Pragmatism*, ed. Theodore A. Couloumbis and Sallie M. Hicks, Washington, 1975, pp. 110 ff.; Andreas Papandreou, *Democracy at Gunpoint: The Greek Front*, New York, 1970, p. 134.
6. For the text of this notorious letter see 'Cyprus The Problem in Perspective', ed. Cyprus: Public Information Office, Nicosia, 1969, pp. 36 ff; and Jacob M. Landau, 'Johnson's 1964 letter to Inönü and Greek lobbying of the White House', in *Jerusalem Papers on Peace Problems*, Jerusalem, 1979, pp. 19 ff.
7. President Johnson is worth quoting *verbatim*: 'Then listen to me... fuck your parliament and your Constitution. America is an elephant. Cyprus is a flea. Greece is a flea. If these two fleas continue itching the elephant, they may just get whacked by the elephant's trunk, whacked good.' When ambassador Matsas objected that Greece was a democracy and the Prime Minister could not act contrary to the will of parliament, Johnson exploded: 'Let me tell you what answer I will give if I get that sort of reply back from

your Prime Minister... Who does he take himself for, anyway? I can't have a second De Gaulle on my hands. We pay a lot of good American dollars to the Greeks, Mr. Ambassador. If your Prime Minister gives me talk about Democracy, Parliament and Constitution, he, his Parliament and his Constitution may not last very long.' Philip Deane, *I should have died*, London, 1976, pp. 113 ff.
8. Kadritzke, op. cit., pp. 52 ff.
9. Kadritzke, op. cit., pp. 66 ff.; Christopher Hitchens, *Cyprus*, London, Melbourne and New York, 1984, p. 70.
10. Keesings Contemporary Archives, p. 26, No. 709.
11. Kadritzke, op. cit., pp. 73 ff.
12. C.D. Barkman, *Ambassadeur in Athens: 1969-1975: von Diktatuur tot Demokratie*, Gravenhage, 1984, pp. 160 ff.
13. What follows is based mainly on: Andrew Wilson, *The Aegean Dispute*, London, 1979; Friedrich Sauerwein, *Spannungsfeld Agäis: Informationen, Hintergründe, Ursachen des griechisch-türkischen Konflikts um Zypern und die Agäis*, Frankfurt, 1980, pp. 150 ff.; also Keesings Contemporary Archives. pp. 26, 667 ff.
14. Article of the Geneva Convention defines the term Continental Shelf as applying to:

'(a) to the seabed and subsoil of the submarine areas adjacent to the coast but outside the area of the territorial sea, to a depth of 200 metres or beyond that limit, to where the depth of the superjacent waters admits of the exploitation of the natural resources of the said areas;

(b) to the seabed and subsoil of similar submarine areas and subsoil of similar submarine areas adjacent to the coasts of islands.'

According to the Second UN Maritime Rights Convention islands are defined as follows:

Article 121:

(1) An island is a naturally formed area of land, surrounded by water, which is above water at high tide.

(2) Except as provided for in paragraph 3, the territorial sea, the contiguous zone, the exclusive economic zone and the continental shelf of an island are determined in accordance with the provisions of this Convention applicable to other land territory.

(3) Rocks which cannot sustain human habitation or economic life of their own shall have no exclusive economic zone or continental shelf.'

(Quoted from *The Status Quo in the Aegean*, p. 13.)

15. According to Article 6 of the Geneva Convention if a continental shelf lies adjacent to the territory of two or more States whose coasts are opposite each other, these States must agree the boundaries of their respective continental shelves between themselves. If they cannot agree, then the boundary will be the median line through all points equidistant from the nearest base-line from which the coastal sea of these States is measured, unless special circumstances justify the drawing of a different borderline. (Quoted from Union of Athens Newspaper Editors, 'The threat in the Aegean', Athens, n.d., p. 21.)
16. By Decree of the President of the Greek Republic: 'The Greek Republic, having regard to Articles 2 and 9 of Act No. 5017 regulating civil aviation, published in the Government Gazette, part No. 153 of 13 June 1931, and to Article 1 of Act No. 2569 of 19 April 1921 ratifying the International Aviation Convention (of Paris signed on 13 October 1919), published in the Government Gazette, No. 68 of 26 April 1921, and upon recommendation

of the Minister of Aviation, has resolved and decreed as follows: The extent of the territorial waters referred to in Article 2 of Act No. 5017 shall be fixed at ten sea miles from the coast of the State. The Minister of Aviation shall be responsible for publishing and giving effect to this Decree.' (Quoted from *The Status Quo in the Aegean*, p. 14.)

17. Determined by Article 2 of the Chicago Convention, ibid.
18. The decisive passage reads as follows: 'Turkey would look favourably upon every measure that the Greek Government would consider necessary to take to ensure the security of the islands that are under the sovereignty of Greece. . . The militarisation of the Greek islands that will take place is that of the islands of Samothrace and Lemnos. We absolutely agree to the militarisation of the two islands and at the same time to that of the Straits.' Quoted from ibid., Parliamentary Debates, Vol. 12, p. 309; 5th Legislative Period, 81st session, Friday 31st July 1936. The text reads: The provisions concerning the islands Lemnos and Samothrace belonging to our neighbour and friend Greece, which had been demilitarised on application of the Lausanne Treaty of 1923 are also abolished by the Treaty of Montreux and we are very glad of that. I avail myself of this opportunity to stress once more that one of the characteristics of the policy of new Turkey is to wish for her friends what she wished for herself and not to wish for her friends what we would regard as an injustice for ourselves.' (Quoted from ibid.)
19. Article 13 of the Treaty of Lausanne reads: 'With a view to ensuring the maintenance of peace, the Greek Government undertakes to observe the following restrictions in the Islands of Mytilene, Chios, Samos and Nikaria:
    1. No naval base and no fortification will be established in the said islands.
    2. Greek military aircraft will be forbidden to fly over the territory of the Anatolian coast. Reciprocally, the Turkish Government will forbid their military aircraft to fly over the said islands.
    3. The Greek military forces in the said islands will be limited to the normal contingent called up for military service, which can be trained on the spot, as well as to a force of gendarmerie and police in proportion to the force of gendarmerie and police existing in the whole of the Greek territory.' Ibid., p. 5
20. Article 2 rules: 'These islands shall be and shall remain demilitarised.' Ibid., p. 10.
21. Isabelle Guisan, 'Die letzten Byzantiner gehen in aller Stille unter', in *Pogrom*, No. 123, 1986, pp. 46 ff.
22. Ronald Meinardus, *Die Türkei-Politik Griechenlands*, Frankfurt, 1985, pp. 489 ff.
23. A more detailed account of the developments since autumn 1986 may be found in my book on the Greek-Turkish conflict, *Friede in der Agäis? Zypern- Agäis – Minderheiten*, Köln, Romiosini, 1989.
24. *Athens News Agency*, 21st November 1986.
25. See Ronald Meinardus, 'Die griechisch-türkischen Beziehungen in den achtziger Jahren', *Beiträge zur Konfliktforschung*, 18:2 (1988), p. 91.
26. *Athens News Agency*, 25th February 1987.
27. For a better understanding of the underlying problems here is the text: PROCES-VERBAL SUR LA PROCEDURE A SUIVRE POUR LA DELIMITATION DU PLATEAU CONTINENTAL ENTRE LA GRECE ET LA TURQUIE
    1. Les deux parties sont d'accord pour que la négociation soit franche, approfondie et conduite de bonne foi, en vue d'aboutir à un accord basé sur leur consentement mutuel en ce qui concerne la délimitation du plateua continental entre elles.

2. Les deux parties sont d'accord pour que cette négociation soit, de par sa nature, strictement confidentielle.
3. Les deux parties réservent leurs positions respectives en ce qui concerne la délimitation du plateau continental.
4. Les deux parties s'engagent à ne pas utiliser les dispositions de ce document et les propositions qui seront faites de part et d'autre au cours de cette négociation en aucune circonstance en dehors du context de celle-ci.
5. Les deux parties sont d'accord pour qu'il n'y ait pas de déclarations ou fuites à la presse sur le contenu des négociations, à moins qu'elles n'en décedent autrement d'un commun accord.
6. Les deux parties s'engagent à s'abstenir de toute initiative ou acte relatifs au plateau continental de la mer Egée, qui pourrait gêner la négociation.
7. Les deux parties s'engagent, en ce qui concerne leurs relations bilatérales, à s'abstenir de toute initiative ou acte qui tendrait à discréditer l'autre.
8. Les deux parties se sont mises d'accord d'étudier la pratique des états et les règles internationales en cette matière, en vue d'en dégager certains principes et critères pratiques qui pourraient servir dans le cas de la délimitation du plateau continental entre les deux pays.
9. A cet effet, une commission mixte sera créée, qui sera composé par des représentants nationaux.
10. Les deux parties acceptent d'adopter un rythme graduel dans le processus de la négociation à suivre, après consultation entre elles.

(Quoted from *Athens News Agency*, 28th March 1987.)
28. Details of the US-Greek quarrel may be found in my *Friede in der Ägäis? Zypern-Ägäis-Minderheiten*, Köln, Romiosini, 1989.
29. *Athens News Agency*, 23rd March 1987.
30. *Athens News Agency*, 27th March 1987.
31. Text of speech in No. 14/87 of *Athens News Agency*, 28th March 1987.
32. Ibid.
33. Ibid.
34. *Athens News Agency*, 29th March 1987.
35. *Spotlight*, No. 50 (March 1987), p. 9.
36. See Meinardus, op. cit., p. 93.